VARIETIES
OF WORK

PHYLLIS L. STEWART
MURIEL G. CANTOR
Editors

HD
6957
.U6
V37
1982

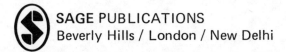

SAGE PUBLICATIONS
Beverly Hills / London / New Delhi

For information address:

SAGE Publications, Inc.
275 South Beverly Drive
Beverly Hills, California 90212

SAGE Publications India Pvt. Ltd.
C-236 Defence Colony
New Delhi 110 024, India

SAGE Publications Ltd
28 Banner Street
London EC1Y 8QE, England

Printed in the United States of America

Library of Congress Cataloging in Publication Data

Main entry under title:

Varieties of work.

  Bibliography: p.
  Includes indexes.
    1. United States—Occupations—Social aspects—
Addresses, essays, lectures. 2. Industrial
sociology—Addresses, essays, lectures. I. Stewart,
Phyllis L. II. Cantor, Muriel G. III. Title.

HD6957.U6V37   306'.36   82-716
ISBN 0-8039-1813-5   AACR2
ISBN 0-8039-1814-3 (pbk.)

FIRST PRINTING

CONTENTS

To Melville Dalton
and
Jessie Bernard
with gratitude

FOREWORD

An earlier volume by Phyllis Stewart and Muriel Cantor was dedicated to Melville Dalton, a sociologist with whom the editors and many of the contributors (myself included) had worked either as students, colleagues, or both. However, that dedication represented more than an acknowledgment of professional and personal ties. It acknowledged an intellectual debt as well. Dalton's work, especially his brilliant *Men Who Manage,* contains some of sociology's most penetrating and subtle analyses of (in Stewart and Cantor's words) "autonomy, power and control as interactive processes." In addition, many of the chapters in the book were inspired by his example and insights.

Dalton stressed that in practicing their occupations, men and women do not only negotiate niches for themselves within organizational "structures of control." They also—and more importantly, from a sociological perspective—vivify those structures, and in giving them life may drastically alter their official shape and purposes. The people whose work lives Dalton studied were shown as truly managing affairs, whether they were formally entitled to do so or not. Not only executives, but also union men and sales ladies, "assistants-to" and secretaries, were all given their due as authors of, as well as actors in, the drama of the workplace. Moreover, Dalton neither romanticized nor minimized the inequality involved in this creative collaboration among people at work. Rather, he saw more clearly than most people that some of us manage more influentially than others, owing not only to formal differences in power and authority but also to informal entrepreneurship.

In the present work, some important structural dimensions have been added to the analysis of work. In particular, the book stresses the fact that interaction at work occurs in the context of historic and economic trends in social structure, paying special attention to the emergence of women as a sizable component of the labor force and to the vicissitudes of labor markets. Equally important, the book urges the adoption of a theoretical model of work emphasizing occupations and organizations more equally. Too often, it is suggested, sociologists treat occupations chiefly as units in the stratification system, regarding organizations as the chief production units. This book's emphasis serves to correct that bias. It calls for more thorough investigation and careful thought about occupations as units of work organization in their own right, and it asks pointedly about the consequences of occupational autonomy (or its loss) both for a society's productive capacity and for the morale and dignity of its workers.

I suspect that Mel Dalton, with his keen sense of history and feel for the fabric of industrial society, would have approved of these additions.

—John Brewer
Trinity College
Hartford, Connecticut

ACKNOWLEDGMENTS

We were encouraged to write this book by some of the contributors to *Varieties of Work Experience.* We wish to thank them especially for their contributions to that work and their ideas on how to write another book building on the same theme. Also, many other colleagues who used *Varieties of Work Experience* in their classes on work and occupations informed us that students found the book useful in stimulating thesis and dissertation research. We want to thank all of our colleagues for their ideas.

Clerical and secretarial work is a female occupation. Mary Alison Albright, Roberta Bixhorn, Audrey Goldman, and Marybeth Hooban typed this manuscript. We are grateful for their superb help. Furthermore, we are glad they are completing their education so that they will have some autonomy to choose the occupation best suited to their aspirations.

Jacqueline Connelly, a Ph.D. student in the George Washington University Department of Sociology, worked diligently editing and checking references. She is an example of the new housewife who is combining the multiple roles of mother, student, worker, and wife. We appreciate her effort in this book.

PART I

INTRODUCTION AND OVERVIEW

CHAPTER ONE

INTRODUCTION

Phyllis L. Stewart
Muriel G. Cantor

THE GENERAL THEME of this book builds on our past work, *Varieties of Work Experience* (1974), in which we focused on the impact of the social structure on the development of occupational norms and relationships. In specific we examined, through a collection of original, descriptive, empirical studies and theoretical essays, four levels of social control which impacted on occupational group and role autonomy—cultural and societal, organizational, occupational, and client control. A broad spectrum of occupations ranging from less skilled work roles to craftsmen, artists, professionals, and other highly skilled work roles were compared on how the levels of control affected the autonomy of each group.

This book continues the above theme. In addition, it places more emphasis on how historic and economic factors enhance or limit autonomy. Changes in the labor force, e.g., the patterns of women working to include a predominance of married women, as well as increases in the number and proportion of unskilled workers, are likely to affect the distribution of power in the workplace. Furthermore, these changes are likely to affect consumption patterns and relations among social institutions and occupations. We attempt to link the concepts of autonomy, power, and control as interactive processes whereby occupations negotiate within the structures of social control to gain and maintain autonomy in the workplace.

Discussion of the historic and economic factors characteristic of occupants in given occupations in their pursuit of group and role autonomy is likely to illuminate to some degree how power is distributed and used in our society. Access to and allocation of valued resources in a society are to some degree determined by the outcome of negotiation between occupations and social structures as the former attempt to create, maintain, and expand their autonomy through various decision-making processes.

We have more studies of craft workers and of nonprofessional occupations than professionals in this book. We have no clear explanation of this phenomenon. We do not know if this reflects an overall decrease in studies on professions. A new publication, *Sociology of Work and Occupations,* began publication after *Varieties of Work Experience* (1974) in which we suggested that a deprofessionalization of occupations may be occurring. An interesting research paper for a student would be a content analysis of this journal with the aim of answering several questions: what is the editorial policy of this journal; has this changed since it was founded; what types of occupational studies are submitted, accepted, and rejected and why; and what do special issues reflect relative to the current state of the art? Answers to these questions may provide some insight into the importance of the sociology of knowledge perspective when applied to the areas of occupation.

This book is not only concerned with the broad issue of *why* to study occupations, but also with *how* to conceptualize the study of occupation as a separate social form. In our previous framework (and in this book as well), occupations could be considered as dependent variables, acted upon by cultural-societal organizations, in addition to occupational and client mechanisms of control. Freidson is arguing that occupation, as a social form, has been a neglected area of study. Furthermore, he argues for clarification of the theoretical status of occupation, separate from organizational and stratification theories.

Freidson is concerned with demonstrating how occupations are able to organize independent of firms and of other occupations in the same social class. A most recent example, the air traffic controllers, serves to demonstrate how this occupation was able to organize support globally, and to tie up transport systems throughout the world, even though only temporarily. Why and how is an occupation able to become an effective control group in and of itself? While these questions are only raised in this book, further discussion of these issues is appropriate for the classroom and even for individual research at a variety of levels.

As in our previous work, we are interested in original, theoretical essays and empirical studies focusing on two sociological questions: (1) how do occupations create, maintain, and extend their autonomy, power, and control at the group and role levels; and (2) how does this change over time within and among occupations? Because our sociological concern is with structure and process, we are not including classical, theoretical, or empirical selections. These are reprinted elsewhere and are often referred to in our chapters on work and occupations.

Many of the contributors to *Varieties of Work Experience* were asked to reexamine their papers on the relationship between social structure and occupational autonomy. Some responded that their intellectual focus had shifted and that they were not interested in rethinking their work. Others were too busy at the time on particular projects that prevented them from addressing this work now. It was difficult for us to decide which papers to redo and which to eliminate. We hope this new book contributes to the student's curiosity as to what factors enter into making some of the decisions on what to include and why.

OUR FRAMEWORK

We are interested in the autonomy, power, and control of occupations at the group and role levels. The sociological literature is filled with definitions of each of these concepts. We are using these terms to guide us in understanding how occupations change over time so that some occupations hold considerably more power than other occupations and consumers. Furthermore, we see autonomy, power, and control as interactive processes whereby occupations negotiate within the structure of social control to gain and maintain autonomy in the workplace. Descriptions of these interactive processes are likely to illuminate how power is distributed and negotiated, and how this changes with other cultural and societal events. Allocation of and access to valued resources in a society are to some degree determined by the outcome of negotiations between occupations and social structures as the former attempt to create, maintain, and expand their autonomy through various decision-making processes.

If some occupations have more power than others, then the labor force should reflect this occupational stratification. To some extent this is empirically visible, because the labor force reflects a large segment of occupations with almost no control over work (low-level service and industrial occupations), and another segment of occupations with almost complete control over work (professional, technical, and managerial). Within the occupations with much control, there is a range of choices possible in which to choose careers, to choose organizations in which to carry out these occupations, and to choose the contents of work (see Cantor, 1980). What emerges is a conceptual distinction where autonomy and control over person (personal freedom) are the distinctive features of certain occupations, whereas control over monetary rewards may not exist. Thus, personal freedom and freedom (autonomy) attached to an occupational role may become blended in such a way that it is conceptually difficult and operationally impossible to separate these two dimensions of autonomy.

We are interested in examining how social controls operate to modify or regulate the degree of autonomy, power, and control experienced by individuals in their work activities. By social control we mean the structures, both formal and informal, which condition and limit the actions of groups and roles. We see autonomy, power, and control as interactive processes between the structure and the occupational role. Informal controls may develop in work groups, or control may come from societal and cultural norms. In addition to these forms of control in the work setting, occupational group and role autonomy may be regulated by any or all of the following structural levels: societal and cultural, organizational, occupational, and client.

Few studies examining autonomy move beyond asking what it is and which occupations hold it or are losing it. One other important question seems to be how much the autonomy of an occupation can be reduced without modifying standards of excellence. Riemer suggests in his study of construction workers that serious problems are likely to arise in the form of shoddy work and the like if the autonomy of this occupational group is reduced.

We are cautious in our statements at this time because we do not have data to directly address this concern. However, new forms and types of bargaining arrangements are occurring among union leaders and car manufacturers who are forced to make changes in worker contracts in order to compete in the larger world market. Ford and General Motors are just two corporations that are appealing directly to workers by asking them to vote for shorter work weeks and less money in order to keep the price of American cars competitive with that of import models. If the voters agree to such conditions, contrary to the advice and pressure of union leadership, new coalitions are likely to emerge. Union leadership will lose some ability to influence its members, and corporate management will gain some power from union leadership. The appeal given by the corporation focuses on convincing workers that the organization belongs to them; they must control it, and only the workers have the power to change the economy favorably. In many companies, the workers have voted to support management's requests and reduce the negotiating position of union leadership. Here is another area of sociological interest in which students of work and occupations can do research at little expense, and possibly even get corporations to fund it.

AUTONOMY, POWER, AND CONTROL

There are many definitions in many literature sources of these three concepts, and their meanings are multiple. In fact, in our studies, these are sometimes considered to be synonymous. Occupation autonomy can be defined for our purposes as whatever discretion is held by occupational groups and roles after other sources of control have operated. Similar to Kanter (1977b: 167), we view power as the ability to get things done, to move resources in the direction of accomplishing some objectives regardless of the work setting. Occupational control is a process whereby the group or role is able to determine what others will do in the workplace, and sometimes outside it as well. Thus, control may be restrictive or extensive.

These concepts are used extensively by sociologists and other social scientists in a variety of theoretical essays and empirical investigations. While we do not want to suggest that we are conceptually lazy, we are purposively avoiding narrow, limited definitions that could become a trap and hinder our general purpose. Thus, we acknowledge the many varying definitions of these concepts and their utility for a variety of efforts. We are interested from an historical perspective in how occupations are able to generate and maintain autonomy, power, and control in a social system that is characterized by rapid national and international social change. As Freidson reminds us, occupation represents the productive activities upon which societies are based.

METHODOLOGY

A similar approach to the methodology of *Varieties of Work Experience* guided the development of this book. We are interested in stimulating students in field work which is systematic in conceptualization, design, and analysis. Good research of this type should spark ideas for discovery, replication, and verification. While no substitute for a research methods text, this book will provide students with examples of how an individual can do research with little or no help from others. Often students begin to acquire knowledge of the assumptions, strengths, and weaknesses of various methodological perspectives and techniques in the abstract. When the challenge arises of actually creating a researchable objective, students often wish to read detailed descriptions of how other researchers began the process of investigation. Some of the studies in this book illustrate various stages of the research process.

Several of the studies included some form of participant observation. Jeffrey Riemer worked as a construction worker (and continues to do so); Susan Martin became a reserve police woman; Peterson et al. drove trucks and cabs; the chapter on nurses was written by two registered nurses (Bullough and Bullough); the professorial role was written by a professor (Herman

Loether); and Jessie Bernard was a housewife for many years. Lewis Mennerick in his study of jail school teachers, and Clifton Bryant et al. in their study of poultry processing workers, also observed workers in their environment but did not participate as workers similar to the others noted above. From a sociology of knowledge perspective, these relationships stimulate several interesting methodological questions for students, including ones concerning bias and error in data collection and interpretation. Such considerations may provide appropriate and interesting assignments for students in methods of research on work and occupations.

Other techniques and approaches were used in the studies presented in this book. Use of the interview (Cynthia Epstein and Rosabeth Moss Kanter) and a mail questionnaire (Marc Silver and Herman Loether) suggest different problems for collection and interpretation, as well as different sources of bias and error.

Some researchers collected new data and compared these to previous studies. Loether's study of professors in the college and university system was a comparison of two time periods, mid-1960s and 1981. While he was not able to match individual responses of the two time periods, he was able to control for several important workplace variables. Some in this book went back to examine the organization, but were unable to carry out new interviews. Such a study was Mennerick's examination of the jail school teacher. He returned and collected secondary data on the same system, and he was able to compare organizational features in the two time periods that impacted on teacher autonomy at the group and role levels. Other studies were updated drawing from a review of pertinent literature (the Epstein and Bernard chapters). All of these studies provide ideas for new and old students on how to develop and test a sociological problem.

Rationale

Why is it important for sociologists to systematically observe and analyze occupations as distinct social forms and as these forms interact within contemporary American social structures? Occupation is important as a separate form economically and politically because it represents the productive activities on which society is based. How occupations are created and maintained and become part of the social structure is part of the overall political, economic, and technologic processes that determine which activities (tasks) are necessary for societies to survive in any form.

Organization of the Book

Because this book builds on *Varieties of Work Experience,* the organization is similar. The conditions under which all occupational groups work are in some way controlled by the client, as well as by the societal, organizational, and occupational norms and structures which interact to define work in a changing society. Thus, we are presenting the case studies according to the kinds of control most influential in determining the way specific occupational groups and roles maintain or obtain autonomy. For all occupations we see these levels interacting, but one or another level has been emphasized in the various studies we are presenting.

Preceding the cases are two chapters: (1) a review of changing issues in work; and (2) a theoretical essay by Eliot Freidson, who develops a basis for the sociological analysis of occupation *sui generis*. The inclusion of these two chapters before the cases provides alternative theoretical approaches that students may wish to ponder before relinquishing themselves to our conceptual constraints. We encourage such intellectual adventure because a convincing argument can be made for both questions: (1) are occupations really of substance as a separate social form making significant contributions; or (2) is it the context of occupations that is really the important independent variable?

THE STUDY OF WORK

Work is an activity which forms the base of every society. As the economic structures and polity change in societies, so does the nature of work. This section has an historical focus to show how work has changed in America over time (especially since World War II) and how these changes depend on changes in the political and economic orders as well as in the ideologies of workers. Examined is the intersection of the evolving nature of work and workers' actions, collectively and individually, with the economic and productive institutions and government policy.

Definitions of Work

The word work has many meanings, but for most people it is synonymous with earning a living. Work, even as a source of one's livelihood, is not simple to define. For our purposes, any activity that is used to earn a livelihood will be considered work (Miller, 1981). Work, then, is any productive activity for household use or for exchange. Work usually means working for wages or fees, but can also include domestic and other activities not done for money. This definition of work will not be accepted by everyone. Labor economists, for example, consider work just those activities which generate income through employment. For most sociologists as well, definitions of work are concerned with the labor force and paid employment (Solomon, 1968; Anderson, 1964). While it is impossible to ignore the economic basis of making a livelihood, it should be made clear from the outset that some people work for a living but are not considered part of the labor force. Others are part of the labor force but do not work for a living; that is, they are unemployed. According to the U.S. government (U.S. Department of Commerce, 1970a), the labor force consists of those people who are working at a job or seeking a job.

Because sociologists and economists have considered work as economic activity, they have usually limited their analyses to the conventional jobs found in offices, farms, mines, and factories. (See Miller, 1981, for an exception.) These analyses exclude workers involved in deviant or underground activities. Although many people make their livelihood from theft, prostitution, the sale of drugs, and related illegal pursuits, such people are rarely included in discussions of work.

In addition, there are people who subsist or make part of their living through a growing, uncharted, subterranean economy. The news media report that a barter economy has developed in the United States where people work, not for money, but in exchange for needed goods and service. A dentist, for example, might provide care for a painter in exchange for having his house painted. This transaction will not involve the usual fee for services, but can be considered work, both by the dentist and the painter. The size and extent of this subterranean economy is not known, but there is strong evidence that it exists and is growing (Schultz, 1980; Trist, 1981).

The above provides examples of work that do not appear in any statistics. If one used the labor force statistics only, approximately 38 percent of the adult population in the United States are not workers (U.S. Department of Commerce, 1979). How do these people make their livelihood? Some, of course, are supported by the government (local, state, or national) through tax dollars. These people are on welfare, in prisons, in mental hospitals, or live in shelters. A few are on the streets and make their livelihood through begging and private charities. Others are students who are supported by their families or again through aid from the state or private and corporate funds. Of course, there are the very rich who live off their investments and inheritances, and finally, there are the retired who live off their investments and pensions. These groups, mentioned above, account for only half of the adults not in the labor force. Although their numbers shrink each year, the largest group of people not considered as workers by economists and some sociologists, are housewives. By the definition used here, the housewife is also a worker but the work is unwaged; running a household is the means of earning a livelihood.

An additional problem with using a solely economic definition of work arises when considering work and leisure as separate activities. Nels Anderson

(1964), for example, explains that work is purposeful economic activity, while leisure is an end in itself. Others point out that work and play have the same common origins and cannot be detached from each other. As the economic conditions of life lighten the burdens of menial work, new possibilities open up for art and play. In the late twentieth century, many people earn their livings at activities that others consider play; the separation of the two is difficult. Sports and the arts provide the most obvious examples, but other kinds of both manual and service work can be cited as well. There are people who spend their "leisure" time repairing their own cars, cooking gourmet meals, and sewing or doing other needlework, while others do the same tasks to earn a living. In addition, as David Riesman (1958) pointed out, it is difficult to distinguish the time spent in nonwork from that spent in work activities, especially among those who earn their livelihood from intellectual or artistic pursuits. In the future, the separation may become even more problematic if more workers make their hobbies also their livelihood.

Occupations and Professions

Thus, work is an activity; and, most work is performed by people as part of their occupational roles. An occupation, as Richard Hall (1975) and others have pointed out, is more than a way of doing work. Rather, occupations are socially organized sets of activities and social roles which are usually achieved through some training and apprenticeship. Because an occupation is a social role, incumbents of that role are treated in specific ways by others and behave in certain ways as well. Physicians act differently from baseball players, both on the job and often off the job as well. Moreover, occupation is the commonly used measure of class, strata, or prestige. Not only does having an occupation alert people to one's social standing, but it often gives meaning and direction to one's life.

Modern societies are noted for their complex division of labor. As knowledge and technology increase, work has become more specialized, requiring knowledge and expertise for performance. Occupations which have monopolies of certain skills are called "professional." Sociologists, especially those categorized as structural functionalists (Parsons, 1968), have placed much emphasis on the professions. There is not general agreement among sociologists about the role of professions in the economy and society, nor is there agreement about which occupations are really professions. There is agreement, however, that the major professions (law and medicine) are powerful. Their key place in the division of labor is reflected in political power, rewards, and prestige.

THEORETICAL PERSPECTIVES

Work from a sociological perspective can be considered in two ways—from the macrosociological perspective and from the microsociological perspective (Parker et al., 1975). Macrosociologists, whether they are conflict theorists or functionalists, essentially study the same phenomenon. Both believe that to understand work in any society, it is necessary to understand the nature of that society, to understand how the society allocates work, how structured differences between classes and/or strata affect the society, and how the society and economy affect classes and strata. In contrast, those who study work from a microperspective (symbolic interactionists and phenomenologists) are concerned with the realities of everyday life, the importance of language, the nature of the self, and the ways in which the self is shaped through group membership and interaction.

There are two ideal types of macrosociology as indicated above. One is the structural-functional approach that owes its origins to Emile Durkheim, and the other is the conflict approach that is Marxist in its origins. Ideally, these two types of macrosociology are diametrically opposite to each other. However, in recent years there has been a convergence of the two in the study of work.

Structural Functionalism. Structural-functional models of explanation are concerned with the ongoing and more enduring patterns of social relationships which constitute society. The emphasis is on the social order and how that order is maintained. However, there are some structuralists who stress the historical aspect of institutions—how they have changed over time, and, in the context of a total societal mode, how changes in one institution relate to changes in all the others.

Marxist conflict theory. The conflict model focuses on wealth and poverty, domination and subjection, property and the propertyless. The basic element which moves society is the class struggle. In Marxist theory, the "sociology of work" is sociology itself. To quote Marx, "With the moment in which civilization begins, production begins to be based on the antagonism between accumulated and direct labor. Without conflict, no progress: that is the law which civilization has followed to the present day. Until now the forces of production have developed by virtue of the dominance of class conflict" (quoted in Dahrendorf, 1959: 6).

Symbolic interaction. Symbolic interactionists also study conflict, especially conflict on the job. According to Everett Hughes (1958), the social drama of work includes the way conflicts are resolved within the confines of the work situation itself. However, symbolic interactionists believe that people live in a "symbolic environment" and that they act in terms of the social meanings that they ascribe to the world around them. People make their own social world. Nevertheless, the existence of society depends upon it being continuously confirmed in the actions of its members. Therefore, when symbolic interactionists study work, they study the meaning of career or inequality rather than the impact of larger historical changes. These studies, especially those done by Everett Hughes (1958) and by Howard Becker (Becker and Strauss, 1956) of many occupations and professional groups, based largely on the techniques of participant observation, have shown what it is like to be a dance-hall musician (Becker, 1963), medical student (Becker et al., 1961), a janitor, and many others. Their sociology of work stresses the concept of "career," the typical series of opportunities and dangers, rewards and disappointments that confront new entrants into an occupation, as well as those working on the job. Such studies emphasize the subjective experience of working in a specific setting at a particular time.

HOW SOCIOLOGISTS STUDY WORK

How work and work roles are affected by the economy, the structural arrangements of the work environment, or the larger social organization (capitalism, socialism, democracy) have been major areas of inquiry by sociologists since the nineteenth century. Karl Marx (Bottomore, 1963), for example, attributed alienation and class conflict to capitalism and industrialization. The questions raised by Marx remain for most sociologists, whether functionalists or conflict theorists, the essence of a sociology of work from a macroperspective. Writing on alienated labor, Marx presents a series of hypotheses and questions based on the major proposition that the product of labor under the factory system is alienation, where workers are separated from the products they produce. Factory work, expecially work on the assembly line, is external to people; that is, it is not part of their nature.

Max Weber (1964) was also concerned with how structures and economy affect workers' productivity and power over the environment. In particular, Weber, like Marx, was interested in the effects of industrialization on work generally, and developed the most commonly used theory of organizations. He contended that capitalism was not necessarily the cause of workers' discontent, but that work under any kind of governmental system, if industrialized, would be much the same. He postulated that as societies became industrialized, "rational-legal" authority structures would be the recurring type of bureaucratic structures. Also, working under a rational-legal bureaucracy would limit the freedom of workers so that people would simply become cogs in the organization.

There are deep philosophical differences in the way Weber and Marx perceived the worlds of work, with the differences far outweighing the similarities. But it can be safely said that both were concerned with the control people have over the work processes, and both recognized the place of values and consciousness in the development of change. The works of Marx and Weber form the foundations of the sociology of work, presenting two important problems for sociologists: (1) the question of power and control over work; and (2) the question of how economies and societies change. Both recognized the importance of class (although each defined classes quite differently), and both recognized the problems of control.

Emile Durkheim (1964) was also concerned with the relationship of modes of organization and the social structure with the performance and well-being of the workforce. However, the problems of society for Durkheim were independent of the system of government and the economy, but rather in the problems of dependence on society itself. The basic dilemma that concerned Durkheim was how people can be more dependent on society and at the same time be more autonomous as the division of labor becomes more complex. Social life under conditions of increased specialization and differentiation of work (the division of labor) is a dynamic, organic entity. Individuals were, for Durkheim, far more a product of society than its determinant. Society, regardless of the stage of development, he saw as more than the sum of its parts. In industrial society, with the division of labor more complex, there is also more interdependence among people and institutions (organic solidarity) than in societies where the division of labor is simpler (mechanical solidarity).

All three theorists have one thing in common: they studied structures and social organizations. During the middle of the twentieth century, their concern with the structure and social organization turned around, in the sense that personality characteristics were newly considered as important, with the structure taken as a given. With the later resurgence of radical sociology and conflict theory in the 1960s, once again researchers and analysts returned to more macro approaches to problems of work.

Regardless of the perspective used, almost all sociologists would agree that a sociology of work is about the structure of society, its inequalities and freedoms, its deprivations and opportunities for self-fulfillment, and the interdependence of work with economic, political, and social lives.

However, the study of work in society is not just a theoretical area for study, but rather a substantive one. Therefore, various and multiple approaches to the study of work are appropriate. Both structural-functionalists and conflict theorists study industries and the work done in organizations. The field of study known as "industrial sociology" is concerned broadly with the study of industrial society, but is also concerned with the analysis of the social organization of work. Workers are seen in the context of the organizations which hire them. Examples of industrial sociology from a structural-functional approach are provided in Miller and Form (1980), who claim that key elements in the approach include history, values, technological change, organizational goals, and organizational complexities. Taking off from Weber and Durkheim, this approach also focuses attention on how structures guide the function of any participant (worker) who is assigned to a given office or status.

Conflict theorists also study the impact of technological change, history, and organizational complexities, but a major difference between the conflict theorists and functionalists is the focus of analysis. Rather than seeing social change as occurring within the context of ends, goals, and norms held by organizations, conflict theorists see change as the result of a power struggle (or "dialectic"). Change occurs when one group is able to impose its will upon another group. History is important for conflict theorists, but is seen as the ongoing dialectical process of conflict leading to synthesis. Conflict in the labor process occurs under definite historical circumstances, i.e., within specific economic and social contexts where the "workers" struggle with the "owners" over control of the "means of production" (Edwards, 1979; Arnowitz, 1973).

Another area where conflict theorists and structural-functionalists disagree is in the study of the "division of labor" and of occupations. Both recognize that all societies have a division of labor. Labor is divided according to structure and function for the followers of Durkheim, while it is divided according to who owns the means of production for conflict theorists. Both agree that the division of labor reflects the inequalities in society. For structural-functionalists, this inequality is the result of the needs of society. They believe that hard work, talent, and skill result in some people having more important roles and occupations than others (Davis and Moore, 1945). Conflict theorists, in contrast, do not see occupational stratification as the essential divisions in a society, but see classes as social groups with distinctive interests which inevitably bring them into conflict with other groups with opposed interests.

CHANGING SOCIAL AND ECONOMIC CONTEXT OF WORK

To understand work in any society, it is necessary to understand the nature of that society. The United States is an advanced, capitalist, industrial nation. What does that mean and how did industrialism happen? Three broad historical developments have influenced the way people work in modern society: urbanization (the growth of cities), industrialization, and capitalism.

Economic historians began using the term "Industrial Revolution" to refer to the series of dramatic technological and economic innovations made in England during the period from about 1760 to 1830 (Lenski and Lenski, 1978). In their view, the mechanization of the textile industry and its movement from a cottage industry to factory production, the expansion and technical advances in the manufacturing of iron, the harnessing of steam power, and other related developments of that period revolutionized the English economy and the nature of work and family life. What had been essentially an advanced agrarian system in the middle of the eighteenth century became an industrial system by the middle of the nineteenth.

The first factories, of course, were different from the modern factory because this type of shop lacked large-scale machinery and mechanical power (Schneider, 1980). According to some analysts, it was the factory system that created the conditions for the use of machinery and mechanical power, not vice versa. Factories were capitalist enterprises organized for profit. Profit depended on having a free labor force willing to work for wages. The development of the factory system of production caused a social as well as economic revolution. The nature of the family, the standard of living, and the status of women were different under the factory system, and certainly the nature of work changed. It is the factory system of production that has been labelled by some the Industrial Revolution.

In the United States, the growth of the factory system and industrialization are synonymous with the history of the country itself. From its beginnings, the Eastern seaboard of the country started to become industrialized. The first textile mill opened in 1791 and from its beginnings as a major industry, women and "Mill girls" were employed (Foner, 1977). However, it was not until the Civil War and the decades immediately following the War that the United States (or at least the Eastern part) could be considered industrialized. An agrarian America visualized by Thomas Jefferson only 60 years before was no longer a viable ideal. Some have suggested that the Civil War was not a battle over freeing the slaves, but rather a battle between agrarianism and industrialization. An industrial, capitalist society needs workers free to sell their labor.

Before the growth of industrial capitalism, common ideas about work were nonexistent. There was no such thing as employment and unemployment as we know it today. These terms and even the term occupation are part of the politics of work in both capitalist and socialist economies. Today there is a debate which has been going on since the nineteenth century about which form of government and economy best provides work for its citizens. Both socialism and communism in their modern forms are part of the outgrowth of this conflict and debate.

Capitalism. Some people believe that the economic system in the United States is not true capitalism, because the government regulates workers and inventories, and also assists those who are unable to work. Workers are guaranteed the right to collective bargaining through unions and employees' associations. Through social security and other legislation, the government provides aid to dependent children and adults who cannot work, and it provides unemployment insurance, Social Security, and some health care, especially to veterans and the aged. Civil rights laws aid women and minorities to gain employment and pay equality in the workplace.

However, there is another side to this story. Capitalism will once more be modified if Congress and the President approve laws which will cut drastically some of the benefits passed in the last fifty years. Also, in the last several decades, there has been a growing tendency for the return of monopolies or oligopoly through the growth of conglomerates and multinational corporations. Certain political economists, such as Paul Baran and Paul Sweezy (1966), Harry Braverman (1974), and Richard Edwards (1979) have written extensively on the growth of monopoly capitalism. They suggest that the marriage between capitalism and political democracy may be more fragile than formerly believed. They and others point out that class divisions in American society not only remain, but are growing more extreme.

Whether their pessimism is warranted should be seen as an open question. Their studies of the workplace and the change in relations between capital and labor, and between the government and the economy provide political, economic, and legal analyses of work. As administrations change, so do the laws governing workers and the workplace. As the economy changes, various groups solicit support for their constituencies. Unions, associations, and volunteer groups all have lobbyists in Washington. The involvement of government in labor relations and in protecting capital has increased substantially since 1880, and especially since 1930. Although policies may change, and groups in the political struggle may become less or more powerful, the role of the government is an essential ingredient in the analysis of work in America.

Socialism. The goal of socialist economic systems is to free workers from dependency on the wealthy few and to provide a decent standard of living for *all* members of society. Socialism (and there are many forms) is the economic institution most prevalent in western European democracies (Sweden and France, for example). As in capitalism, consumers are free to spend their income as they please, and workers still sell their labor to the highest bidder. Socialism differs from capitalism not in the marketplace, but in what happens to profits and how they are used. Profits from private industry are heavily taxed, and essential industries such as public utilities, transportation, and others are run by the state. Private individuals are also heavily taxed for the purpose of equalizing wealth. The goal is to provide jobs for everyone.

In Sweden, for example, socialism has eliminated the widest extremes of economic classes. There are few (some claim no) poverty-stricken people unable to find work, barely existing on government welfare payments as in the United States. Sweden is a class society, but few are very wealthy and most work.

Communism. Modern communism is both an economic theory and a political system, built on the theories of Karl Marx. The ideal goal of a communist system is to have the people own the means of production, rather than individual capitalists, with each individual thus sharing in the economic rewards. Communism seeks an even distribution of wealth—a classless society—with both the means of production (capital) and the goods and services produced belonging to all the people. The government becomes the sole producer, distributor, and employer. Although the ultimate goal of communism is a classless and stateless society, no "communist" nation exists approximating the ideal stage that Marx and Engels (1959) had predicted in the "Manifesto of the Communist Party."

Whether people are "better off" in communist countries, such as the USSR, the People's Republic of China, and other countries of the Eastern Bloc than in the other industrialized countries becomes a political question. It is clear from the data available that industrial work is somewhat similar; that is, working on an assembly line is the same, regardless of whether the government is socialist, communist, or a capitalist democracy. However, there are great variations in how wealth is distributed, in definitions of equality, in individual freedom, and in the meaning of work in various countries. The system of government is but one variable in a complex maze of variables that influence how work is distributed, how it is organized, and how opportunity is dispersed among the various elements of a population.

Changing Laws and Labor Force Participation

Following the Civil War there was an enormous influx of immigrants, and the rise of heavy industry took place. From 1880 to 1920, an average of five million immigrants entered the United States in each of the four decades, and the total population grew at a rate of one-fifth to one-quarter every ten years. Many of these newcomers went into the iron, steel, and other basic industries. The new workers were largely male and were willing to undertake heavy and dirty work (Kerr, 1979b).

The next great change followed World War I. In 1920, 30 percent of the population still lived on farms, compared to just about 5 percent today.

Movement into the cities was accelerated by the Great Depression and then by World War II. The migrants at first were largely white and later largely black. The new workers were still mostly male, but not entirely, and oriented toward blue collar, manual jobs. The automobile industry, which still employs about one out of every seven workers in the United States, had been based substantially on a labor force rural in origins. During the same period, however, single women were also leaving the small towns to work in the growing service sector of the economy, especially in the clerical jobs that went along with the growth of monopoly capitalism.

During the period between the two world wars and the decade following World War II, the United States became highly urbanized, and patterns of life were greatly affected. Suburbs grew, ghettos spread, and labor became unionized.

The greatest changes that occurred in the world of work in the United States since the 1950s were not in the laws governing the workplace (although these laws are important), but in three areas which are interrelated: the growth of monopoly capitalism and multinational corporations; the adoption of new technologies; and the decline of work in the agricultural sector with increase in service industries. These changes resulted in an extraordinary increase in female employment. The proportion of women in the labor force jumped from 28 percent in 1947 to 42 percent in 1980. At one time the United States produced most of the products it used, but by 1975 many of these products were being manufactured in the developing nations or in other industrial nations where production was more efficient and labor costs cheaper.

These changes in the economy, in production, and in the structure of the labor force are causing some people to reevaluate the meaning of industrialization. Some suggest that we have entered a post-industrial, high technology era, in which the processing of information, services, and knowledge are the major sources of employment and where routine work will be done by automation or robots (see Bell, 1973 and Toffler, 1980). The beginning of this post-industrial, high technology society (or "third wave" as Toffler [1980] calls the new changes), cannot be pinpointed. However, it is our position that work is constantly affected by some of these changes causing a subtle revolution in American society, changing the ways workers are controlled on the job and off.

CHANGES IN THE LABOR FORCE

The terms "occupation," "labor force," "employment," and "unemployment" have technical meanings. These meanings also have both political and social implications for policy decisions. For example, measures of employment and unemployment are related to the way the law provides for training and retraining of individuals and groups. Having an occupation is defined as being gainfully employed in a job. To be unemployed, one must be seeking work. The labor force consists of those employed and unemployed (but not discouraged) workers who have not given up trying to find a job.

The U.S. Department of the Census (Edwards, 1943) is responsible for classification of occupations and industries. Officially, people can be classified into 400 occupations. In reality, the Dictionary of Occupational Titles (1977) in its fourth edition lists over 20,000 different jobs, but these are compressed into broader categories for record-keeping purposes. Through a monthly survey (Current Population Survey) and the Decennial Census, the Bureau of the Census collects data on who is working for pay, at what, in what industries; whether people are working full-or part-time; and whether, if not working, they are seeking work. From this information, most analyses of the class structure in the United States are derived, and employment and unemployment figures are generated.

From these data, one can find out how the labor force is stratified by age, sex, and race. These data, however, should be used with caution, and the categories used should not be accepted at face value. Investigators using the same data often come up with different interpretations of what the figures mean. However, there is little question about the reliability of the measures if one can accept the assumptions and concepts used; the figures are replicable.

The division of labor is so complex in the United States that to get a holistic picture of labor force participation, it is necessary to make assumptions about work and about the ways workers are stratified. The Census classifies 10 major occupational categories under which 400 jobs (occupations) are listed.

White	1.	Professional and technical
Collar	2.	Managers and administrators
	3.	Sales workers
	4.	Clerical workers
	5.	Craft and kindred workers
Blue	6.	Operatives, equipment operatives
Collar	7.	Transport equipment operatives
	8.	Nonfarm laborers
	9.	Service workers
	10.	Farm workers

These categories are used essentially as both a function code and for status categories, with "professional and technical workers" assumed to be highest in the status scale and farm workers the lowest. According to Theodore Caplow (1964), this type of scale contains important assumptions. The first is that white collar work, work done in offices and demanding mental processes, is better than manual work, working with one's hands. The first four categories are the ones frequently called "white collar work" and the next four, "blue collar work." The last two, "service workers" and "farm workers," are not classified. Another assumption is that "clean" work is valued more than "dirty" work.[1]

The census classification was designed so that occupations can be summarized into homogeneous categories in terms of socioeconomic standing, but many have questioned whether these categories really do reflect social class. Difficulties in placement of some occupations, lack of real homogeneity within the occupational titles, and the overlapping of socioeconomic characteristics among occupations make the scale less than perfect. For example, all salespeople are categorized together whether they sell computers or work as salesclerks in department stores. Computer sales people are often highly trained as engineers, mathematicians, or technicians, while department store clerks are usually not. Another example is that dancers are considered professional and technical workers whether working in Las Vegas revues or in ballet.

The most valuable use of the labor force data is the information provided about how the labor force has changed over the decades. Following World War II, there have been some remarkable changes in work in America. More of the adult population is in the labor force (working or seeking work) than ever before, with the proportion rising every year. More women are working and seeking work, as are more teenagers. More students also combine work with study. The proportion of men in the labor force has also gone down, with many entering the labor force later in life and leaving earlier than those at the end of World War II.

The education level of all workers has increased dramatically. Table 1.1 summarizes some of these changes.

Women. The outstanding change in work since the end of World War II has been the increase of women in the paid labor force. This change has been called a "subtle revolution," affecting all aspects of family life and social life (Smith, 1979).[2] The percentage of women in the labor force has been rising throughout the present century; between 1900 and 1940 from 20 to 26 percent, and between 1940 to 1979 from 26 to 51 percent. Thus, although the two periods of time are roughly equal, the increase since 1940 has been four times greater than the earlier period.

The greatest portion of this increse has been from women now at work, with husbands at home and with preschool or school age children. Tradi-

TABLE 1.1   Selective Changing Characteristics of the American Labor Force

	Characteristic	Period of Time	Change
1.	Proportion of population 16 and over in labor force.	1947-1979	58.9 to 64.1
2.	Percentage of women 16 and over in labor force.	1950-1980	33.9 to 51.2
3.	Percentage of married women in labor force (husband present).	1950-1979	21.6 to 49.4
4.	Women as a proportion of labor force.	1950-1980	29.6 to 42.5
5.	Men as a proportion of labor force.	1950-1980	70.4 to 57.5
6.	Proporation of black and other minority group women in labor force.	1955-1980	46.1 to 53.5
7.	Proportion of black and other minority group men in labor force.	1955-1979	85.0 to 71.9
8.	Median years of education of members of labor force.[a]	1910-1979	8.1 to 12.6
9.	Percentage of labor force who completed 4 or more years college.	1965-1979	11.2 to 17.3
10.	Percentage of employed labor force in white collar occupations.	1960-1979	43.0 to 51.0
11.	Percentage of employed labor force in blue collar occupations.	1960-1979	37.0 to 33.0
12.	Labor force participation rates for all men 55-64 years of age.	1947-1978	90.0 to 72.5

(a) 1910 median years of education of population 25 years and over, which is slightly lower than education level of members of the labor force.

SOURCES:
1. U.S. Bureau of the Census, 1979, p. 392.
2. U.S. Department of Labor, 1980, p. 3
3. U.S. Department of Labor, 1980, p. 22
4. U.S. Department of Labor, 1980, p. 3
5. U.S. Department of Labor, 1980, p. 3
6. U.S. Department of Labor, 1980, p. 62
7. U.S. Department of Labor, 1980, p. 63
8. Kerr, 1979b, p. xv and U.S. Department of Labor, 1980, p. 43.
9. U.S. Department of Labor, 1980, p. 43
10. U.S. Bureau of the Census, 1979, p. 392.
11. U.S. Bureau of the Census, 1979, p. 392.
12. Kerr, 1979b, p. xv

tionally, labor-force participation rates of women have been inversely related to their husbands' earnings—the lower the earnings of the husband, the greater the likelihood that his wife would be working. In other words, women tended to work out of economic necessity, with most jobs available to women being unattractive, ill paid, and socially demeaning.

If low incomes drove women to work, how, then, can we explain the upward trend in female labor-force participation in a period of rapidly rising real incomes (1950-1980)? The answer to that question is not simple. Some say the answer lies chiefly in the growing availability of jobs that, at least in contrast with those of the past, are more attractive, better paid, and involve shorter hours of work or can be held on a part-time basis. The many studies of women in the labor force since the early 1960s tend to confirm the positive influence of favorable employment opportunities. Studies also show that educational attainment is positively related to labor-force participation, because women's educational levels have also risen with their labor force participation.

In the 1970s, women continued to enter the job market in large numbers, although the economic conditions had changed. The largest increase of women workers was among married women with young children. These women, both college and high school educated, increased the proportions of women in all job categories. By the end of the 1970s, women accounted for 56 percent of all people employed in eating and drinking places, 43 percent of employment in business services (almost 99 percent of all secretaries are women and 97 percent of all typists), 31 percent of people in manufacturing, and 81 percent of health service employees (as nurses, nurses aids, other subsidiary medical jobs, and providing the domestic labor in hospitals). Not all women are in high paying jobs. In fact, the opposite is true; although 40 percent of workers in the professional category are women, most are in the semi-professional categories—nurses, school teachers, social workers, and librarians—occupations traditionally seen as women's work (Gross, 1968).

A real division exists within the female work force between the semi-professionals (professional service workers) on the one hand and the rest of the women workers on the other. Female professional service workers are far better paid and are often unionized or belong to professional associations. Other female workers, those in sales, clerical, and other low-level white collar work, have more in common with women in the blue collar service sector. These women are employed in the industries that grew the most during the 1970s: food service, retail trade, and the public sector, state and local governments. Most of these jobs are not considered "good" in the traditional sense. At best, they are clean, but dull and routinized (data processing and low-level clerical), and at worst, dirty service jobs in hospitals and restaurants with little job security, low wages, and almost no chance for advancement. Whether women are in the higher paid, higher status professional jobs or in the lower paid, less secure clerical and service jobs, they are also likely to be paid less than their male counterparts. Women in the United States, on the average, earn 59 cents for every dollar men earn.

Minorities. During the past several decades, minorities (blacks, hispanics and Asians) experienced uneven gains in the labor market (Anderson, 1979), with the proportion of black men in the labor force steadily declining, while the proportion of black women remained stable. All age groups have shown similar trends, but black men of middle age and above have dropped out of the labor force at rates significantly greater than those of whites of comparable ages.

Historically, black women have had higher rates of labor force participation than white women, but the gap between the two groups has narrowed as more women enter the labor force. The occupational distribution of the black work force did improve somewhat during the 1960s, but the magnitude of change was not sufficient to equalize the job status of blacks with others in the labor market (U.S. Department of Labor, 1980: 74). On the plus side, more blacks are categorized as professional, technical, managerial, and clerical workers than earlier. Blacks have also experienced upgrading in the blue collar fields, moving out of the unskilled labor and domestic service jobs (being replaced by illegal immigrants and Hispanic nationals) into semi-skilled operative and skilled occupations. However, within the broad occupational categories, blacks still tend to concentrate in the least prestigious and most poorly paid jobs. Among professionals, for example, blacks are disproportionately concentrated in the teaching and social service occupations and have made only minor gains in fields such as engineering, sciences, and management. In addition, black occupational gains in the white collar fields, especially management, have been concentrated in the public sector rather than the private sector.

The employment picture for blacks improved modestly in the 1960s and 1970s when the economy was expanding. The trends in unemployment reveal most clearly the difficulties faced by the black work force. Between 1961 and 1969, the number of unemployed blacks declined by 400,000, a reduction in line with the overall improvement in job opportunities associated with the expanding economic activity during the decade. Since that time, however, unemployment among blacks has moved steadily upward. During the 1970s, blacks accounted for almost 20 percent of the increase in unemployment. Since late 1976, the black unemployment rate has remained at 12 percent or above, while the rate for whites declined steadily to 5.2 percent in April 1978 (U.S. Department of Labor, 1980).

In 1980, the census classification was redesigned in order to make it easier to match up census data with the Dictionary of Occupational Titles. The following categories have been developed resulting in *six* summary groups and *thirteen* major groups (PC 80-1-C series, *General Social and Economic Charac-*

teristics, U.S. Dept. of Commerce, Bureau of the Census, to be published mid-1982):[3]

Summary Groups	*Major Groups*
1. Managerial and professional	1. Executive, administrative and managerial
2. Technologists and related support	2. Professional specialty
3. Service	3. Technical, sales, and administrative support
	4. Sales
4. Farming, forestry, and fishing	5. Administrative support, including clerical
5. Precision production, craft, and repair	6. Private household
6. Operators, fabricators, and laborers	
	7. Protective service
	8. Service, except protective and household
	9. Farming, forestry, and fishing
	10. Precision production, craft, and repair
	11. Machine operators and tenders, except precision; fabricators, assemblers, inspectors and samplers
	12. Transportation
	13. Handlers, equipment cleaners, helpers, and laborers

This classification raises some problems and interesting questions for those who interpret and use these data. Comparisons between the 1980 data and other years may present difficulties for some. Detailed code categories have been written showing how the old codes fit into the new classification. While these are available, there will be sources of bias and error that might be introduced in making translations. Researchers may have to make decisions in translating codes that could affect reliability.

A question that many will ask is how the assumptions have changed in the new scale, if at all. Do we assume that managers, administrators, and executives are higher on the status scale than professional and technical specialists? Perhaps, assuming a status scale is no longer applicable. These are questions that many social scientists will be asking and evaluating when the new code and data appear.

THE WORKPLACE—CHANGING ORGANIZATIONAL FORMS

Although the nature of work changed during the 1970s, many people still work in large organizations, and many paid work activities take place in complex organizational structures with hierarchies, largeness of scale, and other features of the ideal-type bureaucracy.

The workplace is usually an organization, and the way work is organized may affect actual working conditions more than individual characteristics of the workers. To understand the nature of work in the United States (and elsewhere), it is important to realize that industries provide the jobs, and that these industries are organizations which determine through their formal and informal structures how the work and workers will be controlled. The most elemental example of organizational power is that the organization, through its representatives, controls the hiring of the workers. Although the U.S. government, through law, has established that people must not be discriminated against because of age, sex, religion, or national origin, these laws work just moderately well in actuality. In our society, gross pay and employment inequities in organizations and industries for major groups still exist.

Organizational controls over workers are not absolute. American industry and organizations are characterized by rapidly expanding technologies which require a highly skilled, knowledgeable workforce, making certain other skills and knowledge obsolete. The advancement of science and technology has provided some autonomy for certain workers in scarce occupations in organizations, but as Braverman (1974) and others have pointed out, the adoption of newer technology has also led to the deskilling of still others, thus lessening the control workers have had over their work process. For example, it has been suggested that the introduction of automation and electronic technologies such as the word processor may contribute to great unemployment in some white collar occupations (Trist, 1981: 50). In addition, British trade union leaders have forecast "the collapse of work" in the year 2000, which could result if high-risk areas are not identified and controlled (Jenkins and Sherman, 1979).

It has become a general proposition about modern industrial society that more and more of paid work activity takes place in large-scale organizations. Even those areas of the economy where the workers do service work or return to a domestic mode of production, the work is likely to be controlled by large conglomerates or corporations. For example, many of the new jobs of the 1970s were in service industries providing direct service for consumers. While fast food restaurants and direct sales work jobs have increased, these jobs are controlled to a great extent by large organizations such as McDonalds and IBM.

Some writers suggest that this may change as we enter the post-industrial or third wave society (Toffler, 1980). Others predict the end of the big multinational corporation and state capitalism as these are known today. Macrae (1976) suggests a process of organizational devolution. This process will occur as employees become educated, and as the world economy shifts (and becomes more interdependent) along with the effects of high tech-nology. Peterson (1981) extends these ideas by specifying several forms of entrepreneurship underlying an entrepreneurial revolution: franchising, con-tracting, and entrepreneurial departments and organizations.

Parallel to the growth of large organizations has been the growth of organized labor power. Union leaders have continued to negotiate contracts for workers with relatively good benefit packages. This was possible in an economy that was expanding. Today, large organizations, through manage-ment, are asking workers directly to give back some of the negotiated benefits. Certain industries, automobile, airlines, steel, and others, are expec-ting workers to reduce their expectations from the companies because of a reduced economy. In order to avoid significant numbers of layoffs, com-panies are telling the workers that they will have to be willing to work a shorter week at less pay.

Union leaders are advising workers not to accept management requests. Workers in some companies have, however, agreed to less return for their wages. It is likely that further changes will be needed in large organizations which compete in the world system because of the shifting global economic patterns. It is clear that workers will not do all the adjusting, and that organizational innovation will continue to be required.

NOTES

1. For a detailed review of occupational categories and analyses, see Montagna (1977: ch. 2).

2. This is not a completely new phenomenon. Women have moved in and out of the labor force as societal needs have required. An example of such movement was evident during World War II. Women were employed in large numbers doing a variety of difficult and physically demanding jobs. After the war ended, women left the labor force; men returned to it. If the current participation pattern continues, with increased numbers of married women in the labor force, important changes are likely in consumption patterns, time use, and mobility patterns of families.

3. The broad categories of blue collar and white collar are not built into the new categories.

CHAPTER TWO

OCCUPATIONAL AUTONOMY AND LABOR MARKET SHELTERS

Eliot Freidson

THE CONCEPT OF occupation has been curiously neglected in sociological theory. In empirical studies of members of occupations, attention is devoted to issues of career, contingencies of work, interaction with clients, colleagues, employers, and the like, while taking the idea of occupation for granted. And in the large body of macrosociological work on inequality and status attainment, where occupation plays a critical role in identifying people's positions in the social structure, occupations are typically lumped together by the use of broad governmental classifications which are not remarkable for their consistency or their theoretical import. Occupation represents much too critical a concept in sociology to be taken for granted, for it represents the productive activities upon which societies are based. Furthermore, it has the special potential for linking the microsociological world of everyday experience and activity, which is explored by most studies in the tradition of Everett Hughes, with the macrosociological world of social structure, which is explored by most studies of class, stratification, and social mobility. It is unlikely to be able to serve that function, however, until its theoretical status is clarified and a systematic strategy for its analysis created.

In this chapter I hope to contribute to a clarification of the theoretical status of occupation. I shall argue, first, that the two major bodies of theory most closely connected with the concept of occupation—organizational theory and class and stratification theory—cannot explain parsimoniously in their own terms certain features that occupations may display. Thus, I shall argue that a theory of occupations must be developed separately, and not as a mere derivative of other bodies of theory. I will then argue that a useful focus for such a theory lies in the capacity of occupations to become organized groups independently of firms and of other occupations in the same class or stratum. It is by becoming an effectively organized group that an occupation can gain for its members a modicum of autonomy from control by others. Finally, I will argue that both as a mechanism by which one can explain how relative autonomy can be established for an occupation, and as a concept which can provide the resources for connecting the microsociological experience and activities of individuals with the macrosociological realities of political economy, the notion of a special kind of labor market segment—the shelter—may be a fruitful point of departure for theorizing about occupational organization and experience. I shall conclude with a sketch of the interrelations of major variables to illustrate how it is possible to reason systematically from the shelter in the political economy to occupational organization, training, career, identity, and the like.

OCCUPATION AND ORGANIZATIONAL AND CLASS THEORY

In principle, it is possible to argue that a theory of occupations is not necessary because between them, organizational and class theory can both explain how occupations are created and sustained, as well as make sense of occupations as part of an organizational division of labor which is itself linked into the broader political and economic environment that provides the resources for and otherwise surrounds and conditions organizations and their policies. And indeed, it is true that in all developed industrial societies, many "occupations" are simply formal work roles or positions in complex organizations created and controlled by managerial power being exercised on behalf of either private or state capital, or a mixture of the two.

But not all work roles have such characteristics, either here and now or in other times and places. Many have characteristics which cannot be explained or analyzed adequately by reference to the organizations in which they may be found. Some occupations exist and thrive in the external labor market outside of administratively constituted firms. Other occupations, even when carried on inside firms, are noted as "exceptions" (e.g., Piore, 1975) because they can establish, as Stinchcombe put it (1959: 186), "continuity of status in a labor market" in such a fashion that while their members may hold positions in firms and depend for their livelihood on employment in them, they control the supply of specialized labor and even contribute to increasing the demand for their services. They become the source of defining, controlling, and evaluating the work roles in the organizational positions they fill, a source that is exogenous to the firm. Since, as Moore (1970: 9) has noted, "it is extremely unlikely that an occupation will be able to set itself apart from, and above, mere tasks set by the administrative wisdom of superiors without making common cause in a formal organization," such occupations can be conceived of as groups organized independently of firms, and must be conceptualized as something other than a mere derivative of the firm or the formal organization.

The same conclusion may be drawn for both stratification and class theory, though for different reasons. As in the case of the firm, occupation is an essential empirical component of both stratification and class theory. However, what is generic to occupation—its existence as an organized form of differentiated productive activity—is at worst ignored and at best blurred and obscured by the analytic focus of both class and stratification theory. The latter are concerned with the unequal distribution of the goods of life, including as some of the goods of life both the jobs that people have and the economic, political, and symbolic rewards that are attached to them. The distribution of people into various occupations which are rewarded in various ways thus constitutes a central issue of class and stratification theory. But apart from having the potential for explaining who has what jobs and their attendant rewards, class and stratification theory is poorly equipped for explaining how the work of those jobs is performed—how the process of production takes place. Production takes place through the medium of *individual* occupations. To see production, one must see occupations, and not merely broad classes or strata. The intrinsic rationale for class or stratification analysis lies in the *aggregation* of different occupations by some criterion of inequality. The intrinsic rationale required for the analysis of how concrete empirical instances of productive work take place lies in the *differentiation* of occupations in a specialized division of labor. While for class or stratification analysis a file clerk and a typist are the same, they do not do the same things in a productive process which, if we are to understand it, must be conceptualized in terms of those occupational differences.

Finally, I may point out that it has been a persistent problem of class theory to explain the absence of consciousness and organized action in what is defined as a class by theorists (see Mann, 1973). Considerably less of a problem exists for the concept of occupation, for that is the way by which individuals today readily and consciously identify themselves and act in their roles as productive workers. An even more intense collective consciousness and action may be found in empirical circumstances in which occupations have organized as groups independently of productive organizations or firms, and independently of other occupations ostensibly of the same stratum or class (see Krause, 1971: 85). While not all or even most occupations of the entire working population today have these characteristics, it is the demonstrable potential of occupations to become conscious, acting, organized groups that poses a serious problem of explanation for both organizational and class theory. That potential might be addressed more satisfactorily by developing a mode of analysis based on the notion of occupation itself rather than by attempting to derive concepts from theories designed to address and explain different issues. The problem is how the concept can be developed, what criteria of salience should form the focus for empirical analysis, and how the elaboration of theory can be accomplished.

THE PROBLEM OF FOCUS

At present, occupations tend to be conceptualized in terms of two criteria, neither of which is theoretically appropriate to them. First, there is the conception of occupations as tasks or functions. In the simplest and most obvious way, we distinguish those people who do welding from those who diagnose diseases, blow glass, or whatever. Superficially, this does make sense. After all, is not that what occupation is all about? However, looked at closely, one cannot usefully conceive of occupation by its technical tasks. Machines also weld and blow glass; computers diagnose disease. Should we really conceive of occupations strictly by the tasks or functions associated with them, without covertly smuggling in unacknowledged assumptions, then we would not be able to make any distinction between occupation and technology.

The second major conception of occupation avoids that difficulty by emphasizing the differential positions of occupations in a class or stratification system. Thus, in conventional stratification and social mobility studies, and in official labor statistics, occupations are distinguished by their location in a hierarchy of prestige, income, power, or control over production. Those with the same broad *quantity* of imputed skill, income, prestige, or education are considered the same, irrespective of the different tasks they may perform. So also does Marx-inspired class analysis group all occupations together that share the same very general social relations of production, irrespective of differences in task (see Wright, 1978: 1370).

But while self-employed physicians and self-employed lawyers, for example, share the same very general social relations of production implied by self-employment in a capitalist political economy, and while they belong to the same social stratum, each has a distinctly different social identity and each does different work. The work they do is not subject solely to organization by broad social relations of production, nor can it be understood solely as a function of a given level of skill, responsibility, prestige, or whatever. The particular contingencies of being a doctor rather than a lawyer have consequences of their own for the character of the work setting and the performance of work that cannot be ignored if one wishes to understand and explain the labor processes of doctoring and lawyering. Class theory, with its emphasis on relations of production, cannot tell us much about how and why those productive tasks are performed in the particular way they are, and what the relations of the workers are each to the other, and to other workers. Indeed, what Turner and Hodge (1970: 34) called the "macro-statification assumptions" underlying the class approach to the analysis of occupations dissolve what is distinctive about occupations and the work they entail. On the contrary, work is predicated on task differentiation into particular occupations: the socially organized performance of differentiated tasks has specific implications for the social organization and the social psychology of work which cannot be explained in broad class terms.

But if we cannot satisfactorily conceptualize occupations solely by their different tasks, or solely by their place in a class or stratification system, how *can* we do so? I suggest that a fruitful focus lies in analyzing the circumstances in which occupations become organized as social groups, in classifying them by the source, type, and degree of their organization, and in analyzing them in such a way as to explain both how and why their form of organization came to be and could be maintained, and what the consequences of that organization are for the productive division of labor of which they are part. Such an approach has manifest ancestry in Durkheim's discussion of occupational groups in *The Division of Labor in Society* (1947: 1-31), and *Professional Ethics and Civic Morals* (1957: 4-41), although Durkheim was neither concerned with nor in fact developed a systematic method for analyzing occupations as groups.

It is of course impossible to pursue such a focus fruitfully if we deal only with occupations that are exclusively organized groups, for that would exclude the vast majority of all occupations today. Lack of organization must be included among the varieties of organization. Many occupations have no organization beyond that imposed by the market and its consumers of labor (e.g., Morse, 1969; Olesen and Katsuranis, 1978). Others are not exclusively organized as individual occupations, but rather are organized into a transoccupational association like a trade union. Other occupations may be exclusively organized groups whose members share a common occupational identity as well as broad solidarity and commitment, the most obvious being some of those often called professions and crafts.

Clearly, in our ordinary discussions of labor we always pay some attention to occupational organization, for organization is one major connotation of such conventional terms as casual labor, trade unions, professions, and crafts. But those words are unfortunately so vague and imprecise, overlain with so many other connotations that they have collected over their linguistic histories, that they are unlikely to be useful as conceptual tools. What is needed are more precise, logical concepts of occupational organization, rather than fruitless attempts to use those "folk concepts" more precisely or to abstract some essence out of them. Logical notions of differentiation in occupational organization can be created by developing a coherent theoretical conception of the critical parameters underlying the *possibility* for occupational organization and autonomy, influencing both the form they take and their consequences for work and the worker.

As the direct link between individual and economy, a link which can be seen to be mediated by productive firms and by class but which can on occasion stand by itself, occupation must be conceptualized in such a way as to allow us to understand how it can stand by itself, autonomous of class or firm. What may be an anomaly to organizational theory and a contradiction in class theory must be the focal issue for direct explanation by occupational theory. Taking as the central issue how occupation can stand autonomously by itself, linking individuals to economy without firm, and standing separate from other members of their ostensible class, how can that link be made; what mechanism can represent it?

The notion of an occupational group, and particularly that of an occupational community, is quite useful for organizing the data one gains from traditional studies of members of relatively distinct occupations, or segments of occupations (see Salaman, 1974). It allows one to deal with important issues of personal identity, of social relations outside the workplace, and the like. In and of itself, however, it cannot link occupation to political economy because it does not contain the conceptual resources by which one can understand how it can come to be within a particular political economy. Essentially, it takes occupational organization more as a given than as something to be itself explained. If an attempt is made to explain it, it is done by reference to the characteristics of the members of the occupation and their relations to each other (e.g., Lipset et al., 1962), which does not establish effective links to the political economy.

MARKETS AND SHELTERS

A fruitful way of establishing such links has been explored by M. S. Larson in her study of the rise of the professions in England and the United States as a "market project," most particularly a project which "constitute(s) and control(s) a market for their expertise" (Larson, 1977: xvi). Such a project involves, as Larson notes, a number of activities, including the delineation and standardization of a distinctive commodity, the formation of a training program and inducing recruits to accept the sacrifices of going through it, the establishment of supportive relations with the dominant class, and the like (Larson, 1977: 9-18, 47-48). In a rather different analysis, Kreckel casts a wider net and delineates five social mechanisms "affecting bargaining strength" between employers and employees in their dealings in the labor market (Kreckel, 1980: 540-541). Occupational success in such a project may be seen, structurally, as the effective monopolization of opportunities to perform a particular bundle of tasks and, furthermore, to perform them under desirable conditions and on favorable terms. In essence, the successful occupation establishes an "exclusionary social closure" in the labor market (Parkin, 1979: 44-73), or a "sinecure" (Collins, 1979: 55-57).

The pejorative connotations of those terms, however, attest to their origin in class theory and to their concern with inequality. Such concern, I have already argued, diverts attention from the analysis of differentiation that is intrinsic to the concept of occupation. Indeed, both major sources of class theory—classical (or capitalist) theory stemming from Adam Smith, and critical (or socialist) theory stemming from Karl Marx—are at bottom hostile to the very idea of a stable, organized occupation. Their notions of inequality are predicated upon implicit conceptions which allow no room for the social organization by which an occupation can be stable enough to allow long-term careers for those who practice it, or to allow the possibility for an occupational community. The utopian model underlying the critique of mercantilism by classical theory is a labor market unconstrained by "combinations," a fluid market in constant motion as individuals freely compete in seeking better paying positions or opportunities. The utopian model underlying Marxist theory, while not as clearly specified, also envisages free movement among various tasks without long-term specialization in any single set of tasks. Both bodies of theory seem to share a vision of a system of perfect mobility, with a very fluid division of labor. Occupational groups are seen as conspiracies, or in any case as undesirable constraints on such fluidity. In both, it is difficult to see how complex work requiring long periods of training and practice for effective performance can be socially viable.

There is no doubt that a social closure is a conspiracy against some would-be workers. But it is also protection for those already at work and for those limited numbers they recruit into their ranks. If our emphasis is on how workers gain control over their work, however, we must consider self-protection as something more than mere conspiracy. To avoid the pejorative connotations of terms drawn from class theory to characterize the segmentation of the labor market as "sinecure" or "social closure," I would suggest the term of Marcia Freedman (1976)—"labor market shelter." Its connotation is one appropriate to the perspective of workers who not unnaturally wish to increase their economic security while continuing to practice the same work rather than having to move from one kind of work to another as externally dictated opportunity and demand dictate.

In essence, I suggest that the arena which can link the macrostructure to the microstructure is the *external* labor market that lies outside the employment and personnel policies of firms which are conceptualized in dual labor market theory as the internal labor market (see Doeringer and Piore, 1971). Furthermore and more particularly, I suggest that the mechanism which can be relatively distinct and separate from the broad stratification or class division of the external labor market, which can constrain the influence of internal labor markets, and which can be conceived of as interacting with occupational organizations, is the labor market shelter. In theory, one can visualize the labor market as a collection of occupational shelters through the nature of which one can analyze in an orderly and systematic way the parameters by which we can understand both an occupation and the experience and behavior of its members. (See Caplow [1964: 142-180] for a valuable set of sketches of such shelters, though emphasizing wage theory rather than occupational organization and autonomy.)

Occupations represent the organization of productive labor into the social roles by which tasks are performed. In market economies, workers enter those social roles through the labor market, their position conditioned in capitalist economies by what Kreckel calls "primary asymmetries" between labor and capital (Kreckel, 1980: 529). Within that general position of relative weakness on the part of all workers, however, some are stronger than others by virtue of "secondary asymmetries," which allow them to become stable, organized groups that gain relative autonomy. In order to gain such relative strength in the market, it is essential that they gain some control over the supply of labor entering the market to perform the tasks in which they specialize, and over the substance of demand for the labor they supply. A labor market shelter represents occupational control over supply and the substance of demand. What the perfectly free market is for classical economics (see Kerr, 1950: 279) and perhaps for conventional stratification theory, and what the stratified market is for class theory (see Edwards, 1975), a "balkanized" labor market composed of occupationally differentiated shelters is for occupational theory.

Empirically, there are many different kinds of shelters, as is implied by the clusters found by Freedman (1976). The criteria by which sheltered workers are discriminated (and the excluded discriminated against) are also quite variable (see Form and Huber, 1976: 757-759). Since I am concerned here with identifying and following out the interaction of significant variables of occupational organization and autonomy rather than with exploring each in detail, however, I will emphasize formally negotiated shelters based on some public claim of specialized training and skill—that is, qualification (Kreckel, 1980: 531)—rather than those sometimes less conspicuous shelters which are created by informal and frequently publicly invisible gender, racial, ethnic, neighborhood, or kinship conspiracies. And I will more particularly emphasize the state-sanctioned quasi-monopolies to be found among some of those occupations called professions under the assumption that they will display more of the essential prerequisites and consequences of strong occupational organization than would more hidden and isolated shelters.

CONTINGENCIES OF MARKET SHELTERS

In order for an occupation to establish a monopoly, or even a lesser but stable shelter, it must in essence gain control over determining both the number and characteristics of those who can offer to provide a defined set of productive tasks for which there is a demand. Such control, however, presupposes either binding agreement by all potential consumers to use only members of the occupation for supplying a defined kind of labor (as occurs in the case of some of those occupations called crafts), or the imposition of legal controls by the polity, which either require or make it difficult for consumers to do otherwise than use only the labor of bona fide members of the occupation (as occurs in the case of some of those occupations called professions). In the former case perhaps more than the latter, the practical characteristics of the industry in which a particular occupation is employed—its seasonal character, for example, its geographic concentration or dispersion, the presence of a monopsony, or the industry's vulnerability to interruptions of production—are critical considerations. (For a provocative case study, see Zeitlin, 1979. For a more general discussion of organizational and bargaining factors bearing on shelters, see Freedman, 1976: 39-65.)

In the latter case of legal controls, on the other hand, which the literature on the professions has emphasized, rather more intangible and perhaps ideological judgments figure alongside practical industrial characteristics. Restrictive licensing equally of such professions as medicine and dentistry and such occupations as barbering and tatooing seems to have depended on persuading key members of the polity that the public good would best be served by those who had a defined course of approved training thought to assure a minimally acceptable level of competence in performing a defined set of tasks (see Shimberg et al., 1973). In addition, the tasks themselves are evaluated as being of such importance to the public good that leaving them unregulated would be undesirable. Such notions of public good and functional importance to which occupations seeking support appeal, of course, must be compatible with the larger ideology connected with social control by those classes or elites which are dominant in the political economy of the society (see Larson, 1977: 208-244), although it would be greatly mistaken to assume that in any complex industrial society, with all its nooks and crannies, those relations are simple, or unilateral, or functionally direct for most occupations.

A shelter in a labor market thus presupposes some method for restricting the use of a particular kind of labor by consumers. It also presupposes some method of identifying those bona fide members whose offer of labor is to be sheltered. In such organized occupations as professions and crafts, recruitment, training, and identification of competent members is largely under their control, as has sometimes also been the case of less putatively skilled occupations. Whatever the case, the modes by which members of an occupation are recruited, trained, and labeled bona fide for use by consumers are clearly important dimensions for the analysis of how a labor market shelter can be established and maintained. Recruitment, training, and placement methods also affect the quantity and quality of occupational membership, the shape of the work career, and the quality of work itself. And, by shaping the experience of the member, they also play a part in the generation and maintenance of occupational identity and commitment.

THE OCCUPATIONAL CORPORATION

Another dimension presupposed by a secure shelter in a labor market is the capacity of an occupation to negotiate collectively as an entity with either labor consumers or the polity, and to organize the institutions of recruitment, training, and work placement. This capacity presupposes at the very least some corporate organization on the part of the occupation—a union, guild, association (see Millerson, 1964), or whatever—that can be taken to represent the occupation collectively. It further presupposes a limited number of officials who can testify, lobby, and negotiate legitimately on behalf of the entire membership with the reasonable expectation that the membership will ratify and conform to any agreements reached with significant agents of the economy. The relationship of the collective membership to the formal leadership may be taken to be always problematic, however, not only because of the compromise of varied interests intrinsic to representation rather than direct participation, but also because of the division among members by varying interests due to seniority, prestige, income, and other elements of stratification present in every stable occupation, and by the varying interests and internal demarcation disputes stemming from specialization within the occupation (see Gilb, 1966). Critical to the analysis of the success or failure of an occupation to gain and maintain its shelter is the analysis of its internal stratification and segmentation, and the bearing of those cleavages on the structure of its formal organization and on the effective capacity of its leaders to undertake binding negotiations concerning its place in the labor market.

THE INDUSTRIAL DIVISION OF LABOR

Another dimension that is implied by the very notion of occupation is also critical to establishing a labor market shelter: the composition and characteristics of the division of labor in the industry or situs of which the occupation is a part, and the relation of that occupation to others in that division of labor (Morris and Murphy, 1959). To attain a strong shelter requires carving out firm demarcation boundaries—both horizontal and vertical (Kreckel, 1980: 530-531)—in the face of potential overlap or encroachment on the part of contiguous occupations in a division of labor which may not be expected to accept exclusion without resistance (see Goode, 1960b). Less trained occupations must be prevented from being able to claim automatic ascent on the basis of practical experience, thereby swelling the labor pool beyond the limits of security, just as puddlers attempted to prevent helpers from ascending to their position in the U.S. steel industry (Elbaum and Wilkinson, 1979: 288-289), while occupations with similar tasks and skills must be either firmly excluded or, as medicine dealt with pharmacy, securely coopted (see Kronus, 1976). Most powerful and secure is the uncommon but typologically valuable position of being dominant in a division of labor; that is, of ordering and coordinating the technical tasks of other occupations (Freidson, 1970b). In coping with these issues, both the organization and the content of the division of labor, as well as the number of occupations composing it, may be taken to be variables which have important bearing on the possibility of both establishing a secure shelter in a labor market and maintaining it successfully. Part of the efforts of a successful leadership must address the relation of its members to those of other occupations composing the division of labor of which they are part, and negotiate secure jurisdictional boundaries within it (e.g., Akers, 1968; Orzack, 1977).

TASK, SKILL, AND THEIR CONTINGENCIES

The dimensions I have discussed thus far are directly connected with the process of establishing a stable place for an occupation in an economy. Insofar as they refer to the occupation's relations to the sources of ultimate control of the polity in general and the political economy in particular, they also link the occupation with the larger class system and the firms of the industry in which it works. Those dimensions are not adequate in themselves for explaining satisfactorily the organization that an occupation has or has not gained, however, for they tend to gloss over both the task and its technical contingencies, as well as the social relations of task that are generic to occupation and give it a place in industry. They furthermore gloss over the characteristics of the settings in which work actually takes place, and therefore do not provide adequate linkage between the general agreements constituting the macrostructure and the everyday life of the real people who actually perform productive labor. Without such linkage, we might be able to understand how work gets organized in a general and formal way, but we could not understand how and why it gets done in a particular way; we could chart how an occupation is organized formally, but we could not understand the source and nature of the cleavages and threats that weaken that organization, nor could we link occupation to the everyday experience of its members.

Task forms the link between organization and experience, and must be a key dimension of analysis. However, it is so laden with ambiguities as to present formidable obstacles to any fully satisfactory method of analysis. One problem with it as a variable lies in the fact that except in the most extremely detailed division of labor, members of occupations perform a *set* of tasks rather than merely a single task (Hughes, 1971). The ambiguities of the set of tasks of even such presumably concrete manual occupations as glazier, metalworker, and the like may be seen clearly by inspection of the "Green Book" which collates the agreements arising out of jurisdictional disputes among occupations in the construction trades (e.g., Building Trades Employers' Association, 1973). Ambiguous or not, we cannot avoid the necessity of delineating occupation in part by its tasks, and of accepting those tasks as in some sense objectively determinable even though we must recognize that the choice of tasks to emphasize and the evaluation of tasks are inevitably arbitrary and may rest on an ideological foundation (see Jamous and Peloille, 1970). Of importance for negotiating a secure shelter in a broader occupational division of labor is the capacity to single out for emphasis concrete tasks by which encroachment can be unequivocally identified—as medicine can single out and monopolize prescribing controlled drugs and cutting into the body, for example, but cannot single out "counselling" or "diagnosing." In the absence of defensibly concrete delineation of an exclusive task, an occupation can only defend the exclusive right to a title or a place on a register.

Equally important as defensible delineation of task is the claim that task is of such a character that only members of the occupation possess the skill or qualification, by virtue of their occupational training, to perform it properly and reliably. It is difficult to sustain a claim to the exclusive right to perform a task that anyone might perform just as well. But while there can be no doubt that skill and prior training or experience play some irreducible part in the capacity to do many kinds of specialized work, the problem is that their part is so overlain with social claims and meanings that the precise outline of the irreducible contribution of skill and prior training and experience is always likely to be somewhat unclear.

Workers have to know more and do more on a job than outsiders, and superordinates are inclined to believe (e.g., Kusterer, 1978). But so are workers also inclined to exaggerate the amount of knowledge, skill, and judgment that is involved in some of their everyday work (see Freidson, 1970a). Like task, we must treat skill, training, and prior experience as *claims* which have indeterminate truth value, but which figure significantly nonetheless in the negotiation of shelters and in the interaction of members of an occupation with superordinates, members of contiguous occupations, and clients. From the lessons taught by the historic crafts and professions, we may presume that one condition for successful formal organization is gaining acceptance of claims to the unique qualification of members to perform important kinds of tasks requiring specially trained, esoteric skill.

By naming the tasks of an occupation, and the skill and training said to be prerequisite for their performance, one can begin to delineate the substance of the industry in which it works, its place in the division of labor of that industry, and some of the sources of its success or failure at generating an organized labor market shelter. Additional understanding of the character of its shelter stems from examining the contingencies connected with those tasks and skills. The technical contingencies of task—such as the problems of work stemming from the nature of the physical materials on which work must be done, and from the available tools and knowledge by which work must be done—not only define some of the problems of performing work, but also are invoked by workers to legitimize both their sheltered position as specially trained persons, and their resistance to the use of precise and simple criteria by which to govern the supervision and evaluation of their work (see Jamous and Peloille, 1970).

Apart from the technical contingencies of task, there are also what might be called the social contingencies or *the social relations of task*. They are linked with technical contingencies insofar as the task requires parallel or complementary tasks performed by other workers, and they are intrinsic to tasks which "technically" involve working on human beings or providing them with services. To go into detail about the social relations of occupations' tasks is not possible here, particularly since a large body of empirical material on those social relations and their variations has been built up by case studies of "industrial relations" and by those following the work of

Hughes in studying individual occupations (Hughes, 1971). For the actual analysis of a real occupation, however, details are precisely what is necessary in order to build up a picture of what members of an occupation must cope with during the course of their work, how work is actually performed, and how attitudes toward work, occupation, labor consumers, and others are built up independently of formal training, the broad outlines of the occupation's shelter, and formal occupational ideology. They can also go far toward explaining rank-and-file deviation from the agreements and understandings of the formal leaders of their occupational organization by revealing the grounds of experience at work on which differences get generated.

Everyday work life is not uniform, for what is in theory the same set of tasks for many occupations is practiced in a variety of settings in which the social and even the technical contingencies of task can vary, and in which the actual substance of tasks chosen out of the whole repertory claimed by the occupation can vary. Part of this variation is a function of differentiation into specialities and segments within a complex occupation (see Bucher and Strauss, 1961), but part also is a function of differences among different work settings serving different labor consumers with different powers (see Strauss et al., 1964; Laumann and Heinz, 1979). In fact, within any reasonably large and complex occupation there are likely to be major divisions among the membership reflecting the fact that work goes on in distinctly different kinds of settings, with different social contingencies of task. Having to cope with different technical and social contingencies in different work settings, plus having to perform different tasks for labor consumers of different powers and needs both create deeply felt differences in work experience and interest which can pose a serious challenge to the unity of the occupation and therefore its capacity to maintain its shelter in the face of occupational encroachment or consumer initiatives.

Variations in the social contingencies of task may also be seen to influence the degree and type of shelter an occupation can attain. When labor consumers are composed of a large number of heterogeneous and unorganized individuals, as is the case for medical patients, for example, the occupation can more easily organize itself for its own ends (see Johnson, 1972: 51). When, on the other hand, the consumers are rather few in number and powerful and knowledgeable as well, it is less likely for an occupation to be able to organize itself, though a monopsonist can deliberately choose to provide an occupation with a monopoly (Lees, 1966: 13), even if not allow it to pursue goals of which it disapproves. Surely the predominately corporate consumers of engineering services have something to do with the weak organization of the "profession" in comparison to that of medicine (see Larson, 1977: 19-31).

THE SOCIAL PSYCHOLOGY OF OCCUPATIONAL MEMBERSHIP

Thus far, I have dealt with a number of well-known dimensions of occupational analysis, showing how it is possible to deal with them systematically by connecting them more or less directly with the process by which a labor market shelter is created and maintained by an organized occupation claiming jurisdiction over a particular set of tasks, practiced in particular settings with particular contingencies. I assume enough has been said to show how it is possible to make sense both of an organized occupation's relation to the macrostructure and of the patterned character of its members' experience and performance at work. It remains to show how those dimensions interact with the social psychology of occupational membership.

In essence, it can be argued that the labor market shelter of an occupation provides the structural resource by which the "absorptiveness" of an occupation (Kanter, 1977c: 25-30) can be established and sustained, and by which the member's identity, commitment, and solidarity can be understood. A primary structural resource is established by an occupational organization when it secures a shelter in the labor market. Once that shelter is given, and labor supply maintained advantageously in relation to labor demand, those who become members of the occupation can count on a relatively secure life career of performing the work of that occupation. This possibility alone tends to generate identification with the occupation on the part of its members; the frequent necessity of investing time and money in a special course of training established by the occupation intensifies the likelihood (see Becker and Carper, 1956). Only when one can count on performing it for a considerable period of time is it likely that the work of an occupation can become a "central life-interest" (Dubin et al., 1976), that the occupation can become a source of personal identity, and that its members can develop some sense of common occupational experience, identity, and interest, some "occupational community" (Salaman, 1974).

As in the case of the other dimensions, it is not possible to dwell on any detail here, but surely a labor market shelter which permits the life-long practice of a particular kind of work with some modicum of security and dignity (but by no means necessarily a high income) provides the "orderly career" which encourages commitment to both the occupation and its particular work. At the very least, it creates vested economic interest in the occupation's shelter and its defense, an interest shared with other members of the occupation and expressed as "solidarism" in collective action (see Kreckel, 1980: 540-541). In the case of the historic crafts and professions, it has also on occasion sustained interest in the intrinsic rewards of the work itself, a preoccupation with the extension and refinement of knowledge and technique, and a sense of responsibility for their integrity (Carr-Saunders and Wilson, 1933: 284-288) or, as Mills (1951) put it, an "ethic of craftsmanship." However rare such an ethnic may be, and however vulnerable to economic interest, it is difficult to imagine it to be equally common among those participating in transient and unorganized occupations. Similarly, while we would expect the latter to feel alienated from their work, it is possible to imagine sheltered occupations to manifest *commitment* to their work.

While its mere existence is insufficient ground for explaining attitudes to work and the quality of work performance, it can be hypothesized that a shelter *permits* the development of commitments and interests that other features of occupational organization and task-performance may then actually stimulate and facilitate. The shelter may thus be seen to be at once part of the broad political economy of a complex industrial society—a special niche defining the boundaries of opportunity for members of an occupation in the labor market of that political economy—and the conditioning ground for the interaction among workers over their problems of work which establishes their consciousness, identity, commitment, and performance as they seek autonomy in the market at large, and in the concrete settings in which they perform their work.

By focusing on shelters, we establish systematic linkage between macro-structure and microstructure, and also preserve the conception of occupation as something more than mere job titles in a firm, or mere particles of class, correlates of income and education, vehicles for social mobility. Occupation can be treated *sui generis* as activities around which groups can be formed as their members seek autonomy and control over their particular and distinctive work. The variety of occupations can be conceived of as a variety of successes and failures in their "market project," some being creatures solely of their employers' demands, others gaining shelters of varying degrees of autonomy. Analysis of the conditions for success and failure links together the conventional variables of occupational analysis which have for far too long remained disconnected.

PART II

CULTURAL AND SOCIETAL CONTEXT

IT IS OUR position that several sources of social control influence occupational autonomy at the group and role levels: cultural and societal, organizational, occupational, and client control. The focus of this chapter is how cultural values and societal norms affect occupation autonomy, i.e., how occupations cope with controls generated from outside the occupations.

Because we are also studying work, a few preliminary issues are first introduced to provide a focus for the examination of occupational autonomy: what are the cultural values associated with work in American society today? Have these changed, and if so, in what directions? Many would answer that the dominant cultural value is: men should work. Others would ask: what is the cultural value associated with women and work? Are these values different, and if so, how? If these values are different, do men and women hold different orientations to work with varying degrees of commitment and involvement? Consequently, do they choose and are they chosen for different occupations?

Not all of these questions can be answered by the two studies in this chapter. They are raised, however, to stimulate students to consider how cultural values about work shape the way occupations are structured and the possible consequences for occupation autonomy at the group and role levels.

Some of the questions are now areas of systematic research, and evidence seems to be accumulating which supports the premise that men and women are rejecting some of the traditional values regarding work and family (see Kanter, 1978b; U.S.A. Today, 1981; Yankelovich, 1981). A recent national study reports that both men and women listed a personal sense of accomplishment as the primary reason for working (Harris Poll in U.S. Today,

1981: 2). This report concludes that in the 1980s, experimentation by employers and families will continue as new modes of adaptation appear which reflect changing views on the responsibilities for care of home and children. Perhaps men will be asking a new question, one frequently raised by women: how do I combine a career and family?

Another set of questions are associated with the cultural value of work: who works, who does not work, and who can strike and when. In his third encyclical, "On Human Work," Pope John Paul II acknowledges the right of workers to strike.

> One method used by unions in pursuing the just rights of their members is the strike or work stoppage, as a kind of ultimatum to the competent bodies, especially the employers. This method is recognized by Catholic social teaching as legitimate in the proper conditions and within just limits. In this connection workers should be assured the right to strike [1981: 240].

Society's need to control certain groups of workers during certain economic periods has sometimes resulted in some groups agreeing to forfeit the right to strike. In 1974, for example, the steel-workers agreed to accept a no-strike agreement in their contract negotiations. The particulars of the negotiation process are unknown. However, such a decision by these workers seems to reflect considerable pressure from those in power concerned with societal needs for economic growth and survival in the world marketplace. In this case, the shared interest was to negotiate so that the steel industry in the United States could remain competitive with those of Japan and Europe.

In 1981, however, another group of workers was unwilling to give up its basic right to strike (if such a right exists somewhere). This group represented professional government workers whose skills were essential to maintain economic stability across nations. The professional air traffic controllers union (PATCO) was unable in the summer of 1981 to renegotiate a contract with the government after the initial agreement was not acceptable to the workers who argued that the government had misrepresented its position.

This case is particularly interesting because it highlights some of the problems of occupational autonomy that emerge when highly skilled workers are employed in large, complex structures, especially government organizations. Also, this case demonstrates where real power resides and how swiftly it can be applied. Furthermore, the legitimacy of government action was widespread in society as most people accepted the position that the striking air controllers should be fired, and probably not rehired. These workers were accused of trying to hold the government and consequently the entire nation as hostages; such an action was perceived by many as workers abusing their power. The public, in general, was satisfied when President Reagan carried out his warning to the workers: work or be fired.

Why the President's threat with "the big stick" did not result in air traffic controllers returning to work is an empirical question. Whether or not the President's decision to fire striking workers will hold is a legal question. At this time, the official organization, PATCO, has been "decertified" by the Federal Labor Relations Board.

Another interesting facet of the same case is related to who works and who does not. Because of the impact of the strike on other workers in the airline industries, e.g., pilots, the demand for workers has shifted and in some cases decreased. While the pilots did not support the controllers' strike and did not openly argue against their dismissal, the pilots have been affected adversely by the controllers' actions.

One of the effects is a temporary reduced need for pilots because of decreased airline schedule demands and capabilities resulting from the controllers' strike. As organized, professional workers (American Pilots Association), pilots have a great degree of autonomy to negotiate in the workplace and thus, to a great extent, to determine who will work. Several airline companies at this time have agreed to pilots' requests to reduce their flying time (and payment) in order to prevent unemployment among them.

A further question emerges from the above case: is the right to strike and the right to autonomy in the same decision area? Pilots have autonomy and can strike. They, however, have the major responsibility for the safety of passengers, cargo, and equipment. Similar to the physician role, the pilot is the captain of the team at the role level. While there are a variety of pressures on the pilot and rules and regulations from the Civil Aeronautics Board, it is the pilot who decides whether the wheels leave the ground. Similarly, it is the surgeon who decides if the operation will be done and how.

Both of these occupations, medicine and aviation, have considerable autonomy grounded and legitimated in their professional organizations. Both of these occupations are legitimated through license and mandate to conform to a set of occupation norms which reflect cultural values. The right to strike exists for these occupations. However, because of the autonomy available at the group and role level for the majority of such workers, such a right is not often exercised.

It would be interesting and enlightening to study the societal value attached to the right to strike, its meaning and implementation across cultures, by comparing occupations within nations and across nations. As in the case illustrated above, air controllers from countries outside the United States supported the American air traffic controllers' strike against the government. While the support was short-lived, important sociological questions can be raised: does one occupation have the power to economically, politically, and structurally change the power relationships of the entire global social system? What is the significance of occupation as a type of social organization in and of itself? How does separate occupational analysis link occupations to the larger class system so that we understand further why some occupations are granted autonomy at the group and role levels?

While the two studies in this section are primarily about norms and values which are reflected in the whole society, their scope is limited relative to the questions raised previously. These are up-dated essays drawn from *Varieties of Work Experience,* and demonstrate, to some extent, that norms and values may change and that these changes affect occupational roles.

Law as a profession is organized, as Cynthia Epstein notes, so that women are underrepresented in proportion to their numbers in the labor force. Because women are systematically structured out of law (as well as medicine, academia, and so forth at the higher levels), the organization of the occupation itself reflects the cultural values concerning the woman's place. The internal organization of law as an occupation reflects the larger society, in that few women will attain the same prestige, rights, and duties as their male counterparts. The idea of universalistic standards which are supposed to apply to occupational members obviously do not apply to these women professionals. Nor do universalistic standards apply to all males who enter law as a profession. Informal structures develop in all occupations which systematically reward certain qualified people more than others equally qualified; the social control system of the profession itself operates to undermine a variety of groups and individuals.

Epstein notes that some changes occurred during the 1970s, but women in professions today are still deescalating their ambitions. One explanation she offers is that people still perceive it to be ideologically incorrect for women to aspire to high status professions. The ideological debate continues between radical feminists, who oppose the assumption by women of what they label "male" values, and the old-timers, who believe it is "unfeminine" for women to seek success in "male" terms.

Today we are beginning to observe changes in this cultural norm, and we will perhaps see changes in several occupations and industries. However, these changes will come slowly until there is tolerance in society for women in authority positions in the work role. As Epstein notes, the current, normative occupational structure is functional to the degree that social interaction is easy and competition among males and females at work is reduced. But changing this aspect of the role network will likely affect other work and non-work-related roles between males and females. The conflict is likely to be covert since control coming from cultural norms and social values requires some degree of support from existing institutions. In work and nonwork roles, women will need to develop a set of ethics whereby autonomy and discretion seem appropriate.

But more importantly, the acceptance of women into elite professions and positions in organizations requires tolerance by male members of these professions. They regulate the opportunities that allow mobility into the key positions. The degree to which change can result will be determined significantly by male acceptance of competition with women. However, another condition is required. The "consciousness" of women must be raised so that unification occurs and women help increase this tolerance.

Epstein is focusing on women. However, she is presenting a societal problem which can be generalized to other occupational groups. How the societal values work both on women and men to help them define their own roles and how such values are reflected in a variety of occupations and their organization should be explored further by students. Epstein's study provides clues for this further investigation.

Whereas women are systematically structured out of law, medicine, the ministry and academia, and other occupational groups, housewifery by definition and in actuality could not exist in its present form without women. Jessie Bernard is presenting two models in Western thought which have been reflected in policy. She argues that our thinking is handicapped by the incompatible assumptions, values, and goals of the two models—economic versus societal, pre-industrial versus industrial. In the actual operation of the housewife role with its low prestige, isolation, and lack of tangible rewards, the satisfaction for women may be negligible. Yet the institutions of society still provide intangible rewards. The role of the housewife is seen as "normal" and appropriate for women. On the other hand, the housewife role, though autonomous, is by itself low in prestige and has no economic rewards except through the husband's status and position. Jessie Bernard is suggesting that social norms can be changed and that the role of housewife can and should be brought into the economic world. By her definition, housewifery at this time is not an occupation. But by our definition, the housewife role *is* an occupation because it is a social role with economic ramifications and, for many housewives, it occupies most of their time. This is not a disagreement, because all agree that the labor performed as a housewife is not rewarded by the same standards as other similar occupations. The dilemma facing the housewife may be reflected in her role performance. More important is the larger problem of whether the functional differentiation of work roles by sex is indeed disappearing and whether such differentiation should disappear.

Jessie Bernard, in her discussion of the post-industrial housewife, argues that the emerging occupations in the technological revolution are not yet sex-differentiated. The communication industry will be a significant one, especially as it affects service requirements and products. Business service will be a dominant product and especially open to female employment, particularly to the housewife, who will be able to perform her work at home because of the revolution in communication and computer industries. Whether house-wives will elect to choose an alternative work place, home instead of office or factory, and what the impact of this decision will be on occupational role autonomy are interesting questions for further sociological inquiry.

CHAPTER THREE

AMBIGUITY AS
SOCIAL CONTROL
Women in Professional Elites

Cynthia Fuchs Epstein

OVER THE PAST decade, social and legal attention has been focused on the underrepresentation of Blacks, Puerto Ricans, Mexican-Americans, and other disadvantaged groups of Americans in law, medicine, science, and other elite professions. This concern was extended to the underrepresentation of women in this period.

The exclusion process in the professions has always been more than a simple matter of quotas on new recruits. Even today, as formal quotas have been eliminated through changes in the law, the professional community embodies a social control system, a system of rewards and punishments, that sifts recruits on their entrance to careers and their way to the top. The present analysis asserts that the social control system undermines the motivation and participation of persons who possess statuses viewed as negative by the gatekeepers of the professions;[1] our inquiry focuses on the control system as it affects women in particular.[2]

Membership in an elite profession is synonomous with "success" in American society. Although the number is growing, the proportion of women in the professions remains low, and the larger society, which until recently has not especially noted their absence, does not believe that women aim for occupational success or that it is fitting for them to do so. Even when women do attain professional success, they are usually judged by a set of standards very different from those applied to men.[3]

Success in the professions is more than a matter of membership or even commitment and talent. The "real" world of the professional—the area in which he or she will battle for recognition and success—begins with legal, medical, or academic training, but does not end there. In the "community" (Goode, 1957) of profession into which the graduates enter, women find themselves unwelcome and unable to perform to their full ability or even to learn the norms for performance.

Of course, all such systems do reward talent and hard work for many of their members. In addition, since not all who enter are equally endowed, many men and women will achieve no more than a modest success. It has been suggested that women do not do well in certain professions because they lack talent for specific types of work, or perhaps because they cannot or do not work hard.[4] But some of the evidence suggests that the women in some professions are at least equal to their male colleagues in potential at the *early* stages of their careers.

L. R. Harmon (1965) and Jonathan Cole (1971) have assembled data indicating that women graduate students and professionals in the social and physical sciences have, on the average, higher IQs than their male peers.[5] In my first study of women lawyers (Epstein, 1968), close to one-third of a randomly picked sample had been law review *editors* while in law school (until recently, only those students ranking in the top 10 percent of their class were invited to join law review staffs). Further, women who have carried out preliminary, unpublished investigations for feminist groups report that college administrators have admitted privately that higher grade averages have been required for women's admissions. And over the years, many law schools have imposed quotas on female entrants, thereby assuring that female students were more rigorously selected than the men.

These data suggest that, at least up to the time of beginning their professional work, women are not conspicuously deficient. What happens afterward?

SOCIAL CONTROL IN THE PROFESSIONS

Analysis of the problems women face is instructive in identifying the "holding operations" of the society's stratification system; the mechanisms which ensure women's poor representation in the professional elites are generally the self-maintaining mechanisms of the stratification system. This analysis suggests that these mechanisms facilitate passage into the elite for those who are preferred, and hinder or exclude those regarded as inappropriate.

For the preferred, those with desired status-sets, the path to success is made clear. The status-sequence from recruit to full member is outlined, and the person who deviates is rerouted with further information about how to perform on course. The messages are direct, instructive, and motivating. For the recruit who is defined as inappropriate and regarded as outside the system and incapable of becoming part of it, the messages are less clear, often ambiguous, and contradictory.

No doctor becomes a brilliant diagnostician simply by going to school, nor can a lawyer become a persuasive courtroom advocate by taking courses. There are no objective tests for competence at high levels. Here, the status-judges of the profession, and to some extent one's clients, bestow the crown of competence. Lawyers do not really learn law until they have had the experience of handling real cases and courtroom situations.[6] They learn some things through trial and error, but learn more from the tutoring of an older partner who sees it as a duty to guide the neophyte through the maze.

In medicine, law, and the academic world (and this is true for business as well), competence is created by exposing the new professional to the task, giving him or her the opportunity to learn the tricks and avoid the pitfalls. The professional is given access to persons who can help and information about the important people in the system. The accepted newcomer learns by observing and performing, because he or she is put in a position in which it is possible to observe, and where he or she must perform. Important colleagues will watch and give feedback vital for improvement as a professional.

Those who teach the young professional and those who lead the profession usually agree that the "appropriate" candidates are competent and will later become more competent in important ways beyond their talents and formal training, and the "inappropriate" candidates cannot become competent. It is believed that those with the "wrong" statuses cannot be part of the subtle, informal collegial system, will be unable to catch the messages, will be ill-prepared in the necessary etiquette of professional behavior and rules of reciprocity, and will be incapable of proper behavior toward a hierarchy that may not be clearly labeled (see Epstein, 1970a). Cleverness is not sufficient, nor is a medical or law degree, even from a "proper" school. Because failure is presumed, few will act as sponsor to prepare the unwanted professional for a successful career.

The person with the "wrong" sex status or social status may succeed, idiosyncratically, as a "deviant," and without the systematic set of rewards and punishments by which the professionals within the system acquire standards and professional taste and learn to identify with the occupational status so that it becomes a defining part of the self. The latter enlists the person in the elite social control system by socializing him to monitor his own behavior, his professional commitment and aspirations, by reference to the norms of the profession (Goode, 1957).

The general socialization process and the control system which further socializes professionals within their profession give them a different orientation toward work than people in lower level occupations. Typically, professionals rank high on scales of work satisfaction (Richard Hall, 1975) and job commitment, and they have high aspirations and personal involvement in their work (Gross, 1958: 78). This is predictable not only because their material rewards are great[7] and their work is interesting,[8] but because they are also subject to a social control system which reinforces this commitment (Goode, 1957: 194).

Furthermore, the social control system of the professionas usually interacts with the social control systems of the larger society in a harmonious way. Performance to high professional standards is highly regarded and respected, and often the professional is asked to serve on public committees and to aid in decisions affecting the larger society. Similarly, poor performance by a member of the professional community typically means that the larger community will also regard the person as a failure and not worthy of respect, although he may be a decent person and community member. Indeed, the community will often grant the dedicated professional exemption from community responsibilities in the belief that he is serving the community better by performing his occupational role.[9]

The standards of professionalization are usually left by the community to the professions to decide. Thus, the measure of the individual's worth, criteria of performance, and recruitment selection are all set internally. The profession's elite are the norm-setters and the gatekeepers of the profession (Oswald Hall, 1946). Their standards and their evaluations determine who rises and who falls.

Until recently, the selection mechanisms of the professional elites have remained largely unquestioned, even though they have not been devoted to judging the functionally specific capacities of recruits. The professions have usually limited their selection to recruits of like kind, insisting that they come equipped not only with the techniques of craft but also the preferred statuses of class, ethnicity, race, and sex.[10]

Discriminatory professional recruitment has not been considered unjust by the outside community, but rather as part of the natural order of things. Furthermore, because of their high place in the outside community, elites in the professions and other decision-making spheres have been able to maintain control and counter challenges to their legitimacy. There is no doubt that the acceptance of this system by the outside society, including those who are excluded, comes not only from lack of power or resignation, but also from acceptance of the idea that those who are rewarded *are* worthy, that some are "suited" to enter these spheres and others not, and that *what is, is right.* Certainly, women as a group have typically believed in their own inadequacy to compete for high positions in society, thus becoming conspirators in their own exclusion.

The mechanisms of exclusion affecting women are similar to those affecting *all* disadvantaged groups. But women do constitute a special situation.

My interviews with female lawyers and other professionals in the 1960s and early 1970s were filled with experiences of differential treatment stemming from the fact that they were women as well as lawyers. Remarkably, the victims showed little sense of outrage. They were often aware that the definitions of justice for female professionals varied substantially from the definitions applied to men, both within the professional community and outside of it.[11] As a group, for lawyers of their age, ability, and experience, they voluntarily chose to work at levels beneath their capabilities and expressed lack of commitment to the profession by taking part-time jobs. A few women who had strong aspirations early in their careers radically reduced them. Although men do this as well, it is clear that the overwhelming majority of men in similar positions (for example, with three or four years' investment in their career) push hard to get ahead. The paucity of striving was evident in the cases of the women studied, but what was more striking was their belief that reducing aspiration was entirely appropriate and that they did it without regret. This situation changed somewhat in the 1970s, as female law students and lawyers revised their images of self and their images as professionals; yet enough residue of the pattern remains to note the process which still tends to keep women on the lower end of the professional hierarchy.

TYPES OF REWARD-PUNISHMENT AMBIGUITY

The manipulation of rewards and punishments in the professions and in the larger society creates ambiguities for women which often cripple their larger professional attainments.

A positive relationship between work, approval, and advancement is construed by society as "justice"; conversely, a lack of reward for excellence is seen as "injustice."[12] But the clarity of this equation does not appear to extend to women with regard to reward for work. It is clear that women who go into law practice have had a tougher time in developing a "successful" career than have men. In the past, 2 to 3 percent of women in the field managed to pass through the hiring grid. My 1960s study showed that, among those who got jobs, certain discernible patterns evolved. Many went into government service (as did Black professionals), or they entered family practices with husbands or fathers. Some who married men with good incomes—and most who married, married lawyers—chose to do voluntary work for the Legal Aid Society or other community organizations. A few actually were hired by large firms. Some had the idiosyncratic experience of encountering a "sex-blind" hiring partner who was merely looking for talent. World War II also created opportunities as the young men went away. Some women were hired on a temporary basis for special work assignments and managed to stay on because they had become specialists in areas of work which the firm had come to depend on. Most women who were lured by the "big" firms staffed the back offices, however, doing "blue sky" research (keeping account of state securities law changes), trusts and estates, and less often, tax law.

Some women "made it" to the highest prestige careers on Wall Street, but not many. In his now classic book, *The Wall Street Lawyer,* Erwin Smigel (1964) reported counting 18 women in Wall Street firms. In 1968, I estimated a universe of 40 women and interviewed 6 with Wall Street experience.

The climate of the country began to change in the late 1960s. As part of this change, the women's movement was developing and having its effect on women's entry into the occupations dominated by men. But, although women were doing better than before, only 2 percent of partners in large firms today are women, an increase in *absolute* numbers over the past, but still a tiny proportion.

High-ranking jobs attained by female lawyers in the past decade are still few, and even those who became the 2 percent of judges or partners may not be as successful as the men who constitute their reference group. Many judges, for example, feel they could have gotten an appointment to a more prestigious court had they been men.

The rewards of female professionals may also be more closely linked to their female status than to their status as professionals. These situations are not uncommon in other elite systems in which women are rewarded in terms of their female status rather than their own occupational status or roles. Bright female graduate students are often satisfied with gifts of approval and attention from professors for whom they work, and are content with the vicarious pleasure of contributing ideas as an ancillary partner.

Like wives who act as research assistants for their husbands (without benefit of title), they are seldom given co-authorship or even footnotes acknowledging specific contributions. Like the wives, they are given florid acknowledgments in prefaces. But professional reputations are built on publication and citation, not on dedications.

Because women are typically considered to be outside the exchange system, the rewards for their efforts may not correspond to normative exchange rates. Furthermore, if they accept love instead of money where money is appropriate, they are conspirators in driving their own price down or in accepting alternative definitions of the worth and kind of performance they are rendering, and the goals they are seeking. Instead of becoming a true disciple, entitled to the senior person's sponsorship for launching her career, the woman is defined as being outside the system. I suspect that women's talents in professional activity often go unnoticed because of this phenomenon. On the other hand, their work is still utilized and "waste" is reduced.

Women's talent is probably tapped in this way more than the talent of any other group of "outsiders." The others' prices may be too high in that, unlike women, they would insist on being brought into the system.

Despite the ambiguities of the reward system, women, like their male colleagues, are "punished" by the profession for violating its norms. The women in my studies who worked part-time and had discontinuous career lines made less money on the average than their male colleagues and were not awarded high-ranking jobs. Since they did not aim high and exhibited little assertiveness, they were not given career-line jobs or assigned clients who could assure them positions of power. Their histories illustrate that there are certain absolute professional standards which, if not met, result in negative consequences.

The ambivalence-producing mechanisms which reduce women's representation at the top of the elite structures are shown clearly in the cases of women who are *not rewarded for good professional performances* and who are *punished for good professional performance.* The latter is the result of role-conflict stemming from expectations that fulfillment of professional role obligations will entail violation of role obligations attached to the woman's sex and family statuses.[13]

Many of the female lawyers interviewed felt they were underrewarded for good professional performance. Many had the experience of seeing men in their firms rising to partnership while they were frozen at associate rank despite demonstrably equivalent competence. Even women who could be considered successful by male career standards often feel relatively deprived; that is, they believe they should be regarded as *great!*

Part of the problem stems from women's lack of power in the bargaining process. Power is itself a reward, but a degree of power must somehow be attained to bargain successfully for more. No powerful client will permit an important case to be handled by an associate, and many associates achieve partnership for this reason, but women do not often have powerful clients who will press the firm to make them partners. One lawyer interviewed who had long waited for partnership pointed out that if she had brought a substantial number of clients to the firm, she could not have been refused partnership because she could have threatened to leave and take them with her.

The female attorneys I interviewed felt that they had to "be better" than male lawyers. But being better only gave them the opportunity to be where they were; it was needed to cancel the disadvantage of their negative sex-status, and they did not feel it necessarily gave them an entree to career advancement. Some felt that since more effort did not win them promotion, there was little sense in commitment to hard work, and they refused extra or overtime assignments.

The case of the woman who succeeds in her profession but is punished for supposed violation of her female role obligations—a violation which is presumed if she is a success—is equally destructive. Here the woman is the object of sanctions, both from those in the professional sphere who believe that success detracts from a woman's feminity, and from those in her family who feel that her success makes their relationships insecure or uncomfortable.

Although men acquire added ranking in *all* spheres when they are rated a success in their work, at times the woman seems to be subject to a zero-sum evaluation in which the greater her occupational accomplishment, the more likely she is to be rated lower in her performance of female roles. This evaluation is usually not based on whether or not she can take care of both her clients and family, but is due to cultural *assumptions* that she is neglecting her family.[14]

The successful woman lawyer continually meets expressions of ambivalence in the evaluation of her role performance. Respondents reported being told that they were taking work away from less successful male lawyers. They were told that they "thought like a man" by their colleagues, who offered it as a compliment but implied that they were less of a woman for it. Successful women who did trial work claimed that opposing attorneys complained that they often won by female "wiles"; but other respondents were told by male lawyers that female attorneys who do not use wiles are "masculine." Here, women are subjected to the "damned if you do, damned if you don't" syndrome experienced by other people with negatively evaluated statuses (Merton, 1957b: 426).

Some women today find that they have to deescalate their ambitions because other people find that behavior ideologically incorrect. Most radical feminists as well as moderates of all persuasions oppose the assumption by women of what they call "male" values. Ideological lines were drawn in the early 1970s and continue today between women who feel it legitimate and appropriate to work primarily for high status and money, and those who believe it morally wrong and ideologically incorrect. This latter group differs from the old-timers who believe it was "unfeminine" for women to seek success in "male" terms. They believe that women have been prevented from achieving success, which has the *benefit* of removing them from the corruption of the "rat race." They argue that a movement of women toward internalizing "establishment" values would mean capitalizing on the opportunity presented by an illegitimate opportunity structure.

To some extent women have the same experiences as men who are being phased out of the running for important jobs. The messages, for example, are disguised as protective "concerns." One respondent reported that an employer denied her promotion because "it would be too demanding of her energy"; another because she would be hurt by hostility in a truly male domain. Some women saw through such explanations and experienced them as sanctions, but many accepted them at face value. This was especially so when it was a husband-partner who was "protecting" her from her profession.

The sanctions attached to violation of female role-performance are often relevant where women are experiencing professional success. The women who make high professional incomes rarely seem to view these as a desired symbol of success or an unmitigated reward. There is evidence that some respondents would view a sharp gain in income as an intolerable burden on their relationships with their husbands, whereas few men view a rise in their incomes as a burden or destructive to their other roles.

These professional women's "sense of reward" was related to their husbands' incomes. They reported a sense of accomplishment from their earnings, but it was true that those reporting the highest incomes generally were married to wealthy men and conceded that their personal earnings had ceased to matter. For women, financial reward may not have the consequence of motivating them for future performance in the same way it does for men. Significantly, as many high-income respondents dropped out of practice as stayed in.

The case of the woman who does not comply with professional norms but is rewarded anyway is sociologically interesting because it runs counter to common sense and arouses the cultural distaste reserved for those who "get something for nothing." This involves two sets of phenomena: too much acclaim for routine performance; and acclaim for little or no performance. In the latter case, the woman typically violates professional norms by her lack of commitment, working only occasionally or dropping out altogether at the peak of her career; yet she continues to enjoy prestige in her family and community, although probably not in her profession. She is honored for *having been* a lawyer, although a man who leaves the profession and does not work is generally labeled a has-been and a failure.

Women, especially married women, settle for lower incomes because having any income gives them a feeling of accomplishment and making too much might cause trouble. Even many single female lawyers in my study who were concerned about providing for themselves did not have high economic aspirations.

For female lawyers especially, membership in a high-ranking male occupation is itself an indicator of great success to the world outside the profession. The women in the study who had a network of friends who were not lawyers felt little impulse to rise within the profession; they had attained sufficient rank by just entering law. The woman's network, whether or not her friends were working women, was always important to her evaluation of her career.

The ambivalence of expectations and rewards faced by women professionals arises from the following conflict:

(1) Normative prescriptions for attainment of occupational success require that the professional demonstrate commitment, talent, and hard work.

(2) But normative prescriptions weigh against women's occupational success because the female role requires a lack of assertiveness and a noncompetitive work role vis-à-vis men, and is assumed to require a fundamental commitment to home and family.

(3) There are also normative prescriptions that women are incapable of conforming to professional norms, with the consequence that different standards are applied to their performance.

(4) Women professionals are subject to a contradictory reward structure which may confer rewards not commensurate with the levels of their performance or contributions to the profession. Further, success may brand them as failures in the larger society, or, concomitantly, failure in a profession may result in rewards from the larger society.

Although the control systems of the elite professions violate the rule of universalism with respect to women, this violation does not undermine the professions' general normative structure. Within the professions, by undermining the motivation of women to engage their talents at the highest levels, this control process maintains the cohesion of the collegial group, makes for ease of social intercourse in the male legal community, and reduces competition.

NOTES

1. As in my other analyses of women's place in the professions, the discussion of the dynamics of status-set interaction draws on the conceptualizations of Robert K. Merton, which have not as yet reached print, but which have reached audiences through "oral publication" (again, his concept) over the past decade in lectures at Columbia University.

2. The analysis presented here developed from earlier inquiries (1965-66) into the place of women in the professions (Epstein, 1968, 1970b). The insights and theory presented derived from intensive personal interviews with 65 lawyers who practice in New York City and environs chosen from the Martindale-Hubbel Law Directory. Although this discussion leans on their accounts, later studies added interviews with female doctors, social scientists, physical scientists, architects, journalists, and administrators. Their career profiles and experiences have given further evidence that the patterns suggested by earlier interviews were indeed institutionalized in other elite professional spheres.

3. Harriet Zuckerman has brought to my attention one example of the different and lower standards used in evaluating the eminence of women as compared with men in American society. Because Americans of achievement listed in *Who's Who*, a directory of prominent people in the United States, tend to be almost entirely men, a separate volume, *Who's Who of American Women*, was introduced in 1958. In establishing criteria for inclusion, the editors noted in their preface to the first edition that they were "scaling down" the *Who's Who* standards because (as they said in their letter to potential listees) for women, "national or international prominence . . . is not a requisite." (See Preface to *Who's Who of American Women*, First Edition, 1958-59, and most recent form letter, dated 1968.)

4. Nor are they equally endowed with personal "connections." Connections can be important, especially in steering the neophyte professional to a promising first job, though presumably they are less important in achievement-oriented fields. It is true, however, that under certain circumstances and in certain subfields of the professions, the well-connected lesser talent has opportunities and rewards denied the greater talent.

5. Cole found that women Ph.D.s, as a group, had higher measured intelligence than men at every level and in every field of science, even when controlling for specialization and quality of doctorate department.

6. At this point I feel I must at least note the constraints of language in using the generic "he" for "the person." Although "he or she" would certainly be more appropriate as a substitute, it is awkward. I will restrict my energies currently toward an identification of processes which result in the cultural identification of "professional" with a male-gender pronoun, and leave it to the linguists to come up with a neuter-gender pronoun resonant with language style.

7. Only groups such as the owners and managers of large businesses consistently attain higher incomes than successful professionals. U.S. Department of Commerce, Bureau of the Census (1960: 325).

8. See Richard H. Hall (1975: 70-137) for an analytic review of the literature in the field of professions.

9. Thus the conditions for the creation of role strain are ameliorated by the activation of a number of social mechanisms which reduce it for the professional person—by insulating him and providing him with a hierarchy of priorities (Goode, 1960a; Merton, 1957a).

10. Abel (1963) and Kucera (1963) reported the results of a survey done by the *Harvard Law Record* of 430 private law firms, of all sizes and throughout the country, which indicated extreme resistance to hiring women, members of minority groups, and those candidates with rural backgrounds or fathers in blue collar occupations. Jews, Negroes, and women were most consistently rated negatively. Of all the "deviant" statuses reviewed, the female drew the most negative rating (4.9 on a scale of from zero to plus ten for those least likely to be hired). *Only poor scholarship drew greater opprobrium than being female.*

11. Homans (1961: 325) poses this "role" of distributive justice as: "a man's reward in exchange with others should be proportional to his investments."

12. If, according to Homans, justice is an equation between investment and reward, and women are believed to make less of an investment (background characteristics such as sex, race, and ethnicity are included with hard work as "investments"), then they should not expect as much reward as a man who has "put in" a *higher* investment (i.e., by being male). Homans (1961: 236-237) further suggests that being Negro or a woman is an *unchanging* value, unlike "experience" (another investment), which increases with time. If one takes the legal profession as the context in which the appraisal of justice is

being made, women are not unfairly treated, since it is true that, on balance, women are believed to have a lesser investment in the structure than do men. If "society" is taken as the structure, the balance scale is not as clearly weighted. If women in law (as a group) are taken as structure, then a different system of weights and values surely emerges. We do not agree with Homans that we are using an "olympian" view of justice when we appraise as "injustice" the situation in which women get a lesser reward for hard work than men. Goffman's (1963: 7) perception of the situation seems to hold more truth, that "in America at present, *separate* systems of honor seem to be on the decline," and that even those with so-called "abnormal" characteristics have come to believe that they "deserve a fair chance and a fair break." See George C. Homans's (1961: 232-264) discussion of the "principle of distributive justice" and its application for behavior.

13. This has as source and consequence two types of sociological ambivalence. The first, specified by Robert K. Merton and Elinor Barber (1963), comes from the conflicting demands of different statuses ordinarily involving different people (e.g., demands of the senior partner versus demands of the female attorney's husband). The second is a type in which ambivalence arises from conflicting expectations of role partners in a role-set attached to one status because of visibility of the role incumbent's other statuses.

14. An example of differential expectations directed toward men and women in political elites in Germany is reported by Harriet Holter (1970: 113). In an assessment of attitudes about women active in political life, those holding political office were considered unfeminine and were believed to neglect their families by a majority of people. No such view was held of the men in political life.

CHAPTER FOUR

BETWEEN TWO WORLDS
The Housewife

Jessie Bernard

THERE IS NO category of workers, male or female, which remotely approaches the category of "housewife" in size. Housewives include more than half of all women sixteen years of age and over in the United States.[1] None of the work they do as housewives has economic value in the general sense of the market. Its societal value, however, is generally conceded to be literally incalculable. It is the purpose of this chapter to explore the nature of this paradox in terms of a conflict between two paradigms—the economic and the societal. Much of our thinking about the housewife is handicapped by a gap between these two models, leaving us with policy choices based on incompatible assumptions, values, and goals. Either of these models alone is inadequate to deal with the problems generated by modern industrial trends, and the housewife remains caught between policies based on two incompatible models.

After a brief overview of several versions of the basic conflict between two kinds of models—economic versus societal, status-world versus cash-nexus, pre-industrial versus industrial—the effects on the housewife of these opposing ways of viewing her work will be examined. For example, viewed from the outlook of the economic model, housewifery is not an occupation; the housewife is not in the labor force, nor is she even in industrial society. Viewed from the outlook of the societal paradigm, the housewife is in a status "love and/or duty" relationship to the "clients" she works for. In the last section, proposals for integrating the housewife into modern industrial society will be examined.

INCOMPATIBLE MODELS

The economic and the societal models have been compared and contrasted by Mancur Olson, Jr. (1968: 114), who concludes that:

> the economic and sociological ideals described (by the economic and the societal models) are not only different, but polar opposites: if either one were attained, the society would be a nightmare in terms of the other. . . . The important question is how much of the one ideal to give up in order to get more of the other when you can't get more of both. . . . The economic and sociological ideals, far from both being destroyed by their contradiction with one another, are in fact expressions of the most fundamental alternatives human societies face.

A related contrast has been made between what Talcott Parsons calls the domestic and the occupational worlds, in which the first is governed by particularistic status norms and the second by universalistic, impersonal ones; the first is characterized by traditional norms, the second by rigorously functional ones (Parsons, 1959: 261).

These two statements of the contrasting models are recent versions of a long tradition of social science preoccupation with the revolutionary change in human relationships that came with the industrial revolution. Sir Henry Maine was among the first to analyze it; he characterized the pre-industrial world as a status world and the industrial one then emerging as a contractual world. Others characterized it as a cash-nexus or money-mediated world.

The terms "status" and "cash-nexus" or "money-mediated" worlds are used here since they highlight the particular aspect of the two models considered most relevant to a discussion of the housewife. The housewife works in a status world in which motivation is expected to be based on love and/or duty rather than in a cash-nexus world in which it is taken for granted that motivation is based on wages, salaries, or other monetary incentives. The old saying, "I wouldn't do that for love nor money" recognizes the contrasting motivations in the two worlds. The housewife is called upon to make all the adjustments demanded by the incompatible models.

The position of the housewife is an excellent starting point for a discussion of the difficulties involved in attempting to deal theoretically with the situation. Parsons, for example, has given us his version of how our society in the past has attempted to deal with the matter of incongruent paradigms: only one person in the family could be dealt with according to the economic model; applying the economic model to the domestic world would be disastrous, but applying the societal paradigm to the labor force would be equally so. So the husband was assigned to the cash-nexus world and the wife to the status world.

THE WORK COMPONENT OF HOUSEWIFERY

The actual, specific tasks involved in housewifery vary widely according to the size of the household, income of family, social class standards, facilities and equipment available, and no doubt many other relevant variables. They usually include at least shopping or "procurement," food preparation, cleaning, and laundering. These are all amenable to the same kind of job analysis as the components of any other kind of work. And, in fact, there is a long tradition of such analyses by home economists. In the nineteenth century, for example, the great state colleges of agricultural and mechanical arts had established, along with agricultural and engineering schools for men, schools of home economics for women. Household management was viewed as a perfectly respectable subject in colleges of home economics.

But not all of the efforts to glorify "women's work" succeeded. A woman could be trained to be ever so competent in household management, quite professional, in fact. But housework remained housework. No amount of scientific know-how or romantic glorification in the women's magazines could finally hide the fact that it was low on any prestige scale. Little by little, a change came over the colleges of home economics. Emphasis on the hard sciences increased while interest in domestic skills decreased. There was more physiology and nutrition, less food preservation and cooking; more chemistry of textiles, less sewing; more social psychology, anthropology, and economics of fashion, less tailoring. The schools were now, in brief, training professional women rather than housewives, producing domestic engineers who could design the most efficient arrangements of kitchen equipment.[2] These highly trained women went into the labor force rather than into the home. The women who went into the home still had to carry on the low-level work.

THE HOUSEWIFE IN THE ECONOMIC MODEL

The only component of housewifery that shows up in the economic model is that of "procurement." The housewife does most of the shopping and marketing for food and clothing; she is therefore salient as a consumer. But as a worker, she has no place in the economic model. Her work does not constitute an occupation, she is not in the labor force; she is not even in industrial society.

Housewifery is not an occupation. The housewife does not, according to the economic model, have an occupation. For although running a household may fully occupy most of her working hours, and even though what she does may be the hardest kind of work, it has none of the characteristics associated with an occupation (Bernard, 1971b: 74). Helena Lopata (1971: 139) states:

> There is no organized social circle which tests a candidate and then admits or rejects her on the basis of proven skills. She enters the role "sideways" as an adjunct to the role of wife . . . In addition, the role is not easily located in the occupational and social structure. . . . It lacks the basic criteria of most jobs. It has no organized social circle which judges performance and has the right to fire for incompetence, no specific pay scale, and no measurement against other performers of the same role or against circle members. It is vague, open to any woman who gets married, regardless of ability; it has no union and belongs to to organizational structure.

Why, then, is the housewife included in the present volume? She is included here because her work is, sociologically speaking, *sui generis.* It is wholly outside of the occupational world, a negative case that, by way of contrast, helps to highlight other occupations.

"To housewife" and "to husband" both once meant to economize, to manage with skill and thrift, one a household and the other a farm. In such a sense, the job of housewifery was, and is, the running of a household. The term as either verb or noun specifies the two characterizing aspects of housewifery as a job: it is done in a house and it is done by a wife. Merely having a house as the place of work does not, however, in and of itself set if off from other kinds of work. The same work done by a hired person of either sex is no longer housewifery but rather household management, housework, or stewardship. What renders the housewife sui generis is that her marital status and hence her motivation is part of the job description; it is these aspects that remove her from the labor force.

The housewife is not in the labor force. The housekeeper or the steward is a member of the labor force, but the housewife who does identical work is not. The housewife does not inhabit the same world as do other workers.

The concept of the labor force came in with the industrial revolution. Before then, there really was no such labor force as we know it today. Jaffee and Stewart (1951: 33) define the workforce as including: "those persons who voluntarily offer their services for hire in the labor market (in exchange for which they receive wages or salaries) and who thereby participate (or attempt to participate) in the production of the gross national product." The operant words are "voluntarily," "labor market," and "wages or salaries." So also is "production of the gross national product." But contribution to the gross national product is definitionally prohibited by the fact that housework is not paid for.

If paid for, the contribution of the housewife would vastly increase the gross national product. One study (Groseth, 1970) reports that it would increase our country's national income by almost two-fifths (38 percent), and a forensic economist (Soo, 1969: 271-284) has computed the value of the lost services to a man if his wife dies.[3] But since the housewife's work is not mediated in a labor market, it does not count, and including it in the labor force would not help economists understand the operations of the economy. "It would serve no purpose . . . to include the housewives in a count of the country's working force," because their work, however socially desired, is extra-economic. Hence, including them in the labor force "would have no relevance for the significant economic problems of our times" (Jaffe and Stewart, 1951: 14, 18). Again, since the housewife's work "is outside the characteristic system of work organization or production . . . for the purposes of analyses of the functioning of the economy, as required for social policy decision" (Jaffe and Stewart, 1951: 14), including their extra-economic services would tell us nothing about the labor market or the way the economy was operating.[4]

The housewife is not in industrial society. Not everyone who worked in the primitive factories and mines of the eighteenth century was in the labor force; some were contracted by overseers of the poor who found this kind of employment an excellent way to deal with paupers. But for the most part, workers, especially adult males, were in the labor force voluntarily and were paid wages determined by the labor market. One may cavil at the adjective "voluntary" as applied to men in the labor force, but for most it was not forced, slave, or indentured labor. One may cavil also at the wages paid, but for the most part it was in money. And one may cavil at the concept of market when the positions of hirer and hired were so unequal. Nevertheless, in the industrializing world, men entered a cash-nexus, a world in which relationships were based on money. This was revolutionary and did revolutionize all human relationships.

Most women, however, remained at home, working as hard as ever at their domestic occupations. They did not enter the cash-nexus world mediated by money. They continued to live and work in the status world of the home in which one related to others on the basis of love and/or duty, not money.

The two worlds are widely different. The differences between a non-industrialized and a modern industrialized society are summarized by Jaffe and Stewart (1951: 28) this way:

Non-Industrialized World	*Modern Industrialized World*
Very low level of technological development	Very high level of technological development freeing many from the necessity of producing the needed physical goods
Almost no division of labor	Very highly developed division of labor
Each worker tends to own and control means of production	Control of the means of production largely concentrated in a few persons or in the state
No exchange economy based on cash	Highly developed exchange economy based on cash
No notion of free contract; the culture determines the person's labor activities	Highly developed notion of free contract; the culture does not predetermine the individual's labor activities; rather he enters into free contractual relationships

Since the eighteenth century, an increasing number of men have been moving into the labor force, the money-mediated or cash-nexus world. And in the twentieth century, an increasing number of women have also moved into this world. But the housewife remains in the love and/or duty status world. Some people look back nostalgically to the time before the cash-nexus replaced the pre-industrial love and/or duty status world. Whether or not the money-mediated world is worse than the status world is moot. But one thing is certain: If half the world is in a cash-nexus system and half is not, the half that is not is at a great disadvantage.

These characterizing aspects of housewifery—that it is not an occupation, that it is not part of the labor force, and that it belongs in a pre-industrial status rather than in an industrial world—are not trivial or superficial but fundamental and widely ramifying throughout the institutional structure of our society. The exclusion of the housewife from the occupational world is more than merely a statistical artifact for the convenience of economic analysts. It reflects rather, as Talcott Parsons (1959: 262-263) tells us, a necessary accommodation of the family to the occupational world. The work of wives has to be separated from the occupational world because it operates on wholly different principles from that of work in the labor market. In order to articulate such different systems, only one marital partner can participate in the labor force, and that one partner has to be the husband:

> Broadly speaking, there is no sector of our society where the dominant patterns stand in sharper contrast to those of the occupational world than in the family. The family is a solidary group within which status, rights, and obligations are defined primarily by membership as such and by the ascribed differentiations of age, sex, and biological relatedness. This basis of relationship and status in the group precludes more than a minor emphasis on universalistic standards of functional performance ... Clearly for two structures with such different patterns to play crucially important roles in the same society requires a delicate adjustment between them ... To an important degree their different patterns can be upheld only by mechanisms of segregation which prevent them from getting in each other's ways and undermining each other. Yet they must be articulated. Broadly this problem of structural incompatibility is solved in the United States by making sure that in the type case only one member of the effective kinship unit, the conjugal family, plays a full competitive role in the occupational system. This member is the husband and father [Parsons, 1959: 263].

Since the focus of our discussion here is primarily on the housewife as housewife rather than on her labor force participation, we pay here only passing attention to the ways in which, once more, "the woman pays." The female worker in the labor market is, in effect, victimized by policies based on the conflicting models. Because the "delicate adjustment" referred to by Parsons calls for a view of women primarily, if not exclusively, as wives, a train of consequences follows. Employers can rationalize discriminatory practices as follows: (1) women have to devote most of their time and energies to their families; they are, therefore, only short-term workers, so there is no point in putting time or money into their training; (2) their domestic obligations will lead to much absenteeism; (3) they are only secondary workers in the family, working primarily for pocket money, so lower pay for them is justified. A great deal of anguish is, in fact, generated by working wives and mothers, torn between their obligations as defined in the status love and/or duty world and in the cash-nexus occupational world. It is generally assumed that all the adjustments required for accommodating these two incompatible worlds should be made by the housewife. Only now is it beginning to seem unfair, and even now only an avant garde is beginning to ask why society should not make some of these adjustments. We shall return later in our discussion to several proposals being offered for integrating the two work worlds.

Before we leave the discussion of the housewife's occupation in the economic model, a few comments on "the economic risks of being a housewife" by Barbara Bergmann (1981), an economist. She reminds us that economic analyses from a male point of view differ from those from a female point of view. Under the impact of the feminist critique, we are coming to analyze the housewife's occupation from a perspective somewhat different from the traditional male one. Bergmann speaks, for example, of intimacy as a fringe benefit in the occupation of a housewife; she notes that changing jobs—divorce—is more painful for the housewife's occupation than for other kinds, for it may involve changing residence as well; she refers to the housewife's attractiveness as human capital, which may suffer depreciation with time; she reminds us that the housewife's identity as a mother is another form of human capital that wanes as children grow up; she finds the housewife's occupation therefore an especially risky one.

A large proportion of accidents, furthermore, take place in the home. There is a considerable risk of abuse by the "employer" or husband, for which legal redress is difficult. The annual risk of divorce, Bergmann tells us, is 2 percent. And finally, the high variability in payoff is itself a form of risk. The application of such strictly economic concepts to the occupation of the housewife highlights some of its salient characteristics which have hitherto been glossed over.

THE HOUSEWIFE IN THE SOCIETAL MODEL

Lip service is universally given to the contribution of the housewife to society. Her work in the home is accorded great importance. Still, in actual practice, it is taken for granted or enormously denigrated. David Riesman (1964: xxiv) has called our attention to the infrastructure that successful men depend on but which they rarely acknowledge. And the long controversy during the nineteenth and early part of the twentieth century about whether or not women should "work," i.e., enter the labor force, revealed the strong feelings associated with retaining their services in the home.

An analysis of housewifery reminds us of the highly artificial nature of the usual economic approach to work that includes only activities of a certain kind, based on certain presuppositions. It reminds us also of the uncertain accommodation between the economic system and other systems as they operate in our society. It reminds us also of the very considerable part of the consumption goods and services which are produced quite outside of the economic system. A strange anomaly emerges: we consume a great deal more than, technically speaking, we produce.

Not only in the home but also in the community, in addition to house-wifery the housewife makes a contribution to the community in several other ways. It has been suggested, for example, that the beautiful yards of homes in the cities and suburbs constitute in effect public parks maintained at private expense but enjoyable to all. If we had to depend on tax monies for their upkeep, we would probably not have them. A large part of such gardening and yard tending is done by well-heeled housewives. A great deal of the work of voluntary agencies is also contributed by housewives, work whose value we will only realize when, as is increasingly the case, they begin to demand pay for doing it.

The contrast between the societal and the economic paradigms has been highlighted in an unexpected area, namely blood donorship, by one of the most distinguished men in the field of welfare, Richard M. Titmuss (1971). He finds that the practice of paying blood donors—according to the economic model—leads to waste, inefficiency, higher costs, and poorer quality:

> The commercialization of blood and donor relationships represses the expression of altruism, erodes the sense of community, lowers scientific standards, limits both personal and professional freedoms, sanctions the making of profits in the hospitals and clinical laboratories, legalizes hostility between doctor and patient, subjects critical areas of medicine to the laws of the marketplace, places immense social costs on those least able to bear them—the poor, the sick, and the inept—increases the danger of unethical behaviour in various sectors of medical science and practice, and results in situations in which proportionately more and more blood is supplied by the poor, the unskilled, the unemployed, Negroes and other low income groups and categories of exploited human populations of high blood yielders. Redistribution in terms of blood and blood products from the poor to the rich appears to be one of the dominant effects of the American blood banking systems [1971: 245-246].

Titmuss is arguing for a return to the nonmarket, the non-cash-nexus world.

But the determinative characteristics of the work of housewives lie in the way our society structures the living arrangements of families in separate, individual, private households. This pattern means that the work is isolating, a fact that has important effects on the woman herself. It means also that her "clients" or "employers" are in a non-economic relationship with her. But there are other characterizing aspects of housewifery. An analysis of house-work made some forty years ago, for example, singled out several especially significant characteristics, namely: (1) it is not, for most women, freely selected as an occupation, but with or without interest in it, it is or has been compulsory, not voluntary, however subtle the coercive pressures may be; (2) it has low status; (3) it is noncompetitive; (4) the timing is not synchronized with the work world; (5) it is, as noted above, isolating; and (6) the housewife is in a non-economic relationship with her "clients."

Housewifery is not voluntary. The Jaffe-Stewart definition of the labor force specified that membership in it was voluntary. Not many women have an interest in housewifery. A generation ago, in fact, L. M. Terman and C. Miles (1936: 209-210, 215-216) reported that only a little over one-third of a sample of women 25 to 65 years of age with high school education expressed great interest in the domestic arts; one-tenth showed little or none. Among college women, the levels of interest in the domestic arts were even lower, with fewer than one-fifth (18 percent) showing great interest and only 8.6 percent little or none.

Yet housewifery is prescribed for all. The vow taken at marriage may not commit the wife to housewifery, but the pressures of the world she lives in, including the law, do. "The legal responsibilities of a wife are to live in the home established by her husband; to perform the domestic chores (cleaning, cooking, washing, etc.) necessary to help maintain that home; to care for her husband and children" (Schulder, 1970: 147). The courts jealously guard the husband's rights to his wife's services in the home. And, until recently, the wife who insisted upon monetary payment for her services was looked at aghast. Some states expressly deny such payment. Even if she has an outside job, the management of the household will still be defined as her responsibility. "The law allows a wife to take a job if she wishes. However, she must see that her domestic chores are completed, and, if there are children, that they receive proper care during her absence" (Schulder, 1970: 141).

Even if, as is increasingly the case, the husband shares some of the household chores, he does this as a favor to the housewife, not as part of his genuine or legal responsibilities. Only recently has this "forced labor" aspect of the housewife's job become an issue, raised primarily by the Women's Liberation Movement. In this nonvoluntary characteristic, the work of the housewife violates the labor force concept.

Housewifery has low status. The lack of money payment for the work of the housewife contributes to the low regard in which her work is held. So too does the undeniable fact that it is menial work, and that in this country menial work has low status. "The homemaker is typically portrayed as someone who needs little intelligence, since the duties are routine and narrow in scope and since her home is not part of the social life (Lopata, 1971: 141).

There has been a long and valiant history of heroic efforts to glorify housewifery. A woman could be ever so competent, quite professional, in fact, but housework remained housework. And no amount of clamor about the dignity of labor could change the low esteem placed on it. No amount of scientific know-how or romantic glorification in the women's magazines or on television could finally hide the fact that it was, in the words of some of the radical women, "shit-work," and as such low on any occupational prestige (and hence, status) scale.[5] To meet this aspect of occupation, housewife Rae André argues that we should work to improve its status. She notes that we are so steeped in the economic model that we can readily recognize the validity of the feminist drive to improve the status of women in the labor force. But to improve the status of the occupation of housework goes against traditional belief systems:

> "People in our society tend to believe that certain kinds of work should earn money, power, and prestige while certain others should not . . . Efforts to gain status for women's paid work . . . conform to our traditional beliefs about the desire to work. Efforts to improve the status of housework, on the other hand, are outside and even antithetical to the traditional belief system" [1981: 254-255]

We are not yet accustomed to the ideas of upgrading the work rather than the worker. She thinks we should reward the housewife for the importance of her contribution.

Housewifery is nonhierarchical and noncompetitive. Lacking in the housewife's occupation are channels for upward mobility. There is no way she can improve her status, since there is no hierarchy to "climax" (Andre, 1981: 256). Her work is therefore noncompetitive. Although competition may have damaging effects when too highly encouraged, as in the male professional rat-race or the factory worker's rate-busting, when it is wholly absent the result, however tranquilizing, is boredom. Laboratory studies a generation ago showed that competition had a stimulating effect on the speed and quality of work done. Since the housewife is not in the workforce and can neither be fired nor promoted, there is little in the situation that creates competition. She adapts to this situation by creating it for herself. Advertisers understand this well. Television commercials show housewives competing with one another as to the relative whiteness or "tattle-tale grayness" of their laundry, the relative shine of their kitchen dishes, the polish on their furniture, and the taste of their coffee. If one bridge club hostess puts whipped cream on the cake, the next one adds a maraschino cherry, the third, nuts, the fourth an ornament, and so on. The whole family has to keep up with the Joneses. There is also maternal competition, each mother trying to get her child to reach certain levels of development—first word, toilet training, crawling—

before the others. Another adaptation to the boredom of noncompetitiveness is the reverse: withdrawal. One characteristic also reported a generation ago was that in noncompetitive situations, irrelevant ideas tended to be more frequent. The housewife may therefore be more likely to daydream or let her mind wander, or escape boredom in television soap operas.

The housewife may adapt to the noncompetitive nature of her work by overcompensating; she may be more compulsive. More than a century ago, this was already being noted as a problem of housewives, with much of their work being labelled as unnecessary (Fern, 1870: 40). A generation ago there was a popular play and motion picture, *Craig's Wife,* on the same theme; the compulsive household manager for whom the house was the major concern in life.

The work of the housewife is isolating. The structure of living arrangements on the basis of separate, individual, private households has the effect of cutting the housewife off from contacts with fellow workers.[6] In spite of modern means of communication and transportation, the housewife is functionally isolated from her peers. "Not only does the housewife lack the stimulus of functional contacts with other people doing the same work or working on a common project, but in addition she is practically isolated in her work" (Bernard, 1942: 533-534). And isolation has been found to "encourage brooding; it makes for more erratic judgments, untempered by the leavening effect of contact with others" (1942: 534). Isolation also heightens one's sense of powerlessness (Seeman and Evans, 1962: 772-782). It also renders one more susceptible to psychoses. These points will be elaborated below in our discussion of the pathogenic effects of housewifery as an occupation.

But the sociological consequences of occupational isolation are equally relevant. Isolation precludes organization, or at least renders it difficult. "The logistics of organizing individuals who work in millions of separate dwellings is enough to daunt the most fervent activist" (Andre, 1981: 256). Individual initiative is all well and good, "but at some point the work of isolated individuals is no longer enough."

The housewife has non-economic relations with her "clients." The "clients" or "customers" or "consumers" of the services supplied by the housewife do not pay her for them. She performs them on the basis of love and/or duty. Although she cannot be fired, neither can she quit, short of breaking up her marriage. The relationship, thus, between the housewife and her "clients" or the "consumers" of her services is extremely delicate. None of the sanctions available to "buyers" and "sellers" in the labor market operate here.

The timing of housewifery does not sychronize with that of the occupational world. The peak loads of work for the housewife do not coincide with the work schedules of the outside world. Her peaks come at mealtimes, when other workers are not working, and her work lulls come when others are working. Her leisure time is thus scheduled when adults to share it with, except other housewives, are not available. She tends, therefore, to have a one-sex social life, or none at all.

On the positive side of housewifery is its autonomy. The housewife has some say about when and how she will do her work. It is, furthermore, one of the few kinds of work in which handicraft can still be practiced (Bernard, 1942: 536).

The housewife as victim: The pathological aspects of housewifery. All of our thinking about occupations, about work, about the labor force, about the labor market on one side and about marriage, family, child-rearing, and the home, and the policies based on such thinking are determined by the models or paradigms—economic and societal—as given. There is little challenge of the presuppositions and assumptions basic to both of them, and yet such presuppositions and assumptions are intrinsic parts of the paradigms. The rejection of the housewife in one model and her preconceived role in the other mean that she is not viewed realistically in either.[7] Her plight is rejected as irrelevant in both.

We noted earlier some of the consequences of this conflict in models for working wives and mothers in the form of discriminatory practices by employers. Here, from a somewhat different angle, we note that the circumstances attending the work of housewives may be pathogenic. The devastating overall effects of housewifery have been commented on for at least a century. It has long been noted that it cuts the housewife off from intellectual stimulation and from satisfying emotional contacts; it is dehumanizing. This is how the housewife's position was described a century ago under the rubric "Hints for the Household":

Need of Change. Women need more change, more variety, than is to be found in the ordinary housekeeper's life. Year in and year out the great body of womankind in our country stay at home, faithfully treading their monotonous round of work and duty; no break in the drudging sameness of their lives only as sickness, or births and deaths, each in its own way, jars on the monotony for a time. We are more careless of ourselves than of our brittania and silver, for we are careful to keep them brightly burnished, but our intellects are dulled with lack of friction with others, and our minds narrowed for want of broader channels in which to widen. With all of us the dearest spot on earth is home, sweet home; yet do we not all admit that always staying at home leads to narrow, unhealthy views and nervous prostration? Change of air, change of surroundings, change of thoughts—oh, for more of it for our over-worked, nervous women! [Unsigned, 1886].

As late as the first third of this century, the Lynds (1929) were still noting how eager the women in Middletown were to talk, even if only with a researcher. Their wishful comments illustrated the continuing isolation of housewives. Still today, commentators speak of the fundamental vacuity of the housewife's existence, of its emotional as well as intellectual poverty. Her isolated workshop is a prison that needs no walls. This is especially abrasive in the case of women who have been exposed to the stimulation of college life: "The emotional and intellectual poverty of the housewife's role is nicely expressed in the almost universal complaint: 'I get to talking baby talk with no one around all day but the children' " (Slater, 1970).

In the 1920s there was already a book on *The Nervous Housewife,* and by 1963 Betty Friedan was still documenting the problem that had no name. By 1970, a public health survey provided clear-cut evidence that the "housewife syndrome" was indeed a reality, and not a figment of the imagination. A fairly extensive research literature had shown that, as compared with unmarried women, married women showed up poorly as far as mental health was concerned (Bernard, 1972: 3). A great many aspects of marriage might well contrive to bring about this result, but the trauma of housewifery seemed to be among the most crucial. One study reported that whereas more working than nonworking wives were neurotic, almost twice as many nonworking mothers as working mothers were psychotic (Sharp and Nye, 1963: 316). And even the findings with respect to neurotic symptoms are controverted by other studies, one of which reported that "working mothers are less likely than housewives to complain of pains and ailments in different parts of their body and of not feeling healthy enough to carry out things they would like to do" (Feld, 1963: 344).

The most spectacular documentation of the destructive effects of housewifery was provided by a Public Health Service study in 1970 which showed that housewives had far greater vulnerability to symptoms of psychological distress than did working women, more than half of whom are married and living with their husbands. The "housewife syndrome" was far from a figment of anyone's imagination: "White women who were keeping house had higher rates than expected for eleven of the twelve symptoms" of psychological distress (United States Public Health Service: National Center for Health Statistics, 1970b: 9). Housewifery seemed, literally, to make women sick. (See United States Public Health Service: National Center Health Statistics [1970b: 30-31] Table 18, entitled "Psychological Distress in the United

States."[8] Agoraphobia, a neurotic fear of open spaces, has been called a housewife's syndrome. And employment out of the home, part- or full-time, has been found to be a protective factor against depression (Brown and Harris, 1978). Thus, although a wide variety of factors might be invoked to explain the poorer health of married as compared to never-married women, these studies seemed to pinpoint the work factor of housewifery as salient.

RETHINKING THE SITUATION

It is becoming increasingly clear that the old functional differentiation of work by sex is being eroded. The assumptions that underlay the old paradigms are less and less valid, for example, that housekeeping was intrinsically a female function. Women are less and less inclined to take housewifery for granted as an exclusive lifework. There has been a renewed interest in the problem of the housewife in the current so-called "second cycle" of feminism in this century. The old definitions and conceptions are no longer accepted without challenge. Some of the thinking is a restatement of nineteenth-century ideas; some of it is revolutionary. Some presuppose a continuation of present-day lifestyles; some envisage quite different ones. Only five lines of thought are discussed here: (1) return to the old status world in as many ways as possible; (2) revamp our lifestyles by moving away from individual, privatized households to more cooperative or even communal living styles; (3) pay for the services performed by the housewife; (4) retain present lifestyles but professionalize and industrialize housewifery, thus moving it into the industrial or cash-nexus system; (5) retain present lifestyle but make possible more sharing by husbands of functions presently performed by the housewife.

Return to old status relationships. Despite the feminist critique of the current role of the housewife, and perhaps as a backlash against it, is the position advocating a return to the "traditional nuclear family" rather than acceptance of current trends. There has even been legislation proposed to ensure such a return. The so-called Family Protection Bill, for example, would withdraw federal funds from any school which taught anything challenging traditional sex roles. The ideal of those advocating such a return is minimizing labor force participation by married women and encouraging them to remain in the home as housewives. This position characterizes the New Right and the so-called Moral Majority. Whether it is feasible may well be doubted.

Cooperative or communal living arrangements. During the nineteenth century there was a considerable amount of criticism of the waste involved in separate, individual households, each with its own separate kitchen, its own separate heating and maintenance problems, its own procurement system, and its own garbage pails. Such an arrangement was contrary to all the tenets of efficiency. It was also contrary to the tenets of a movement of so-called "material feminists" who saw the individual household as oppressive to the housewife who ran it. Their goal was to "socialize housework." Dolores Hayden (1981) traced the efforts of these women to develop cooperative housekeeping arrangements, public kitchens, and cooked food services. Scores of proposals were made for cooperative living arrangements of one kind or another, common dining facilities, and shared housekeeping chores. But despite numerous attempts to establish such common, even communal living arrangements, they did not catch on. Families continue to prefer individual, private living arrangements, whatever the cost in efficiency and female effort. This is an interesting example of the family's imposing its preferences on the economy rather than on the family's adapting itself to the economy.

It was not "socialized housework" but fast-food eateries and frozen dinners and dining rooms in apartment buildings that finally came to reduce the housewife's food preparation obligations. Labor- though not time-saving technologies have greatly reduced her drudgery. But at least some of the weight is lifted from the shoulders of the housewife. It is interesting to contemplate what would have happened if the tenets of economic efficiency had won over the preference of families for private, individualized living arrangements.

Communal solutions, when they have occurred, especially in rural and religious communes, have implied that the housewifery involved should be done by women. But in the urban communes which arose in the 1960s, the direction was different. Rosabeth Kanter and Marilyn Halter (1973), for example, found in their study of urban communes that there was a trend toward equal participation in the central household tasks by both sexes. Even childcare was sometimes shared, although it tended to remain a primarily female function.

Pay for services of housewife. Another tenet of the "material feminist" ideology was to pay for the services provided by the housewife (Hayden, 1981: 3). It is an idea whose time had not yet come, nor has it fully arrived as yet. But it may be on its way. Proposals that the services performed for the economy be paid for, even if performed in the home by the housewife, are now put forward by individuals as far apart as congressmen (Senator Long) and academic economists (Bergmann, 1981). From this point of view, the function performed by the housewife is one of keeping the workforce in good condition. When or if the work environment is such that these services can be supplied by housewives, industry itself or employers must supply them. On a ship, for example, in a lumber camp, a military camp, or a mining town, on an exploring or scientific expedition or an engineering assignment—in any work situation in which living arrangements must be taken care of by industry or employer or other personnel—the work traditionally done by the housewife is done by specialized personnel. When a corporation employee has to leave home, he is provided with a per diem to pay for the maid, valet, and the meal preparation services his wife provides at home. It is, in brief, the work situation and not the work itself that determines whether it is done by housewives or by others and whether it is paid for or not. There is no logical reason why the housewife should not be paid for services that are paid for when performed by others, why she should be obliged to perform them out of love and/or duty rather than for money.

The idea is not in fact totally novel, although as presented in the past it has been from a male rather than from a female point of view. The family wage system, for example, in a curiously biased way, recognized the services performed by the housewife. A married man was paid more than an unmarried man since he had to support a wife. The blind spot was that the married worker was getting services from the wife for which the unmarried worker, male or female, had to pay. (Professional women often note laconically how much they need wives, too.) The married worker was thus being paid to "hire" services for which he did not have to pay. (The part of the family wage that was meant for the care of children raises altogether different questions which are not relevant here.)

In general, the idea of a family wage has never been congenial in the United States, where the emphasis has been on "equal pay for equal work," and women workers especially have objected to the idea that because a man was married he should be paid more. Still, in some cases there has been a curiously accepting attitude. Some fellowships allow extra funds for dependents, itself a kind of "family wage."

The logic of paying housewives for keeping the workforce in good condition is not likely to appeal to either employers or to husbands. And certainly there are many hurdles to overcome. But, who knows, by the twenty-first century employers may be contributing to a fund to pay for the services supplied to their workers by wives in the home as routinely as they contribute to Social Security funds, or unemployment accounts. It may be simply a matter of getting used to the idea.[9] Such a system would require conceptualizing housewives as part of the labor force and counting their contribution to the gross national product. It would constitute a major shrinkage of the segment of social life for which the societal model was relevant. With what "unanticipated consequences," we cannot yet say. But if such a system were inaugurated, it would entitle employers to impose standards of performance, the implementation of which would no doubt be rejected by most housewives.

Industrialize and professionalize housework. If the "material feminists" sought to socialize housework, market forces tend to industrialize it. The major premise here is simply that housewifery is technologically no different from any other kind of work, and there is no reason why it cannot be taken over by industry like any other service. A company contracts with households to perform whatever services are called for keep the household clean; provide laundry service; provide meals; provide valet services for wardrobes; keeping clothes mended and clean; and so forth. Such industrialized services are already coming into operation. In Washington, D. C., for example, there were eighteen firms advertising their wares. They had names like: Rent-a-Wife, Maid-to-Order, The Handyman, and Family Maintenance. One could contract for regular—weekly, bi-weekly, or seasonal—services. These ranged from floor cleaning and waxing to wall washing, as well as the commonly shunned task of cleaning windows.

Industrialization requires "professionalizing." That is, workers have to be trained, learn how to handle the tools of their trade, work on time schedules, and meet certain standards. The advertisement of one agency states that the work is done under strict supervision. The price for such regular services is far too high for most housewives. In the case of women who do housework by day, there has been a movement in the direction of "professionalization" for some time. They are trained in the care and operation of the increasingly complicated household appliances.

Before we leave the subject of the takeover by industry of many of the work components of the housewife's occupation, an insightful comment on the reversal of this trend suggested by Nona Glazer (1981) deserves comment. She notes that many of the services formerly supplied by industry have been thrown back on the housewife. The old-time grocer, for example, found the shopper's items for her, and even took her order by telephone and delivered it. Now the housewife finds her own items, takes them to the checkout counter, and delivers them herself. Automatic tellers ask the individual to do much of the work formerly done by human tellers. All kinds of self-service forms of shopping shift work from business or industry to consumers, most of whom, in food and clothing stores, are housewives. The procurement part of the occupation of housewife takes over much of the work of marketing.

Shared roles. A fifth line of thinking with respect to housewifery has to do with the sharing of its responsibilities, not with other women, but with husbands. The separate, individual, private household is still envisaged by proponents of shared roles, but not as the responsibility of the wife alone. This idea is at least a hundred years old. In the 1890s, the *Women's Journal* "ran articles supporting male involvement in housework and child care" (Hayden, 1981: 117). One of the results was "a dawning consciousness on the man's part that it is just as illogical to assume that all females should do the housework as it is to assume that all males should be farmers." In 1930 there was a revived interest in shared roles, and more recently, the idea has been that both husbands and wives should have the option of performing both the provider and the housewife functions rather than having to specialize in one or the other. Such an arrangement would require more flexibility in the organization of industry with respect to scheduling hours of work. Such a reorganization is seen by some industrial engineers not only as feasible, but even as profitable. With genuine flexibility, both men and women would be able to hold jobs in the labor force and also to contribute to the work of the household (Bernard, 1971a: 272-275; 1971b: 21-28; 1972).

Careful research on the actual impact of flexible working hours on male participation in household work is equivocal (Bohen and Viveros-Long, 1981). More than merely economic changes are involved. Participating in "women's work" seems, in the case of many men, to threaten their identity as males (Bernard, 1981b).

So much, then, for some of the major current issues dealing with the conceptualization and practice of the occupation of housewife. But no formulation of issues can be viewed as permanent. At this point, it may be in order to glance at some of the factors now in the process of emerging that will impact on the housewife's occupation.

THE POST-INDUSTRIAL HOUSEWIFE

One of the few areas in which there is wide consensus among students of work has to do with the impact of technology on its nature, rewards, penalties, organization, and position in the general societal system. At this moment, we are told we are undergoing a major technological revolution comparable to that of the one that began in the late eighteenth century and introduced industrialization and urbanization. It had to do with heavy industry—steel, power, transportation, manufacture—on a grand scale. It was a kind of industry in which productivity could be measured. It called for a certain kind of labor force. The current revolution inaugurates a new era which is called post-industrial. It has to do with high technology; communication is one of its major industries; services constitute its most salient product. Productivity of services is harder to see, let alone to measure, than productivity of automobiles or tires. And it is harder to improve the delivery of services than the output of mines or factories. The new kinds of occupations generated by the new high technology are not yet so sex-typed as the old ones. In them, women do not have to face age-old traditions of what is suitable work for them. Much of it has to do with business services, a long-time major area of female employment.

Even more relevant for the housewife, however, is the scenario that high-technology specialists are beginning to write about: the locus or site of some of the new kind of work. Much of it may be performed at home. And, it may be performed by housewives. At her console in her own home, the housewife of the future, we are told, will be able to perform a great deal of the communications work she used to do in a downtown office, while keeping an eye on the toddler on the other side of the room. Whether we should look with favor on this trend or not is not clear, because so far it has not been widely enough implemented. When it was described to a group of women, they groaned; they did not want to return their work to the home. They wanted the release from the home offered by an outside job. Others, students of industrial history, looked with a foreboding at such a return—at however high a level—to cottage industry, to "sweat-shops," to work that could not be easily reached by protective labor legislation. True, it might well integrate the two housewife paradigms but, they argue, at too high a cost.

Whatever the housewife herself may think about the inroads of high technology, the chances are that they will be profound, ramifying, and extensive. The occupation of the housewife will never be the same again if the current technological revolution has the effects now being predicted.

NOTES

1. Most women, whether or not they are in the labor force, continue to be homemakers. In 1979, about 42 million women were not in the labor force and most of them spent their time housekeeping. Of women living with their husbands, 55.5 percent were in the labor force and, if separated women are included, the proportion approaches 75 percent. If single, divorced, and widowed women are also included, there would be few women who were not homemakers, for themselves if for no one else.

2. This trend was in line with the same kind of trends in other types of work. Nurses have been upgraded to become "para-medical personnel" while the old servile components of their work are taken over by aides and other low-level workers. Social workers are relieved of the time-consuming legwork and are free for more prestigious treatment services. So too with teachers who are assigned aides. The situation was not the same in the case of the housewife. There simply were not enough "aides" to turn the menial work over to when she became highly trained. Housework or domestic service declined from 51.2 percent in 1870 to 6.3 percent in 1968. The implications of the disappearance of household service is one of the least researched aspects of the study of the family today.

3. If a woman with secretarial skills, married and mother of three sons, died at the age of 41, when the youngest child was 11, her replacement value would be $105,546. A Chase Manhattan bank estimate of the value of the work performed by the housewife as of 1972 was $257.53 a week. For the costs of motherhood to mothers, families, and the economy, see Bernard (1974: 288-293).

4. Still, if all housewives went on strike, withholding their services to those in the workforce, it would impact seriously on the way the economy operated.

5. A comparison of the work components in the housewife's job with similar work done in the labor force by Wilma Heide Scott found it to be on about the same level as a restroom or parking lot attendant, a public bath maid, pet show attendant, or hotel clerk (unpublished source).

6. One of the most interesting examples of the effect of isolation is reported in a British study of apartment-style living among servicemen in Germany (Fanning, 1967). The incidence of psychoneurotic disorders was almost three times higher among women living in flats than among those living in houses, but the most interesting finding was that psychoneurotic disorders increased the higher up the apartment was. The confinement of mothers of preschool children within the walls of the apartments added another irritant to the monotony and boredom of their lives. Even the children suffered: they had a higher sickness rate (Hurtwood, 1968: 12).

7. Hayden's discussion of the "material feminists" of the nineteenth century shows that many of them were, indeed, trying to bring the two paradigms into some sort of relationship to one another. In 1898, one of the most outstanding leaders among them, Charlotte Perkins Gilman, stated it this way:

> "When a man marries a housemaid, he makes a wife of his servant, he alters her *social* status; but if she continued in the same industry he does not alter her *economic* status. When he makes a servant of his wife, or she of herself by choice, whatever her social, civic, mental or moral status may be, her economic status is that of domestic service. What she is entitled to receive from society for her labor is the wages of the housemaid. What she gets more than that is given her by her husband without any economic equivalent. She is supported by him on account of her sex." [Gilman, 1968: 177].

8. This report presents figures on various symptoms of psychological distress, comparing employed women and housewives. For example, employed women were less likely than housewives to experience nervous breakdowns, trembling hands, nightmares, dizziness, heart palpitations, and other related symptoms.

9. Senator Russell Long, Chairman of the Senate Finance Committee, has been exploring the idea of admitting housewives into the Social Security system in order to make them eligible for retirement benefits: "Senator Long believes, in principle, that housewives deserve equal recognition for their work. But he is still stumped over how to finance a housewive's pension plan. One possibility would be to deduct the wife's social security tax from her husband's salary. Another idea would be to require husbands to pay their wives a weekly wage, from which her social security contribution would be deducted" (Anderson, 1971).

PART III

ORGANIZATIONAL CONTEXT

IN THIS SECTION we focus on the features of organizations which affect occupational autonomy, power, and control at the group and role levels. Organizations share certain features which differentiate them from other social forms, e.g., hierarchial structure, high goal specificity, and high formalization. While social control mechanisms occur in all social groups, there are specific control mechanisms in formal organizations that derive from the structure of the workplace.

Occupational power, status, adaptation, and integration are likely to vary depending upon the structural relationships within and between organizations. Organizations must share some autonomy with occupations if organizations are to survive. The conditions under which organizations will grant this autonomy to occupation groups and roles will vary from occupation to occupation. To some extent this interaction will vary, depending upon the degree to which society values the occupation, accepts it, and the degree to which the occupation is organized with the intention of self-regulation.

Even though organizational forms are diverse and may be changing, occupations find their viability and permanence in complex organizational structures with elaborate hierarchies, largeness of scale, and other features of the ideal-type bureaucracy examined by Weber. Usually it is assumed that organizational purposes are distinct from the purposes of the occupational groups and roles that occupy it. The continued interface between occupations and organizations today reinforces further the need to examine, theoretically and empirically, across occupations and organizations, how each controls the other. The studies in this section are by their structure predominantly influenced by the work setting of the bureaucratic environment. We are primarily interested in how organizational settings and environments create and sustain particular occupations. Because organizations need to control and coordinate participants' services such that authority over members flows down rather than up, the way specific occupations and roles are granted autonomy and power at each level is important to study.

These studies examine the types and degree of control exercised by organizations on occupations to control their autonomy. Organizational control of role performance may be extensive, as in the case of policewomen doing patrol work and of the jail school teacher role, where survival of the organization is predominant in regulating goal activities. Both occupational roles are acted out in organizations based on a paramilitary model, with security of the broader community as a primary objective. On the other hand, the nature of the work of both roles requires the exercise of considerable discretion when performing the job. Thus, while policewomen and jail school teachers are limited in the degree of role autonomy permitted by the organization, they are expected to take control and to exercise the "right degree" of discretion when completing daily assignments.

Bureaucratic control is most evident in the public sector of the economy, as in government agencies, controlled by regulation and law. It is here that Weber's rational-legal authority is most clear and developed. Any autonomy government workers have is limited to the roles they occupy and by the rules set down by their organizations. Although some rules are generated with the best of intentions, they still function as a means to control the work that people do in the organization. For example, Susan Martin (1980), in an analysis of a metropolitan police force, shows how impersonal rules make "breaking and entering" into police force work different for male and female police officers. Many of the problems women face entering police patrol work can be related to the structure of the work system itself and to the rules generated by officials. Although problems arose from other sources, her study found that opposition to women's presence from individual policemen and conscious attempts by departmental leaders to undermine or limit the opportunities or freedom of women on patrol were far less important than already established policy and rules. By applying the same rules to men and women and officially treating them as equals, the police force adopted an "assimilation" model, implying that women are exactly like men and that it is the women who would have to change to overcome any handicap from prior experience or other physical or psychological "irreducible" differences. In addition, upon entering a foreign domain, i.e., assuming a token status, policewomen are required to cope with the limitations imposed upon them by the dominant group. This negatively affected their opportunity to achieve success—promotion in the police department. The source of the conflict was grounded in the powerless position of the "token" women who comprised such a small segment of the group.

For policewomen, such powerlessness is most significant because of the nature of police work and because of the organizational structure of the police department. Susan Martin and others point out that the authority over life, liberty, and the use of violence tends to isolate police officers from the community. Strong ties of solidarity among the workers are a consequence of the nature of the work and the paramilitary model of organization adopted by the department. These conditions create difficulties for the policewomen entering and remaining in the police force, who experience a socialization process quite unlike their experiences in life to this point. How policewomen learn to adopt and survive are important elements of this study. The ideas for organizational change are carefully derived.

The study of jail school teachers was updated for this book in 1980. (The original study was done in the late 1960s.) Several changes occurred since the original study: (1) The faculty grew in size, including teaching area; (2) thus, more inmates were served by the faculty and the problem of student turnover increased; (3) new criteria were used to assign students to classes, e.g., IQ, reading ability, and social adjustment test scores; and (4) the educational materials designed for remedial students have increased.

How did these structural changes impact on the role autonomy of the jail school teachers in 1980? Because the organization environment is still a highly controlled one (due to the nature of the client), teachers are still adapting to authority measures. Violence and tension continue despite the efforts at structural reorganization into a "humane" system. Teachers no longer define themselves as often in the role of agent, because this role has been filled by social workers. For some of the teachers, this reduces the visible "success" features of their work because while acting as agent, teachers were able to help their clients solve immediate problems which interfered with teaching and learning.

Why do jail school teachers remain in this work environment? Lewis Mennerick suggests that these teachers experience considerable personal freedom and control over the day-to-day teaching activities within their classrooms. Conventional teaching methods can be replaced with innovative methods, and to some extent are required, considering the client. This autonomy, along with financial security (12 months employment as compared to 9 months in non-jail school settings), provides considerable challenge and job satisfaction. Thus, similar to policewomen, jail school teachers may experience considerable discretion, and in fact may exercise this when actually doing the job, even though they are employed in bureaucratic structures. Organizational control processes can be understood by examining their effects at the occupational role level.

The next two chapters in this section focus on organizations characterized by features which are likely to provide these occupations with more autonomy than the previous two studies. The two models examined are collegial and entrepreneurial.

Herman Loether postulated that professors would adapt their role expectations and behavior to meet the organizational context of the workplace. His first study was completed using data from professors during the 1960s. At that time, universities were expanding because of the increased number of enrolled students. During that period, the university and college system in California developed an elaborate bureaucratic structure to administer the system.

Faculty participated with the administration in trying to resolve some of the tensions created for them by the elaborate bureaucratic system. Even though faculty interacted among themselves on the basis of a collegial model (a company of equals), the administration was able to make decisions which reduced faculty power and autonomy at the group and role levels.

In 1981, a second set of data was collected from some of the same faculty, and new ones as well, which makes comparison somewhat problematic. However, the organizational context of the workplace had changed. Enrollments were not increasing; in fact, some were declining. New faculty were not being recruited when necessary. Some programs and majors were discontinued. A further significant decision was the advent of collective bargaining. When these data were collected, the state of California had enacted a collective bargaining law, but the agent had not been selected.

Loether's findings comparing faculty role-orientations in the two time periods raise some interesting questions about the relationship between occupation autonomy and labor market conditions. When the latter were good for faculty, many perceived themselves as mobile and expected to experience autonomy. When labor market conditions were not so good, faculty perceived their mobility and autonomy to be decreased considerably. Collective bargaining did not generate power for faculty in 1981, especially not for those who were unhappy with their positions and wanted to leave. Collective bargaining from a weak position in a bureaucratic environment was an indication of decreased occupation group control. The essence of the conflict between the university administration and the faculty was resolved on balance with the faculty losing power by choosing collective bargaining when in a weak position. In 1981, the university gained more control over faculty at a time during tight labor market conditions, and thus were able to exert power and reduce autonomy at the group and role levels.

As mentioned earlier in this section and elsewhere, new kinds of organizations are beginning to appear in considerable numbers. Some examples of these are QWL-based work units, entrepreneurial departments, and entrepreneurial organizations (matrix management) whose prime product is the marketing of a good idea (Peterson, 1981). In these organizations there is no clear-cut, hierarchical authority structure with a unitary chain of command which directs managers on how to sell an idea or project. If this is so, how do managers adapt to this changing, ambiguous environment, characterized by a variety of uncertainties? How managers become effective entrepreneurs is the basic concern of Kanter's chapter.

Data for answering these questions were collected through a series of pilot, lengthy, in-depth interviews with "entrepreneurial" and "bureaucratic" managers who worked in entrepreneurial and bureaucratic settings. The findings of this preliminary study of entrepreneurship are interpreted in terms of the accomplishment process, which is described in three phases: (1) initiation; (2) coalition-building; and (3) action. Successful entrepreneurial managers persist in a continued effort to accomplish the task even under conditions of adversity and resistance. However, persistence is combined with discretion so as not to provoke the participants.

The development of political skills, in addition to managerial skills, is necessary for managers who want to be successful in emerging forms of organizations characterized by loose authority structures. This suggests that only successful managers will be promoted in these new structures. The risks involved for these new managers in building a career structure are likely to be high. The development of these skills takes considerable practice and has to be learned in the workplace to a great extent. It is possible that this human resource will be a scarce one for some time, because most middle-level managers have learned to "manage" in structures with a hierarchical authority structure where activities are delineated and managers coordinate many tasks.

In summary, the chapters in this section examine how organizations control workers in the workplace. The types of autonomy and power available at the group and role levels vary among occupations, with low-level service workers having the least, and professional, technical, and managerial workers having the most.

Finally, while most occupations are carried out in complex organizations with a unitary chain of command through a hierarchical structure, innovation in the design of organizations is occurring. Several forms include: QWL work units, entrepreneurial departments, and a variety of matrix organizations. It is too early to know if these new designs will be around permanently.

CHAPTER FIVE

EQUAL VERSUS EQUITABLE TREATMENT
Policewomen and Patrol Work

Susan E. Martin

THE POLICE PATROL officer faces a variety of organizationally imposed barriers to work autonomy. Many of these arise because the officer has enormous power over the life and liberty of citizens, and departments have attempted to regulate behavior through a paramilitary organization and detailed rules of behavior. In addition to these organizational attempts to restrict police behavior that affect all police officers, policewomen face further limitations on their occupational activities. Some of the restraints on policewomen's work autonomy derive directly or indirectly from organizational policies; others emanate from interpersonal dilemmas rooted in the wider culture. It is these organizationally generated structural barriers that limit the work autonomy and mobility opportunities of female officers that are the focus of this chapter. Of particular interest are the differential impacts of organizational policies regarding the socialization of new officers and the distribution of assignments to male and female officers that make "breaking and entering" into police work more difficult for a woman than for a man.

The particular structural barriers that affect policewomen illustrate several general dilemmas faced by many work organizations in our society: first, how to recognize that women are different from men without implying that they are inferior; and second, how to treat women as equals and simultaneously provide equitable treatment to all officers. In brief, if men and women are different or behave differently, a formally "sex blind" policy that treats the women just like the men may, by ignoring these differences, create a situation that disadvantages women by putting the burden of being different on them. It is the women who are expected to assimilate into the policemen's world, on the men's terms, and to change to overcome handicaps arising from their prior experience, the attitudes of male co-workers, existing informal channels of power and opportunity within the department, and departmental policies.

THEORETICAL PERSPECTIVES

In her study of men and women in a large corporation, Kanter (1977b) observed that the organizational variables of power, opportunity, and numbers shape and constrain possibilities for autonomy by pressing employees to adapt to their circumstances and providing or limiting possibilities for action. People of both sexes, when placed in powerless, low-mobility situations, respond by lowering their aspirations and adopting patterns of occupational behavior different from those of people offered wider opportunities and greater power. The powerless and low-mobility workers tend to impose self-limitations on their motivation which then trigger a downward cycle of deprivation and discouragement. Conversely, relative power and opportunities produce self-fulfilling prophecies of achievement and advancement. Thus, the structure of the work situation produces organizational behavior that further limits or accelerates opportunities in a circular fashion as opportunity and power shape work values which in turn affect future power and opportunities.

Relative numbers also affect the manner in which women are treated in an organizational setting. Hughes (1944) observed that specific auxiliary characteristics tend to become associated with an occupational status and become interwoven with groups' values and procedures. The entry of an individual with different characteristics leads to discomfort for members of the dominant group, who then focus on the "wrong" (i.e., irrelevant) status in their interaction with the minority or "token" individual. In her examination of the consequences of token or minority status, Kanter (1977a, b) observed that tokens are highly visible, which results in increased performance pressures. Their presence leads to polarization of the differences between tokens and dominants, with a consequent heightening of dominants' group boundaries against outsiders. And dominants tend to distort and exaggerate the characteristics of tokens to fit the former's generalizations about people or about tokens' social types, with the result that tokens get trapped into stereotypic roles appropriate to someone of the token's type, thus limiting the flexibility of their role performance. As tokens in the predominantly male world of police work, policewomen must cope with the handicaps posed by their token status as well as the limitations imposed by their "outsider" status on their opportunities for exercising power and attaining mobility into desirable positions in the police department. How department policies perpetuate rather than break down these obstacles will be the focus of this chapter.

THE NATURE OF THE WORK

The division of labor and the nature of police work affect the formal and informal distribution of power and opportunity within the department and district to the disadvantage of women. Most police officers spend their entire careers as patrol officers, at the lowest rank in the paramilitary hierarchy of the department. The officer's work can be classified into three primary areas of activity: law enforcement; maintenance of order; and provision of a variety of services to the public. (For a discussion of the nature of police work, see Banton, 1964; Bittner, 1967, 1970; Wilson, 1973; Rubinstein, 1974; Manning, 1977; Black, 1980.) The feature underlying and unifying these diverse police activities, however, is the potential for violence and the need and right to use coercive means to enforce the officer's definition of the situation. The police act as the representatives of the coercive potential of the state and the legitimate users of force in everyday life (Bittner, 1970). Although most of police work does not involve crime fighting, this is the aspect of the work most visible to the public, most highly rewarded by the department, and felt to be most satisfying by the officers. The reality, generally carefully hidden, is that most time is spent in the peace officer role, requiring skills in understanding and manipulating people rather than bravado and heroics.

The nature of the work requires vast discretion that is built into the officer's job and leads to ambiguities regarding its use. The possession of vast discretionary authority over life, liberty, and property, plus the potential of danger and the use of violence, tend to isolate police officers from the community (Banton, 1964; Westley, 1970) and have, as a result, led to a highly developed occupational subculture. Conformity to its informal norms and acceptance into its informal social networks are the keys to acceptance and mobility within the police organization.

The importance of informal ties is heightened by the paramilitary organizational structure of the department. Attempts to limit potential abuses of authority by patrol officers have led to the adoption of a military model of organization, detailed rules of behavior, and close, punitive supervision. But because police work requires the exercise of discretion, departmental attempts at control have resulted in an unmilitary, informal set of arrangements for the distribution of system rewards and strong bonds of solidarity among officers.

The work and work culture handicap women in two ways. The fiction of military discipline and the emphasis on rare instances of the need to physically control others lead to the belief that women are inappropriate for the job, thereby affecting their recruitment, training, and promotional opportunities. The informal power structure, based on close personal ties, makes it difficult for an outsider to gain the acceptance or sponsorship necessary for "success" and advancement.

ORGANIZATIONAL POLICY DILEMMAS

The policies of work organizations have a major impact on the way new employees perform their occupational roles. The organization selects and trains workers and is responsible for creating the environment and opportunities which enable them to learn and perform their work. It *can* establish effective training patterns, actively seek to limit discrimination against and harassment of minority or "token" workers, ensure opportunities for mobility and power for all workers, open channels for redress of grievances, and adopt policies that vigorously address problems that arise, or it may fail to do so.

The training and placement of female officers in assignments which affect subsequent opportunities for mobility, achievement, and autonomy pose particularly difficult problems for a police department. How can it provide equality of opportunity and meet the needs of both male and female officers? Treating a women as "just another officer," in fact, is treating her like a man and puts a woman, who is likely to be physically smaller and have been socialized differently, at a disadvantage. But singling women out for "special" treatment leads to difficulties: it heightens their visibility, often implies "inferiority," and leads to resentment of double standards by male coworkers, which may retard acceptance of women as officers.

The findings reported in this chapter are based on a study of a single department—the Metropolitan Police Department of Washington, D.C. (MPDC)—but the dilemmas are common to the approximately 15,000 police and sheriff's departments around the nation.[1] Because the MPDC has voluntarily introduced a large number of policewomen into patrol work, the barriers faced by the women in this department are likely to be fewer and smaller than those in departments that have resisted the introduction of women.

In 1969, a new police chief adopted a policy of fully integrating policewomen into policework. Between 1969 and 1971, more than 100 policewomen were hired and assigned to all units of the department except patrol. Late in 1971, the "experimental" Policewomen on Patrol program was initiated. In all, 30 policewomen were reassigned, and about 100 newly recruited female officers were put on patrol duties in two of the department's seven districts. When a preliminary outside evaluation of the women's performance, on the basis of an average of four months of patrol experience, indicated that women could function adequately (see Bloch et al., 1973a, b), the eligibility lists for men and women officers were merged, the experiment was declared a success, and more women were hired and assigned to all districts. By 1975, there were more than 300 policewomen out of a total of about 4,700 officers (about 6.5 percent of the total force), and the extreme forms of harassment faced by the initial group of policewomen had subsided. Other problems remained, emanating from the nature of the work and the contradictory expectations facing the female officers as officers and as women. The department's officially "sex blind" policy formally ignored the particular needs of the women, while it informally permitted different expectations and treatment of the women.

SOCIALIZATION

Becoming a police officer is a gradual process, through which an individual is socialized into the attitudes, values, skills, and knowledge that are part of the job. The process has several stages: anticipatory socialization, including recruitment; formal training in the police academy; the period of certification for street patrol during the first few months an officer is assigned to a district; and the final "metamorphosis," which generally occurs by the sixth month of street experience (Van Maanen, 1975).

Anticipatory Socialization

The process by which an individual "tries on" a role and/or adopts the values of a group to which he or she does not yet belong is termed anticipatory socialization. It eases adjustment into a new group by permitting imaginative (although sometimes erroneous) rehearsal of the activities, responsibilities, and problems of membership, thus easing the future "reality shock."

The anticipatory socialization of women to police work tends to be shorter and less intense than that of male officers. Boys are more likely to play "cops and robbers" than girls. As teenagers, boys usually spend more time than girls thinking about a career and their occupational options, including police work. Many boys fantasize about acts of bravery, heroism, and physical combat. For young males, actual and media police heroes provide role models which were virtually unavailable to young girls until the mid-1970s.

Prior work experience also better prepares men than women for police work. More than a quarter of the men, but none of the women, in my sample had previously served in the military, thereby gaining experience with military discipline, the chain of command, and the definition of themselves as "men's men." Other male recruits came from jobs traditionally viewed as men's work such as construction and truck driving, through which they acquired the values of blue collar men. Most of the women, on the other hand, were recruited from the white collar world of the female office worker.

Recruitment policies of police departments have traditionally selected as officers men whose views of their own masculinity identified them as possessing "the mark of affinity" (Gray, 1975) that enabled them to "fit" into the informal social world of the police. The mark of affinity standard, or conception of masculinity, served to disqualify women from consideration for police patrol work. Female recruits were selected according to different informal and formal standards.[2] When women were integrated into police patrol, recruiters faced a dilemma with respect to standards for female recruits. As yet, no comparably clear standard for women has emerged since, by definition, women do not "fit" existing standards, and neither their conceptions of masculinity nor femininity are an appropriate test of their aceptability for policing. Instead, the department has relied heavily on a self-selection process to eliminate the most inappropriate potential female recruits and has accepted a more heterogeneous group of female than male officers.

The males and females who enter the police academy have different amounts of anticipatory socialization and work experience which, as will be shown, give the male recruit an early advantage that tends to be magnified rather than reduced when it is simply ignored.

The Training Academy

Formal socialization to police work begins at the training academy. New officers in the MPDC spend about four months at the academy prior to assignment to a district. There they receive formal instruction on the D.C. Crime Code and the law of arrest, departmental regulations and procedures, the communications system, community relations, court and judicial procedures, general patrol techniques, first aid, the use of weapons (including firearms), and self-defense. The rookies participate in a physical training program and must pass physical, driving, firearms, and written tests before graduation. Beyond the formal curriculum, recruits are exposed to the covert curriculum that emphasizes actual police standards and values, paramilitary discipline, and the importance of group solidarity. Training is geared to providing newcomers with a new identity as members of the police fraternity. Like basic training in the military, the training is a rite of passage, designed to break down civilian attitudes and behavior patterns and replace them with new perspectives and habits, including the sense of group membership and loyalty.

Prior life experiences benefit male and handicap female recruits in several ways. Boys are encouraged to defend themselves physically (or face the stigma of being labeled a "sissy"). Girls, particularly those socialized to be "little ladies," acquire skills in verbal manipulation, but learn not to be physically assertive. Instead, in the face of physical threat, they are encouraged to turn to a protector (usually a parent, teacher, or brother), use tears, or demand respect for themselves as "ladies." In interacting with males, girls have learned to follow rather than lead, to suggest rather than command, to manipulate politely rather than confront directly or risk insulting another. While each of these behaviors can be useful at times on police patrol (see Martin, 1980: ch. 7), police officers cannot rely on these devices and patrol effectively. They cannot turn to protectors; they must protect others from danger or violence, by coercive action if necessary.

Because guns and cars are regarded as symbols of masculinity, more teenage boys than girls have tinkered with cars and learned to use a firearm. These prior experiences make acquisition of the driving and shooting skills in the academy easier and more rapidly acquired by male recruits.

Prior athletic and body building activities magnify the physical differences between males and females that again give male recruits an advantage. Experience on the playing field introduces participants into elements found in the police subculture: controlled use of violence, the ability to endure pain, willingness to inflict it on others, an emphasis on teamwork and a group effort, and uniform behavior (Gray, 1975). Few of the female recruits to police work have participated in team contact sports. This is due to the limited number of sports for which there have been girls' teams, and the fact that popularity and prestige for teenage girls do not emanate from being an athlete, but from being the leader of those cheering for the boys' teams or having a boyfriend who is a sports hero. Smallness and delicacy rather than size and strength are esteemed for girls. Thus, adolescent social values and activities magnify differences in physical development during adolescence, increasing the differences between the sexes in such a way that women entering the police academy are at a disadvantage they must be helped to overcome.

Both physical training (p.t.) and the formal and informal classroom curriculum affect the effectiveness of subsequent role performance of both male and female officers. There was near unanimity among officers that the academic aspects of the academy training are unbiased, due largely to the individualized module system of instruction and testing. The content of the curriculum and the informal "lessons" taught by instructors, however, do foster inequality in a number of subtle ways. The focus is on the physical, violent, and dangerous crime-fighting aspects of the work, and the need for a "manly" response to threats rather than on human relations in difficult circumstances. This emphasis on the coercive rather than the interpersonal skills necessary in police work heightens the men's belief that women are inappropriate as officers, and fails to call attention to or build on skills in which women generally surpass men. When scout cars were racially integrated, the department initiated a training program for all officers that addressed the prevailing prejudices, myths, and stereotypes, and gave officers an opportunity to deal with their feelings about the changes that were thrust on them. A unit on race relations remains in the training curriculum. No analogous effort to address tensions and misunderstandings was made when sex integration occurred. Yet men and women are socialized differently, live in different cultural worlds (Bernard, 1978; 1981a), perceive life differently, and often fail to recognize gaps in understanding and communication that occur.

The problems arising in physical education and training pose the most visible dilemma for the police department. Should they maintain a single training qualification standard for men and women, who are physically different in size and strength (on the average)? If so, what should it be so as to be equitable to both? Initially, the department had a single standard for the academy physical training; p.t. requirements subsequently were altered so that women do modified push-ups, fewer pull-ups, and are allowed more time to complete the obstacle course than the men. P.t. requirements are problematic because it is not clear just how much physical training is really necessary to prepare officers for their work and what are valid, job-related measures of fitness and physical skills.

Physical fitness tests have had a long history as a mechanism for screening out women and others as "unfit" for police work. The academy p.t. program probably has been more useful as a hazing mechanism to create solidarity among those suffering the rigors of the training than as a way of ensuring fitness for patrol officers because, in the MPDC, officers are not required to maintain their fitness.[3]

The MPDC physical training program divides the women with respect to what standards are appropriate, how existing standards were actually applied at the academy, and how women should cope with the requirements. Some believe the standards are too high and not job-related, and that it is acceptable for women to seek exemptions. For example, one woman stated:

> They wanted us to do men's style push-ups. That's ridiculous! J _____ wanted to compete with the men but we couldn't, so it didn't bother me not to keep up. . . . We weren't physically able to do what was required of us.

Other women are determined to meet all requirements and compete with the men. They bitterly resent the efforts of other women to seek lower standards and respond to the exemptions given to some women by feeling obliged to become standard bearers and "overachievers" to prove to others that "all women aren't like that." One woman observed that all recruits had to run a mile a day. Many women protested that they could not keep the pace and were permitted to run far behind. She and three other women in her class "refused to accept different standards for women. . . . I felt that if I could do it, and I was smoking a pack a day, there was no reason any other woman couldn't keep up with me." Another asserted:

> Some women tried to be treated differently in p.t. That pissed me off because it reflected on me. I tried to keep up with the men. I can't run but I kept trying. The other women were angry at me because they wanted an excuse for not trying and didn't want any woman to excel because they'd lose their excuse.

The exemptions granted by male instructors to some women had several negative consequences for the women as a group. The women who were simply "passed on" by instructors unable or unwilling to deal with the women's manipulative efforts were generally less well-prepared for the realities of street patrol. Furthermore, they had failed to learn the lessons of group loyalty and suffering in silence as part of the initiation ritual, which undermined the men's confidence in the ability of the women to adhere to the norms of the department. The instructors who may have believed that they were helping the women in fact perpetuated the women's reliance on traditional female behavior, employed a double standard, and fostered a division among the women over appropriate occupational role attitudes and behaviors. By permitting some women to be "different," they subtly fostered the male officers' existing resentment of policewomen as a group because of the high visibility of the relatively few female recruits and the men's tendency to negatively label the token women, particularly when they displayed behavior characteristic of their existing stereotypic image.

The tension and communication problems between men and women, and the division among the women were exacerbated by self-defense exercises. When exercising with a woman, were the men merely preparing the women for the realities of street fighting, or were they being particularly rough as a way of embarrassing and hurting their female partners? Were some women complaining about normal or excessive treatment? The "truth" is impossible to determine (and probably varied under different individual circumstances), but the outcome was clear: divisiveness rather than a sense of group solidarity and shared toughness that other recruits got from the police academy (Harris, 1973; Van Maanen, 1975), and an undermining of men's (already limited) confidence in the ability of women to provide adequate backup.

Certification and Street Patrol

Upon completion of academy training, rookies are assigned to a district in which they undergo an apprenticeship period known as certification. During this period, usually lasting 8 to 14 weeks, rookies learn to adapt to the "reality shock" of the street and the informal norms and procedures by which policing is actually done. As their bodies are adjusting to the rigors of shift work and irregular hours, and their families are adapting to mid-week days off and job-related tensions that often get brought home, they are learning the geography of the district and how to handle situations on the street, as well as how to survive in the department ("don't make waves") and evade certain rules. They may work exclusively with one training officer or "float" among different scout cars and experienced officers.

The initial months of street patrol are very important because during this period an officer "makes" a reputation that follows him or her through his or her career, and cycles of motivation and success or of discouragement and failure are set in motion. Officers viewed as showing good judgment, "heart," and initiative are encouraged, win the trust of trainers and peers, and are provided with support and tips on "tricks of the trade." Rookies who are too retiring, who do not follow the norms, or who get reputations as complainers or troublemakers, get labeled "not police material" and are not likely to get adequate instruction. Those who seek to avoid making mistakes by being passive get reputations as unreliable, stupid, or disinterested, and others are unwilling to trust or confide in them.

Assignments and instruction during certification affect opportunities for learning and gaining self-confidence. Insufficient instruction, limited opportunities to take action, and the feeling that one is the victim of discrimination (whether real or not) are likely to lead to ego-protective indifference and demotivation for most officers. Conversely, "good" assignments are viewed as a reward for performance and encourage those with these opportunities to take further initiative.

Most of the men interviewed in my study were positive about their initial training experiences. Most were pleased to find that they got little hazing, and after an initial period of watching and asking questions "found" their own style. None reported being told to remain in a scout car when difficult situations arose, although several were critical of training officers who taught them little. Several who were shy noted that initially they had gotten insufficient instruction and feedback on their performance and had been viewed by others as disinterested. One male officer, whose certification period had been extended (a sign of initial failure), explained:

> I'm shy and wouldn't speak out or say I wanted to handle a situation. . . . I waited for instructions; they waited for my questions. . . . Now I know a lot better. I missed a lot of things because I wasn't exposed to them.

Other men who may have had similar initial difficulties probably were less forthcoming because such problems are signs of "unmanly" (i.e., passive) behavior and discussion of them is a further indication of "unmanliness."

The obstacles faced by all rookies on entering street patrol were compounded for the initial policewomen assigned to patrol by the largely unfriendly reception they received from male officers. The most blatant discriminatory practices and harassment have been eliminated, but female officers still must overcome the obstacles posed by smaller stature, unfamiliarity with street life, the negative attitudes of male co-workers and supervisors, "performance pressures" emanating from visibility, and a double standard of behavior and evaluation.

The evaluation of the initial phase of the Policewomen on Patrol program (Bloch and Anderson, 1974a: 11) reported that departmental guidelines for the integration of policewomen were "reasonably well observed during the first 6 to 8 months of the program." Several of the "experimental" policewomen, however, noted that women often did not receive the same on-the-job instruction as male officers, that their assignments were changed in the course of a tour of duty, and that a few "favored" women were assigned to the station, while the majority were left to "sink or swim" on the street with little instruction and assistance from partners, who tended to be hostile. One woman reported:

> I was certified when the sergeant came in, handed me a piece of paper and said "sign this." I had been in the district about two months but had never ridden in a training car and did not know the streets. . . . The men who came into the district went into training cars . . . but I wasn't put into a training car or instructed—ever. Yet I was certified because they handed me a piece of paper. . . . I had to learn the hard way— through mistakes—but when I made a mistake they'd come down on me just as hard regardless of whether they'd trained me or not.

At the time, she and others like her feared complaining to their supervisors, many of whom were responsible for the discriminatory treatment. She noted:

> In those days . . . you didn't dare question or say anything . . . there was no union, no EEO officer. . . . Oh, you could say what you wanted, but who would investigate? . . . Besides, I didn't say anything about lots of situations because I couldn't afford any kind of labels; not as a chicken, not as a complainer or crybaby, or anything.

Adjusting to street patrol poses a greater hurdle for rookie women than men, since it represents more of a leap into the unknown for the former. Many girls have been sheltered from street life, kept protectively close to home away from danger and violence. On entering patrol, they find themselves in unfamiliar "tough" neighborhoods, exercising newly acquired authority, and expected to control sometimes unruly citizens. While this responsibility is both frightening and exciting to most officers, it is less familiar and, in some cases, may be overwhelming to female officers.

In the face of a threatening new situation, cultural norms dictate different behavior for men and women. Men are expected to hide their fear; they may not whine or say "I'm scared" to a superior. Those that do not remain silent, master their emotions, and take action face humiliation for failure to "act like a man." Women are permitted a greater range of self-expression and are encouraged to be helpless. They are expected to show fear, and are permitted to whine, cry, or seek exemptions from situations felt to be too difficult or threatening, since "they're only girls." Whereas men learn to act and women to avoid, a police officer, by definition, cannot refuse to act out of fear, although some do. The job requires the officer to deal with situations others cannot cope with on their own. For most policewomen (and some police-men), this means learning new patterns of behavior to perform their job well.

Two contradictory sets of expectations may confuse new policewomen and increase their difficulties in learning new work-related behaviors. On the one hand, they face strong performance pressure due to their high visibility. The women's work is closely scrutinized, and their shortcomings are widely reported within the district and viewed as the failure of all women. At the same time they feel pressured to act as exemplars and meet higher perfor-mance standards, they are protected, expected to act as subordinates of the men and to fail as officers. One woman observed:

> If you're a man and a police officer it's accepted that you can do the job. Nobody's watching to see if you can. . . . But if you're a woman, everybody's watching to see how brave you are, how commanding you can be and how well you can take charge of a situation. You have to prove to the citizens you're a police officer when you take over a scene and you have to do twice as much to prove to your partner and official that you can handle the job.

At the same time, many men encourage passivity and prefer incompetent female partners. Few are so explicit as one man who stated:

> I don't think it's a woman's place [to be on patrol]. I've been taught that women should be treated as queens and I try to treat any woman who rides with me as a queen. Anything we come upon, I take the aggressive initiative. In most cases it's almost mandatory that I do so. . . . Females usually shun being aggressive.

Thus a self-fulfilling prophecy is set in motion. By treating the policewoman like a "queen," she sits back, acting like a queen—and thereby performs inadequately as a police officer, "proving" her inappropriateness for the job. Her behavior reinforces his treating her according to a double standard of expectations for male and female partners.

The competent women, who do not sit back and act like queens, do not avoid problems even though, as several noted, the men do not know how to deal with them and feel threatened by women who reject the double stan-dard. Incompetence is tolerated because it is familiar and, while making the work more difficult, preserves the man's sense of male superiority and dominance. By acting assertively, like a police officer, the policewoman fails to act like a "lady"; men do not know how to deal with or evaluate such women and often pin negative labels, including "bitch" and "lesbian," on those who fail to conform to traditional female stereotypes.

The women of the MPDC studied their reception in the district and responded to the performance pressures and double standard in different ways. Some felt they were coddled and protected, and resented this; others acknowledged the double standard and either welcomed or were unable to overcome it. A few asserted that they were subjected to tougher rather than sheltered treatment, but dealt with it by redoubled effort and resolve to "make it." Others subjected to similar pressure appear to have transferred out of patrol or to have left police work. One "experimental" woman explained that she was able to overcome the performance pressures of the initial entry period by adopting the attitude "I'm going to make it regardless," over-conformity to the rules, and gaining the support of a "super gung ho" officer with whom she was assigned to work. From the beginning, "anything he got involved in, I got involved in, 100 percent." This won his confidence and support, which "was like getting the Pope's blessing." Other similarly assertive women were frustrated by what they viewed as "coddling" by male partners and co-workers. One woman repeatedly told male officers not to ride in on her assignments unless she requested assistance; several others transferred to scooter squad, where they could work more independently and develop their own cases.

Other women were more accepting and even appreciative of male protective behavior and did not seek to alter patterns of interaction. The situation of one woman whose probationary year evaluation stated that she was "hesitant to take aggressive action" may have been typical. She attributed her behavior to the reluctance of many male partners to permit her to assume a more active police role. In fact, when they appeared on the scene of a fight, one partner told her to remain in the scout car (which she did). Determined to improve her negative probationary evaluation, she has made an effort, when working with a veteran male, "to get out of the car first and take aggressive action before he does"; despite her effort, however, the men continue to regard her as pleasant but far too unassertive an officer. For this young black woman and many others like her, the difficulties in overcoming behavior patterns "natural" for a woman are compounded by norms regulating relations with respect to age and race.

ASSIGNMENTS

Assignments and Differential Opportunities for Mobility and Success

Within the district, patrol assignments are made daily by the operations sergeant and announced at each roll call. Senior patrol officers usually have permanent assignments to scout cars, foot beats, or the station house. Newer officers may work in scout cars for officers on leave, in court, or on their day off, or they may be given foot beats, special details, or station duties as needed. The daily assignments an officer, particularly a rookie, receives greatly shape the opportunities to develop patrol skills, gain recognition, and make arrests which are a measure of productivity and "success." These, in turn, are the keys to mobility, affect the type of supervision to which the officer is subjected, and shape the officer's attitudes toward the work, the department, and the self.

Beyond daily assignments, permanent assignments affect the amount and type of autonomy experienced by the police officer through altering the working conditions and type of supervision and shaping opportunities for further mobility. There is much horizontal mobility and a variety of assignments available within the district, as well as in other units of the department. In the district, only about half of the officers are on foot beats or scout car patrol at any one time. Others are assigned to investigative (detective) units, casual clothes and crime prevention tasks, print, canine, community services, juvenile, and administrative units. Other officers transfer out of patrol division to other divisions within the field operations bureau that performs line activities (criminal investigation, traffic, youth, and special operations divisions) or into administrative services, technical services, or inspectional services bureaus.

Promotional opportunities are limited, as the departmental hierarchy becomes quite narrow as one approaches the top. After three years in the department, an officer becomes eligible for promotion to sergeant based on two factors: an efficiency rating score assigned by supervisors, and a score on a promotional examination. The written test gives the appearance of promotion based on universalistic or meritocratic principles. The limited number of openings and stiff competition permit supervisors' ratings to preliminarily screen out those who do not "fit." Recent efforts to ensure blacks and women a "fair share" of the top efficiency scores have increased their opportunities for promotion somewhat, but the "buddy system" and informal evaluative criteria that place greatest emphasis on crime-fighting prowess and a high arrest rate, loyalty and conformity, and being "one of the boys" still prevail.

Daily Assignments

The evaluation of the initial 6 to 8 months of Policewomen on Patrol program, during which time the chief's guidelines prohibiting sex discrimination in assignments were in effect, reported that women were assigned to station duty twice as frequently as the comparison group of men, but found no other differences in assignments (Bloch and Anderson, 1974b). By mid-1973, when the guidelines were no longer in effect, new policewomen were assigned less frequently to single-officer and two-officer scout cars and more frequently to station duty and one-officer foot beats than comparison men (Bloch and Anderson, 1974b). Although no comparable assignment data were available for the district in which I worked during my study, many officers asserted (and my observation suggested) that a similar pattern prevailed. Women got more than their share of station duty and foot beat assignments and fewer one-officer patrol car assignments. Women tended to be put in the scout cars with beats in quiet neighborhoods rather than in high crime areas. A study commissioned by the department reported department-wide assignment patterns indicating an unofficial view that "a woman's place is in the stationhouse" (Coleman, 1978).

The sergeants responsible for making daily patrol assignments confirmed these observations and expressed what they perceive to be the dilemma in which they are caught. On the one hand, they are obligated to treat women (as a class, not as individuals) no differently from men and recognize that male and female officers receive the same pay and should do equal work. On the other hand, they are hesitant to assign policewomen to patrol alone, together, or in dangerous areas of the district and feel, as a result, that the women are not carrying their share of the load. But what is equal work? Are assignments to two beats, one of which is busy and the other quiet, "equal"? Is eight hours on a foot beat or in a scout car equal to eight hours of station duty? Because the amount of danger and the likely "results" in terms of arrests are not the same, the sergeants (and many men) feel women are getting "the breaks." But quiet beats and station duty are disliked by many officers because they afford low prestige, are boring, and offer limited opportunities for "success" (i.e., arrests) to the officer.

Sergeants reationalize their avoidance of putting two women together as "bad deployment of personnel" and label their practice of keeping women from dangerous areas as a display of concern for the safety of the woman and her male partners. Two sergeants explained their "dilemma" in the following terms:

(1) I wish I could say I don't treat [the women] differently. I try not to but I suppose I do unconsciously. I tend not to put them by themselves for everybody's good, so they won't get hurt. They're not as good on the street so I put them with more experienced officers.

(2) I try to be as impartial as possible. Women are getting the same pay, they should be doing the same amount and type of work . . . but there are times when we all look out for a girl in a car by herself more than a male. . . . She should be holding up her end but most can't.

Yet these "protective" patterns have a negative effect on the women's opportunities to acquire patrol skills, and to gain praise, commendations, and other desirable assignments. Instead, they set in motion or accelerate a cycle of demotivation and failure.

Permanent Assignments and Promotions

By August 1973, 18 months after the new policewomen went on patrol, only 45 percent of them, but 71 percent of the comparison men, remained on patrol (Bloch and Anderson, 1974b: 12). In all, 31 percent of the women, but only 12 percent of the men, had inside jobs (community relations, administration, and youth-related duties); another 12 percent of the women and 4 percent of the men were assigned to scooter, morals, and tactical squads. Thus it appears that within the districts, the women had greater mobility out of street patrol than the men. The reasons for and implications of these transfers, however, require examination.

Women's gravitation to inside jobs may result both from a push to remove them from assignments where they are most likely to jeopardize the safety of themselves and others, and a pull toward assignments that are more compatible with sex role norms and family life (since most involve regular daytime hours). Because the work is more routine, policewomen with such assignments are less subject to intense supervision and harassment by co-workers than those on patrol. At the same time, they have less opportunity to "disappear" for several hours on the job, to make decisions that affect the life and liberty of citizens, and to win informal prestige and likely future assignments in the "mainstream" of police work.

Throughout the department, policewomen tend to be overrepresented in the administrative, community relations, and youth service units and on the sex squad (which handles rape cases), and to be underrepresented in criminal investigation (except sex squad), traffic, and special operations units. As of 1978, there were no women in canine units or the robbery squad. In these two cases, women applicants were told they could not handle the assignments: in canine because the dogs were too big, and in robbery because the work involved dangerous confrontations with violent criminals.

Women are also underrepresented in supervisory positions for several reasons. First, their newness and the length-of-service requirements limit the number of women eligible for promotion. Second, their aspirations tend to be more limited: a number of the women, particularly those who have sought and obtained assignments with regular daytime hours, are reluctant to return to street patrol and shift work (to which new sergeants are assigned) and to face the discomforts of supervising policemen, many of whom are strongly opposed to female officers. Third, the informal system of influence and sponsorship limits the likelihood that a woman, excluded from most of the drinking and social activities of the men, will gain the support of a powerful official and be perceived by others as "appropriate" for promotion.

In sum, the opportunities for mobility within the department most readily available to policewomen tend to be those that move them back into low prestige duties traditionally regarded as appropriate for females: working with women, children, and typewriters. Many policewomen readily accept these avenues for mobility both for the reasons that policemen do—regular working hours compatible with further education and family life—and as a means of reducing the stresses arising as a result of male opposition to their presence, which are greater for women on patrol than for those in most other assignments due to the uncertain nature of the work and the demand that patrol officers "fit" in the work group. To avoid similar but intensified stresses, policewomen often limit their aspirations and efforts to gain promotions.

THE IMPACTS OF ASSIGNMENTS AND TRAINING: DIFFERENTIAL OPPORTUNITIES AND CYCLES OF SUCCESS AND FAILURE

Patrol officers face a "reality shock" when they begin street patrol. They must master their fears and learn skills that enable them to take control in situations. Initial success in dealing with paperwork, supervisors, and, most importantly, citizens on the street, leads to greater self-confidence, more willingness to take control, and widening opportunities for testing and using their developing patrol skills. Individuals who do not have or take opportunities to develop and use these skills (whether due to inadequate instruction, overprotection by partners, or limited assignments) are likely to be hesitant to take action and fail to behave appropriately. Because an incompetent officer is a danger both to him- or herself and to other officers, many veterans are anxious to get such an officer off the street or to minimize his or her opportunity to take action, thereby perpetuating the cycle of incompetence.

Several young women who did not appear to be "police material" on entry into the district, for example, were frequently assigned to quiet foot beats and scout cars with more assertive male partners with whom they acted in an "appropriately" subordinate manner. Feeling that they were victims of departmental discrimination, they developed "do nothing" attitudes. For example, one stated:

> I'm not gung ho. I just do what I have to. . . . I get disgusted when I get my assignments. . . . Others with less time in the section [the ostensible

criterion governing assignments] get to ride [in scout cars] more often than I do . . . so I'm not going to break my neck, especially when I don't have a radio [on a foot beat] . . . . I'm not that strong and . . . I'm not going to drag myself to a call box.

This woman does not seek to make arrests, takes little initiative, feels little need to be assertive, and, uncertain about her ability to manage dangerous situations on the street, avoids them. Her performance and attitude have contributed to the view that she is not a promising officer and to her reputation as a complainer. She is caught in the cycle of demotivation and failure that makes it highly unlikely that she will obtain the detective assignment she desires.

Self-confidence and willingness to face the unknown are not sex-linked attributes. But patterns of prior and job-related socialization and the differential expectations of male and female rookies affect the ways they adapt to their new jobs. Without actively trying to overcome the unassertiveness of many women and the protectiveness of the men, the department's policies are likely to permit the realization of a self-fulfilling prophecy. Presumed to be unable to handle many situations, women are given either fewer opportunities and less encouragement to prove themselves on the street or else excessive praise and attention for what, to a male officer, would be a routine activity, indicating a double standard of expectations. Without the opportunities to learn to act decisively and confidently, female officers "prove" their unsuitability for patrol. Overprotected and underinstructed, many continue in traditionally female ways rather than adapting their on-the-job behavior. One female sergeant observed:

I saw women crying I didn't even know had tears crying. I guess they knew that crying wouldn't do any good with me whereas with the men they knew it might do some good. . . . Society has reared men to be protectors of women. . . . [When] women come and say, "I want to do the job equally but I'm scared" . . . the men are not conditioned or trained to say, "you have to do it." . . . Some of the men fear sending a woman out because they think, "suppose she gets hurt, am I to blame?"

This situation stems less from individual shortcomings or from deliberate discrimination than from continuation of learned social behavior patterns and the department's failure to try to alter them.

CONCLUSION: ORGANIZATIONAL POLICY, STRUCTURAL BARRIERS, AND EQUITY VERSUS EQUALITY OF TREATMENT

The entry of women into police work raises difficult questions for departments related to the training and socialization of officers and the distribution of assignments in a way that provides equality of opportunity, adopts an even-handed policy, and meets the needs of both male and female officers and the department. While the MPDC took an important first step by accepting a substantial number of women for patrol and vigorously prohibiting sex discrimination during their first few months on the job, it has not taken further action, expecting time and experience alone to lead to women's assimilation. While harassment and open resistance to policewomen has greatly diminished, wide differences in the opportunities, power, and numbers of women and men in the department still greatly handicap the female officer.

Can departmental policies be altered to reduce structural barriers without producing greater inequities? Short-term policies, including greater emphasis in training and retraining courses in communication skills and human relations, including consideration of the ways certain behaviors of both sexes perpetuate sex-typed behaviors and more frequent assignment of women to work alone and together hold some promise. Longer-term, broader changes, however, are required if policewomen are to have the same opportunities and work autonomy as their male counterparts. Some changes, such as reconsideration of the nature of the police role, modification of training to prepare officers for it, and increases in the number of female officers and female supervisors, thus reducing the problems that stem from their token status, are squarely the responsibility of the department. At the same time, organizational changes must be accompanied by altered cultural values and interpersonal patterns of behavior that replace the "male only" ethos of the police world with a heterosexual basis for solidarity among male and female officers.

NOTES

1. To understand the problems and coping strategies of a new group of women in an occupation traditionally limited to men, I undertook a participant-observation and interview study of patrol officers in a single patrol district in Washington, D.C. Approximately 30 out of about 400 officers in the district were women. I joined the Metropolitan Police Reserve Corps, a volunteer citizens' organization, received limited training, a uniform barely distinguishable from that of sworn officers, was assigned to a district of my choice, and was able to attend roll call and patrol with officers not assigned a partner for their tour of duty. During nine months I worked all three shifts on all days of the week with approximately 50 officers, including 8 policewomen. During the last three months I interviewed 28 policewomen, 27 male officers, and 15 officials

from the observation district, as well as several key informants related to the department's policewomen program. The interviews averaged 1 1/2 to 2 hours in length (for further details, see Martin, 1980).

2. The physical size requirements were lower, but the educational standards tended to be higher for the women officers, who were expected to display interest and skill in providing social services to women and children.

3. The only fitness test is an annual weight check to ensure that the officer has not exceeded the departmental weight maximum. Officers over the weight maximum lose their eligibility for promotion and may be punished in terms of assignments until they lose the excess weight.

CHAPTER SIX

EXTERNAL CONSTRAINTS ON OCCUPATIONAL ROLES
The County Jail School Teacher

Lewis A. Mennerick

THE ROLE OF TEACHER encompasses a number of subroles: director of learning, disciplinarian, judge, friend or counselor, and model of middle-class morality. Variations in the fulfillment of role expectations may be due to a variety of factors, including the larger organizational environment in which the school functions. In short, the school's environment may be influential in determining which roles will be emphasized and how role expectations will actually be fulfilled. An extreme example of the influence of the external environment is found in the case of the *Metropolitan County Jail School.*[1] In this chapter, I use data collected in this particular jail to illustrate and explore two key issues: (1) the external environment and the constraints that environment can impose on occupational roles and worker autonomy; and (2) the processes through which role incumbents deal with such constraints and with the resulting role conflict.[2]

THE EXTERNAL ENVIRONMENT

Correctional organizations can be viewed as relatively "closed systems" in which events within the organization are explained by the unique characteristics of the organization. However, such an approach fails to account adequately for potential or actual influences by individuals or other organizations outside the correctional organization. An alternate approach emphasizes that correctional organizations do not operate in a vacuum, and that activities in the organization's environment may have significant consequences for the internal functioning of the organization (see Irwin, 1980; Jacobs, 1977; Rottman and Kimberly, 1975). Elaborating this latter perspective, we can examine both inter- and intraorganizational relations. In the case of the Metropolitan County Jail School, interorganizational relations entail the linkage between the school and the judicial system and broader community. Viewing the school as a subsystem of the jail, intraorganizational relations, in turn, involve the even more direct connection between the school and the larger jail organization. This perspective leads us directly to the question of how such inter- and intraorganizational relations impact upon the functioning of the jail school and upon the teacher's autonomy in fulfilling the role of teacher.

THE JAIL

Metropolitan County Jail is located in a large urban area. The jail population, which includes both sentenced misdemeanants and unsentenced inmates awaiting trial, averages approximately 1,800 inmates, with an annual turnover of roughly 23,000 inmates. The school consists of an academic section with four classrooms, and a vocational section with a print shop, wood shop, shoe shop, and craft shop. The school is located in the basement of two cell-blocks and has a normal daily enrollment of approximately 150 students. Although the jail population is composed of adults of all ages, school attendance is limited to inmates, 17 to 20. The teaching staff consists of ten full-time teachers and an assistant principal, supplied by the Board of Education.

THE JAIL SCHOOL TEACHER

The primary role of the teacher is to teach: to transmit knowledge to his pupils. In the jail school, the teaching tasks involve a blend of instruction in academic, vocational, and social matters. Yet the teaching role in the Metropolitan County Jail School is influenced greatly by the school's external environment: the courts, the community, and especially the jail complex within which the school is located. More specifically, two aspects of the jail school's environment greatly constrain the activities of school personnel and reduce teacher autonomy: the external control of the recruitment of students and the jail's emphasis on security.

External control of recruitment. Most teachers in most schools have little direct control over the number and kinds of students they get. Jail school teachers are no exception. Upon entering jail, all males between the ages of 17 and 20 ordinarily are assigned to the school tiers. Aside from age and sex status, there is no systematic screening (see Newman and Price, 1977: 37). The external control of recruitment illustrates the influence of both inter- and intraorganizational relations. Students are provided by the jail, the courts, and ultimately by the broader community that the jail serves. And the kinds and number of students the school actually gets has important consequences for school personnel as they attempt to fulfill the teacher role.

Like most other jails, Metropolitan County Jail houses a very "transient and heterogeneous population," overrepresented by low-income, poorly educated, and minority group members (Flynn, 1973; Mattick, 1974; Newman and Price, 1977: 40). Thus, one major characteristic of jail school inmates—as well as other jail inmates—is that they will be in the jail for a relatively short period of time (see Stauffer, 1976). While convicted misdemeanants may be sentenced to the jail for up to one year, most jail school sentenced inmates are present for only a few months. And although unsentenced inmates may be held in jail from a matter of minutes to several months or even longer, most are in the school for only a couple of weeks.[3] The relatively rapid turnover of both sentenced and unsentenced inmates in the jail school influences various aspects of the teaching situation: enrollment and classification procedures, curriculum, and teaching techniques.

One consequence of rapid turnover is seen in the initial process of enrolling students. Incoming inmates are not systematically tested, nor are past school records checked to determine the students' proficiency. Rather, inmates are assigned to either the academic or vocational section largely on the basis of nonacademic criteria. Unsentenced inmates are always assigned to a classroom in the academic section rather than to one of the shops in the vocational section. From the teachers' perspective, rapid turnover and unpredictability of length of stay of unsentenced inmates is less disruptive for the classrooms than it would be for the shops. Security is also a factor. The sentenced inmates are convicted misdemeanants and are considered more stable and trustworthy than the unsentenced inmates, who may include persons accused of such violent acts as murder, rape, and armed robbery. Accordingly, only sentenced inmates are allowed access to the shops and to the numerous tools that might be used as weapons.

Within the academic section, assignment of unsentenced inmates to a particular classroom is determined primarily by each student's own report of the grade level in which he was last enrolled. Thus, students in any given classroom are supposed to be of approximately the same grade level. Yet in actuality, the teachers confront students who are extremely diverse, both in ability and academic background (see Reagen and Stoughton, 1976: 114).

A more basic consequence of rapid turnover is found in the teaching plan used by the teachers. The high rate of turnover precludes the use of a conventional lesson plan involving an outline with daily or perhaps weekly designations of topics or subjects to be covered. Jail school teachers have adapted to the constraint of rapid turnover by using a teaching technique consisting of two basic components: short-term assignments that can be completed in one or two days, and individual tutoring. Examples of materials used by the teachers include supplementary instructional periodicals or workbooks and short sections from standard textbooks. The students read an article and then answer questions dealing with what they have read, or they discuss the material as a class project.

> Yesterday, [the students] worked on some exercises in [this periodical]. Today we'll go over them and correct their answers. You see what we do here isn't anything like in a regular school. The kids are just coming and going too fast. . . . I've had a couple of boys here since November, but they are few and far between. So we just try to help them as best we can. But you just can't do anything like in a regular school [Teacher-Richardson; 5-11-67].

Teachers also tutor individual students—usually in arithmetic, spelling, or reading—and they often give their students ten or fifteen minutes of "free" time to look at magazines or to write letters to friends and family. For the most part, these techniques allow students to leave the class as they are released from jail and new inmates to be enrolled without classroom activities being greatly disrupted.

While teacher autonomy is most drastically affected by the rapid turnover of students, the school and the teachers are also affected by the external control of the number of students. It is the courts that control the supply of inmates for the jail and, accordingly, for the jail school. In the academic section, the consequence is great fluctuation in the number of students present on any given day. For example, a teacher may have 5 students one day, 14 the next, and 8 the next day, depending on how many young persons are arrested, how many make bond, how many have their court cases continued, and so forth. Thus, jail school teachers never know from one day to the next how many new students will enroll or how many old students will have been released or transferred. An even more drastic consequence of the external control of the supply of inmates was evident in the vocational section. Changes in sentencing procedures—so that young offenders would be sentenced to other institutions—forced the school to close one shop and threatened the existence of the entire vocational section for lack of students.

Emphasis on security. The second major source of constraints that reduce the jail school teachers' autonomy in fulfilling their teaching role lies in the school's lack of priority within the jail and in the jail's concomitant emphasis on security and custody. The major concern of jail officials is to maintain a secure institution: to make certain that prisoners do not escape and to control violence on the tiers where the inmates are housed. The intraorganizational relationship between the school and the larger jail organization is such that school activities are subordinate to the jail's overriding concern for security (see Stauffer, 1976; Pollack, 1979). Simply stated, the teachers lack significant influence within the institution (see Bell et al., 1979: 70). Like many other jails, major emphasis is on "custodial convenience" (see Flynn, 1973; Mattick, 1974). Thus, the teachers are affected when security-related activities in the jail affect school activities: when inmates are not allowed to attend school, and/or when inmates are troubled emotionally by activities outside the school. The constraint derives from the fact that the school exists in a much broader, maximum security milieu.

The emphasis on maintaining order affects the school most directly when concerns of the larger correctional organization delay or prevent students from attending school (see Bell et al., 1979: 25; George and Krist, 1980). For example, each morning those inmates (both school inmates and other inmates) scheduled to appear in court are brought down from the tiers for processing prior to being moved from the jail to the courts. While this movement—referred to as "court calls"—is in progress, the school inmates cannot be brought down to the school from the tiers where they are housed. The result is almost daily delays in the start of school.

Violence among prisoners and between inmates and guards occurs both in prisons (Irwin, 1980; Jacobs, 1977) and in jails (Flynn, 1973; Davis, 1980; Hart, 1980; John Howard Association, 1973). In Metropolitan County Jail, intraorganizational relations are also reflected in the fact that the school is affected when jail personnel attempt to maintain order on the tiers. Interorganizational relations, in turn, become relevant when we note the importance of characteristics of inmates (such as race and street-gang membership) brought into the jail from the larger community. For example, because of racial conflict between white inmates and black inmates, jail security personnel assigned the two groups to separate tiers and required that one group of inmates attend school only in the morning, the other group only in the afternoon.

Don't get me wrong. This is not segregation—it's for their own protection—and it's not to say that the Negroes don't gang up on other Negroes, because they do. But there were so few white boys on each tier that they didn't have a chance. White inmates even refused to come down to the school with the others—they were scared. . . . So now we have to figure out a way to bring the two tiers down separately [Principal-Meyer; 10-5-67].

Other sources of trouble on the tiers include fights between opposing street-gang members, cliques, or individuals. Sometimes the individual perpetrator is punished. On other occasions, when unable to determine who is responsible, the guards often punish all inmates on the tier by putting the tier on "ban" (see George and Krist, 1980; Mattick, 1974). They deny the inmates such privileges as using the television set, seeing the weekly movie on the tier, purchasing cigarettes and extra food from the commissary, and attending school. When the inmates are placed on ban and are not allowed to attend school, the school ceases to function: sometimes for a couple of days, sometimes for longer.

THE JAIL SCHOOL TEACHER: COPING WITH CONSTRAINTS AND ROLE CONFLICT

The staff of the Metropolitan County Jail School confront constraints that lessen their autonomy in fulfilling the role of teacher. These same constraints contribute to role conflict. Specifically, the jail school teacher occupies a position within the jail organization and also within the school as a subsystem of the larger organization. Due to conflicting organizational goals (custody/security versus treatment), the teachers' situation is tenuous (see Hepburn and Albonetti, 1980: 447-448). Role conflict for school personnel derives from the fact that the teachers must attempt to fulfill the expectations commonly associated with the role of teacher. Yet they must do this in a setting in which custody and security have major priority, and in which security (as well as other constraints) adversely affects their efforts.

How, then, do the teachers cope with the situation? The general response is one of resignation; they tend to accept custody as the jail's primary goal (see Hepburn and Albonetti, 1980: 448). As the jail school principal noted, "All they [the jail administrators] have to do is throw the word 'security' at us, and we're dead." The teachers do not approve of the conditions within the jail, and, indeed, they employ various informal tactics in an attempt to maximize the relatively small amount of influence they possess (Mennerick, 1974b). Nevertheless, in the end, the teachers attempt to cope with this problematic situation on a general level simply by accepting the futility of trying to change the overall work scene in any significant manner.

The dilemma confronting Metropolitan County Jail School teachers is made more explicit when we consider role conflict related specifically to role expectations pertaining to *teaching effectiveness.* Conditions prevent teachers from receiving many of the rewards commonly associated with successful teaching. And the teachers are aware of the problem of measuring how successful, or effective, they have been with their students. There are no grades, report cards, or progress reports. There are no follow-up reports on the students after they leave the jail (see Bell et al., 1979: 83; Reagen and Stoughton, 1976: 86; Pollack, 1979). The teachers seldom know whether they are accomplishing anything, whether or not they are helping the boys either academically or socially. At best, they are probably successful with only a small number of their students.

> In my own way I think that I do help a few of these boys. Most of them are just too far gone, but occasionally you will find one who seems to profit. I think that if I can just help one boy a month, I'm doing well [Teacher-Richardson; 5-11-67].

Two mechanisms assist the teachers in coping with the resulting role conflict. Specifically, the teachers (1) shift the responsibility for failure and (2) emphasize the role of teacher as agent.

Adaptation: shift the responsibility for failure. Given that they can help only a few boys academically, the jail school teachers, like some teachers in certain other types of schools, devise various explanations that locate the reason for that failure in ways that suit them (see Becker, 1952: 453-456; Wax et al., 1964: 67-71). In effect, they redefine the situation. Part of the explanation places the responsibility on the public schools and on the individual student.

> You know, almost all of these boys are high school dropouts. . . . We try to help them as best we can. But most of them are just too far gone. They are too far behind in their schooling and they just don't care. I think the real problem is in the regular schools. I taught in the public schools . . . and the problem is that too many of the teachers just don't care. They don't want to take the time to help these boys—especially in the schools in the ghettos [Teacher-Richardson; 5-11-67].

Another element in the explanation used by the teachers is the boys' home life. The students come from low-income families. Most live on the west side.

Their world is limited to that area of the city. And they have not received the proper amount of discipline and attention at home. If they had, they would not have dropped out of school and would not have gotten into trouble with the law.

> A lot of these boys lack a strong father image—many of them don't even know their fathers or their fathers haven't been around enough. . . . They need someone to discipline them. But they also need to know that there's someone who cares for them—maybe for the first time [Teacher-Lee; 12-19-67].

A final element in the teachers' explanation of their limited effectiveness is the jail itself. School activities are subordinate to the jail's emphasis on security; school activities are delayed when inmates are being transferred to the courts and completely halted when school inmates are being disciplined. These factors, combined with the rapid turnover of inmate students, make "normal" school activities impossible. Given the numerous constraints that they confront, the teachers reason that it is a wonder that anything gets accomplished.

Regardless of the number of factors involved, the jail teachers' explanations for failure appear to serve the same function as explanations used by some teaching personnel in other school settings. Such explanations shift the source of failure away from the school (see Sexton, 1967: 58-62). For example, failure among the disadvantaged is sometimes attributed to the student's low IQ or to cultural deprivation. Thus, the source of failure is shifted from the school to the student and to the student's neighborhood and home environment. Such explanations also serve other functions.[4] The jail school teachers' explanations appear to rationalize the school's lack of accomplishment. Given the failure of the public schools, the inmate's family, and the inmate himself, and given the constraints imposed on the school by the jail and the courts, it is miraculous that the jail school is able to accomplish anything. Viewed from this perspective, helping only a handful of boys a year constitutes effective teaching. Similarly, given these same conditions, anything can be considered useful teaching material.

For the jail school teachers, such explanations assist in legitimizing their role behavior and in reducing role conflict. Further, by redefining the situation so that virtually *any* instructional effort can be considered useful, the teachers, in effect, establish a degree of autonomy in an otherwise problematic work scene. As noted previously, the teachers are constrained in that rapid turnover of students leads to emphasis on short-term assignments and individual tutoring. Yet, within the classroom, each teacher possesses considerable latitude and utilizes considerable discretion in deciding, on a day-to-day basis, the *specifics* of what will be taught and how it will be taught (see Stewart and Cantor, 1974: 194).

Adaptation: the role of teacher as agent. The teachers also cope with role conflict resulting from their limited academic effectiveness by stressing another aspect of the teaching role. How much the teachers can do for the inmates academically or socially is always questionable. However, there is no doubt that they can and do help the students in other ways. The teachers define some students as bewildered and confused when they first enter the jail. More generally, they define their students as having many things other than school to think about. And the teachers realize that by providing information and small favors, they can help their students resolve many important, immediate problems. The teachers serve as agents for the students.

> The unsentenced boys are another story. But it didn't used to be that way. Now all they think about is getting out—calling their parents—talking to a social worker—getting a personal bond. Anymore, the teachers just serve as their agents. They are always wanting you to make a telephone call for them or to help them get a personal bond. They come down here and that's all they can think about: how to get out [Teacher-Scott; 5-26-67].

Also of importance is the teachers' conception of the school as being separate from the jail.

> You've got to keep the school separate. The teachers here aren't just jailers. These guys [the students] know that—and they know that teachers can do a lot of things for them. And we do a lot of things— finding out if they've got a warrant and when their court date is [Principal-Meyer; 10-27-67].

Thus, the teachers frequently assist their students by providing several types of information. The most common is the inmate's "court date"—the date he is scheduled to appear in court. When a new inmate enrolls in the school, the principal usually makes certain that the inmate knows his court date and amount of bond. The principal may also tell the inmate about the possibility of being released on personal bond—recognizance bond. And quite often the principal and teachers give new inmates request forms to see a public defender and/or social worker.

Problems for the inmate may arise later when he forgets his court date, the date is changed, or the guards fail to get the inmate from his tier on the day he is to appear in court. In these instances, either the principal or the teachers inquire about the matter. Finally, while most of the information requested by the inmates is information related to their court cases, other requests are sometimes made: for example, when a discrepancy occurs in an inmate's account with the jail commissary, or when an inmate who is supposed to be on the "sick call" list is not called.[5]

CONCLUDING COMMENTS

Thus far we have been concerned with ways in which the school's environment constrains the activities of jail school personnel and restricts worker autonomy, and with ways in which the teachers cope with the role conflict resulting from these constraints. Under these circumstances, what keeps these teachers on the job? Why don't they seek other types of work, other types of teaching positions? There are several reasons. Because the school operates twelve months a year, the teachers are assured a larger, more stable annual salary than teachers in conventional public schools. Further, while the teachers confront many problems that are unique to the jail situation, they do not confront some of the problems that teachers in conventional schools face. For example, the maximum security environment in which they work essentially eliminates the possibility (or requirement) of meeting the parents of their students, and thereby also eliminates potential threats to teacher autonomy that the parents might pose. Also, despite the numerous organizational constraints, the teachers do have, as discussed earlier, considerable autonomy and control over the day-to-day teaching activities *within their individual classrooms.*[6]

More generally, however, the teachers continue to teach in the jail school, in part at least because they have made the necessary adaptations that make the job more manageable than it first appears to the casual observer. Certainly, jail school teachers do face conditions that make conventional teaching difficult. Yet, having taught in the jail school or in similar types of schools for several years, they have learned to deal with these difficult situations. For example, to cope with problems in the teacher-student relationship, jail school teachers, like workers in other service occupations who confront problems with their clients, define their students as falling into a variety of types. The resulting typology categorizes students in terms of the ways in which they may facilitate or hamper the teachers' teaching tasks. The teachers are then better able to anticipate and attempt to deal with a variety of potential problems caused by the inmate students (see Mennerick, 1971). Similarly, school personnel have devised ways of dealing with the inherent conflict between custody and treatment (see Mennerick, 1974b).

Thus, jail school teachers remain in the difficult teaching situation of the Metropolitan County Jail School for various reasons, ranging from financial reward to the fact that they have learned how to deal with the problems which they confront. But perhaps the most important implication to be drawn is that even when confronted with an extremely problematic work situation, many workers will remain in that situation. They will stay, provided that they are able to bring a degree of order to what they are doing and are able to justify to themselves and to others that their work is in some way worthwhile.

Some final notes. Metropolitan County Jail is currently in a period of transition.[7] In the intervening years since this in-depth study was conducted, the jail and the jail school have been integrated into a city-county correctional system consisting of six different units. While the original jail housed some 1,800 prisoners, the new combined system accommodates approximately 4,500 and processes over 50,000 inmates annually. The jail school program, in turn, has also increased in size and now services inmates in four of the six units. School personnel currently number over 50, including five school counselors and two teacher-social workers.

Despite these changes in the school's environment and in the school itself, basic constraints confronting teachers remain similar. For example, in 1979 alone, over 3,000 students passed through the school program. The school continues to confront a very rapid turnover of inmates—turnover exacerbated by the fact that unsentenced detainees now constitute over 90 percent of the student population. Teachers also continue to face students with diverse yet usually deficient academic backgrounds. Of these, 90 percent have dropped out of public school and 70 percent read below the fifth grade level. IQ, reading ability, and social adjustment test scores now constitute the basis for assigning students to particular classrooms. However, to some extent at least, less formal mechanisms to help deal with the students' diverse academic backgrounds are still employed. The availability of materials designed for remedial education has increased considerably in recent years, and jail school teachers currently use a variety of teaching materials and techniques. In the context of coping with rapid turnover and heterogeneity of the students, these techniques share at least one common feature: primary emphasis on individualized instruction.

Just as the external control of recruitment still constrains the teachers' activities, so does the fact that the school program operates within a highly controlled environment. The process of reorganization of the jail system in Metropolitan County has included the building of new facilities and the renovation of older structures so as to reduce overcrowding and to "provide a more secure, humane correctional system" than in the past. Yet these changes have not totally alleviated the tension and violence that students frequently experience *nor* the difficulties that the students' problems pose for the teachers. "These problems of home, family, court, fear, and ofttimes physical illness occupy the inmate's mind almost all of the time, making teaching and learning the more difficult" (Report, 1980).

Finally, Metropolitan County Jail School teachers continue to confront the dilemma of not knowing exactly how effective they are in fulfilling the role of teacher. Granted, the increased use of more systematic testing and increased emphasis on preparing students to pass the high school equivalency exam do provide some quantitative indicators of academic effectiveness. Likewise, informal feedback is provided by some students after leaving the jail. Yet, as in the past, the school program still lacks a systematic follow-up that would provide "a more objective, accurate, and precise evaluation." Focusing specifically on rehabilitation, school personnel assert that their efforts to reduce recidivism are successful with a "goodly number" of students, but also concede that recidivism continues to "be a problem in spite of everything we do or attempt." As the following statement indicates, major responsibility continues to be shifted to the school's broader external environment.

> Things being what they are, the problems of modern urban living, economics, and sociology—problems over which we have no control— our students return in spite of all the educational, behavioral, and attitudinal gains that they make [Report, 1980].

With the addition of counselors and social workers to the school staff, we can speculate that the teachers employ the role of agent less frequently than in the past. As such, one might argue that while the counseling and liaison services provided by these individuals may benefit the students, the demise of the teacher's role as agent may actually impair the teachers' ability to cope with role conflict. In short, their ability to assist students in ways in which "success" is readily discernible is diminished. The question arises, then, as to what types of alternate coping mechanisms the teachers might employ.

If the jail school were studied in depth again today, it is likely that other changes, some perhaps quite subtle, would be observed. Nevertheless, the data discussed in this chapter continue to be relevant because they illustrate some of the intrinsic constraints that teachers in this jail and in other correctional institutions continue to confront: constraints that impact upon occupational roles and worker autonomy. Further, the data allow us to explore the processes through which teachers in these types of organizations attempt to cope with these constraints and with the resulting role conflict.

While I suggest that teachers in such situations will adopt varying mechanisms, such as shifting responsibility and emphasizing other aspects of the teacher role, in order to deal with the conflict inherent in their work scene, the specific forms of adaptation will likely vary. In the end, it appears that the jail school's public acknowledgement of reduced expectations may be one of the ultimate means of resolving the dilemma of uncertainty about the effectiveness of the school and of the role of teacher.

Our staff of conscientious, dedicated, and trained personnel is pleased even if *one* student in our charge is prevented from a life of uselessness because of our association and assistance. We are proud when only *one* inmate, because of our efforts, is helped in reconstructing his life. Perhaps we can be criticized for our limited vision of the possible or our low threshold of satisfaction, but we reason that even that *one* person would go unhelped were it not for our services. Fortunately, we feel that we are able to help a good deal more than one and that more than justifies our existence [Report, 1980].

NOTES

1. I participated in the activities of the jail school in the role of researcher during a period of approximately 1½ years. I observed the teachers, inmates, and jail personnel as they went about their activities in the school. During this time I engaged in many conversations and informal interviews with people in the jail, especially with the teachers. Attempting to learn as much as possible about what goes on in a jail school, I listened to what was said and raised questions to clarify points or to elicit information on specific topics. In this chapter I use excerpts from my field notes to document and illustrate the analysis. The name (pseudonym) and position of the person speaking and the date of the field work accompany each quote.

2. Before proceeding, two points should be noted. First, since the 1930s, education has increasingly gained legitimacy as an important component of the rehabilitation process (see Roberts, 1971). Yet we need to focus more attention not only on how such programs "should" function (see Alper, 1974; Miller, 1978), but also on the problems that correctional education programs and the teachers within such programs actually confront.

Second, the present study focuses on a school located in a *jail,* as opposed to a prison. Jails and prisons often share certain characteristics, such as a concern for security. Yet, because jail inmates typically include convicted misdemeanants and detainees (rather than convicted felons who are usually incarcerated for longer periods of time), jails experience a more rapid turnover of inmates than do prisons. Thus, jail school teachers confront some problems shared by their counterparts in prison schools, and other problems that are unique to the jail setting.

3. See Mennerick (1972: 84) for additional details on the average length of stay.

4. The following interpretation was suggested by and generally parallels Wax et al.'s (1964: 67-71) conclusions regarding teachers and school administrators on an American Indian reservation.

5. Although the teachers do provide much information, the role of agent can also be problematic for the teachers. For example, some teachers do not usually ask the inmate about his offense, for fear the inmate will think that the teacher can intervene on his behalf. Thus, the teachers provide only general information, not actual legal consultation. In other instances, inmates cause problems when they *constantly* seek information.

6. One might also suggest that the teachers remain in the jail school because they lack the ability or the qualifications to transfer to other types of schools. Yet the jail school teachers meet both the general requirements for teaching in the public school system and the special requirements of additional graduate-level study required of all teachers who teach in the system's "special" schools. Further, several of the teachers have M.A. degrees.

7. The following discussion relies heavily on Department of Corrections and Board of Education publications. Quotations from school personnel come from a 77-page document published by the Metropolitan Board of Education in November 1980. To protect the anonymity of jail personnel, the document is cited in this chapter simply as "Report, 1980."

CHAPTER SEVEN

ORGANIZATIONAL CONTEXT AND THE PROFESSORIAL ROLE

Herman J. Loether

THE ROLE OF the professor has been characterized as a prototype of the professional role (Ben-David, 1976: 874; Goode, 1969: 267). According to Gross (1958), the criteria which distinguish a profession from a job include the following: (1) an unstandardized product; (2) a high degree of personality involvement; (3) a wide knowledge of a specialized technique; (4) a sense of obligation to one's art; (5) a sense of group identity; and (6) significance of the occupational service to society. If these criteria are accepted as valid indicators of a profession, then indeed, professors qualify as professionals.

Certainly, whether the products of professors' efforts are research or lectures, they can be characterized as unstandardized products. Their long, irregular hours of work and their preoccupation with their work are symptomatic of their high degree of personality involvement. Their expertise in their discipline meets the third criterion. Criteria four and five are satisfied by professors' commitments to their disciplines and their participation in professional organizations. And finally, professors perform an important service to society because of their contribution to the education of the populace.

The criteria listed by Gross are generally consistent with those listed by Carr-Saunders (1928) in his classic treatment of the subject. But as Carr-Saunders points out, it has been argued that the *typical* professions or the *true* professions are those in which the practitioners are freelancers who work for a fee. These characteristics of professionals have traditionally been associated with medicine and law, but not with most of the other professions which came later on the scene (e.g., teaching, engineering, and nursing). These other professions typically operate in organizational settings and are compensated by salaries rather than fees. All of the professions, as a matter of fact, are increasingly found in organizational settings. Even the previously free professions such as medicine and law are ever more frequently found in organizational settings, and increasingly are being compensated by salaries rather than fees.

The characteristics of professionalism are most compatible with the work setting of the free professional. Organizational constraints tend to impinge upon the highly valued autonomy of the professional. Because more and more professionals are working in organizational settings, however, it is important to explore the impact that the organizational context has upon the professional role. Questions such as the following need to be investigated: What adaptations must the professional make to the organization? What concessions must the organization make to the professional? What are the consequences of these adaptations and concessions for the professional and for the organization?

Professors are prime examples of professionals who work in an organizational setting and who are compensated by salaries; therefore, they provide a fitting focus for a study of the relationship between profession and organization. It is that relationship to which attention will be directed here. First, the organization of higher education in the United States will be examined. Next, the types of role adaptations professors have made to their organizational settings will be explored. Then, attention will be directed to two contrasting organizational contexts to determine what impacts they have had on the role orientations of professors. Data collected from professors during two time periods will be used to study these impacts.

ORGANIZATIONAL PATTERNS IN HIGHER EDUCATION

The current pattern of organization of higher education in the United States is an amalgam of European, British, and native American influences. Early colleges in America were founded by clergymen and gentlemen who were themselves graduates of Oxford and Cambridge. These colleges were sponsored by religious groups and were governed by boards of trustees, lay or religious, who had the authority to appoint or dismiss presidents and hire or fire faculty. Characterized by classical curricula designed to educate succeeding generations of clergymen and gentlemen, they dominated until after the Civil War.

The impetus for public higher education in the United States was the Morrill Land Grant Act of 1862, which turned public land over to the states to be used to establish colleges. The Act directed that these colleges "would teach courses in agriculture, the mechanic arts and military science in addition to other scientific and classic studies (Lockmiller, 1969: 127-28)."

The Morrill Act stimulated the development of state institutions of higher education throughout the United States—institutions that embodied the ideas of Franklin and Jefferson that education in practical studies should be made available to the people (Perkins, 1966: 15). Here too the authority of lay boards took precedence over administrative or faculty authority. In the words of Clark and Youn:

> By the first half of the nineteenth century it was the chief American mechanism for bridging the gap between public accountability and professional autonomy, in sharp contrast to the assumption on the Continent and elsewhere that a governmental ministry was the appropriate mechanism. With trustees given formal responsibilities, no superior administrative bodies—a state department of higher education or a bureau in the state bureaucracy—developed. Instead, campus administration was subordinate to the trustees [1976: 11].

The guild was the organizational model for the medieval European university. In effect, the medieval university was a confederation of guilds of academicians in which the academic equivalents of masters, journeymen, and apprentices organized themselves around the learning process. The professors were the masters, the junior faculty the journeymen, and the students the apprentices. Such confederations of academic guilds were legitimized by a king or a pope and later by a governmental ministry which had responsibility for all education within a nation (Clark and Youn, 1976: 3).

This form of organization was the basis for the concept of the *community of scholars* which has persisted to a greater or lesser degree to present times. In the ideal sense, the community of scholars is a collegial organization composed of academicians who have dedicated their lives to knowledge and who devote their time, unhampered, to scholarly activities and teaching. Under such an arrangement, decision-making power rests with the faculty and whatever administrative apparatus is necessary is subordinate to the faculty and exists to serve faculty and students.

The concept of the community of scholars received its chief impetus in the United States with the introduction of graduate education and the development of the university in the latter half of the nineteenth century. Johns Hopkins was the first university to be established as such in 1876, and it took as its model the German university. While the concept of the community of scholars was borrowed from the German university, the German model was not borrowed in its entirety. In the German system, students went directly from high schools into professional and graduate programs. In the United States, a two-tiered system developed in which students were required to complete undergraduate work before they could qualify for professional or graduate education (Clark and Youn, 1976: 11).

Because the European universities came under the responsibility of governmental ministries such as ministries of education, it was at the ministry level rather than the campus level that administrative structures developed to handle the affairs of the university. In the United States, the administrative structures developed within the colleges and universities themselves. The trustees appointed the president and, as the institution grew, the president appointed administrators to handle the day-to-day operation of the college or university. By the turn of the twentieth century, bureaucratic administration internal to the institution had become a distinctive feature of American higher education (Clark and Youn, 1976: 11).

At the academic level, the department took hold as the administrative unit responsible for curriculum and personnel decisions. As such, it manifested most clearly the concept of the community of scholars, although there was considerable variation from department to department. Some departments, in fact, were closer to the British model in which one person held the chair of professor and wielded power over lower-rank colleagues and students. The departments were federated in colleges or schools which maintained many of the same collegial characteristics as the departments.

The resulting institution of higher education in the United States has been described by Clark and Youn as follows:

The American structure at this level differs considerably from other countries by combining the presence of laymen as trustees, responsible for general policy and holding ultimate responsibility and power, with the operation of an administrative corps answerable to the trustees and holding delegated authority, jurisdiction, and responsibility. As of the lower levels, the campus-wide structure is relatively flat and considerably federative, because the many departments, colleges, and schools retain impressive powers and degrees of influence in many sectors of decision making, particularly over personnel and curriculum. But the structure is clearly hierarchical, with central administrators and trustees superior. As a result, day-to-day activity entails an intermingling of the respective forms of authority of professors, bureaucrats, and trustees. In sum, *the control structure of the American university is a federation of collegial groups that is bureaucratically ordered and supervised by laymen* [1976: 19-20].

A relatively recent development in American higher education is the multicampus system. A prime example of this level of organization is the California State University and Colleges System, with 19 campuses. This system is governed by a board of trustees at the system level rather than at the campus level, and is administered by a chancellor and his staff. In addition, each campus has a president and an administrative staff. With the exception of the shift of the trustees from the campus to the system level, the campus organization is much as it is described by Clark and Youn in the quotation above.

An even more recent development than the multicampus system is the statewide superboard designed to coordinate all higher education in a state. In California, this superboard is known as the California Post-Secondary Education Commission. The Commission includes representatives from the University of California, the California State University and Colleges, the private universities and colleges, the California Community Colleges, and the public.

These statewide boards often wield considerable power; however, they do not parallel the ministries of education found in other countries. They do not take administrative responsibility for the day-to-day operation of individual campuses. Rather, they direct their efforts toward the coordination of educational programs and the elimination of duplication of effort among the various sectors of higher education.

The current picture of American higher education is an extremely varied one. The approximately 1200 four-year liberal arts colleges and universities run the gamut of organizational types from the small church schools like those of early America to the large urban public universities with their complicated mixes of bureaucratic and collegial organization. It is the latter public universities, however, which are increasingly coming to dominate the scene. The long-term trend has been to bigness and complexity of structure. This trend is particularly exemplified by the development of the multicampus systems and the statewide superboards.

FACULTY ROLE TYPES

In response to the complex nature of the organization of higher education, a number of faculty role types have developed. Several sociologists have identified what might be characterized as polar role types among professors. These polar types have variously been labeled *academic men with professional orientations* and *academic men with organizational orientations* (Lazarsfeld and Thielens, Jr., 1958), *scholars* and *educators* (Wilson, 1964), *itinerants* and *the home guard* (Slocum, 1966), and *cosmopolitans* and *locals* (Gouldner, 1957-58). All of these labels refer to basically the same role dichotomies. The Gouldner cosmopolitan-local dichotomy is the one which will be used in this chapter.

Gouldner contrasts the role orientations of cosmopolitans and locals as follows:

> Cosmopolitans are low on loyalty to the employing organization, high on commitment to specialized role skills, and are likely to use an outer reference group orientation.
>
> Locals are high on loyalty to the employing organization, low on commitment to specialized role skills, and are likely to use an inner reference group orientation [1957-58: 290].

Thus, the cosmopolitans seek recognition and rewards from the discipline rather than from the campus base. The college or university is merely a source of income and a place to legitimize the title of professor. If another institution offers a better package of benefits, cosmopolitans are likely to go because they have no particular feelings of loyalty to the institution employing them. The locals, by contrast, identify with the college or university and immerse themselves in its affairs. Ties to a professional discipline are tenuous or nonexistent. Any rewards or recognition forthcoming are necessarily from the college or university.

To the cosmopolitan and local types, Stewart (1968: 128) has added two more types which fit the academic situation. She has labeled the type who simultaneously identifies with and serves both the local organization and the discipline the *local-cosmopolitan* and the type who identifies with neither the *indifferent*. The local-cosmopolitans are a balanced type who divide their time between the employing college or university and the demands of the discipline. The indifferents, on the other hand, are oriented neither to the local organization nor to the discipline. They do not do anything out of the ordinary for the college or university nor do they establish a professional reputation through publishing or research. Many of these indifferents establish reputations among their colleagues as "deadwood."

These, then, represent the four types of adaptation which professors may choose in interfacing with the college or university with which they are associated.

CONTRASTING ORGANIZATIONAL CONTEXTS

A major premise of this chapter is that the role adaptations which professors select will depend upon the organizational contexts which are current. To test this premise, data collected from professors during two contrasting time periods will be compared.

The first set of data was collected from the faculty of one large campus of the California State University and Colleges system during the middle 1960s (Loether, 1974). This was a period when there was a rapid expansion of student populations across the country. During the decade between 1960 and 1970, the number of students enrolled in degree programs increased from 3½ to over 7 million (U.S. Department of Commerce, 1970a: 126). At the same time, the percentage of high school graduates going on to college increased from 53 to 60 percent (ibid). Enrollments at the campus studied were increasing in a similar fashion, new faculty were being recruited, and the campus was in the midst of a vigorous building program.

Rigid line-item budgets approved by the state legislature and the governor were the life-blood of the system in general and the college in particular. An elaborate bureaucratic structure had developed to administer the affairs of the college, and a similarly elaborate structure had developed in the chancellor's office. The faculty was engaged in a struggle to get as much control as possible, and to develop some semblance of a collegial organization in the face of threats from the chancellor, the trustees, and the legislature.

In the midst of this power struggle it was revealed that the chancellor's staff had made errors in budgeting faculty salaries. An appeal was made to the legislature for an emergency appropriation to maintain the level of faculty salaries for the remainder of the academic year. The legislature, already disturbed by what it considered a lack of forcefulness on the part of the trustees and the chancellor's office, refused. Under directions from the trustees, the chancellor's office "solved" the problem by reducing the salaries of associate and full professors by 1.8 percent.

Within two months after the salary adjustment, questionnaires were distributed to the full-time members of the college faculty. The questionnaire included items about the college administration, the system administration, salaries, teaching loads, research opportunities, facilities, and so forth. In addition, background information such as age, gender, rank, years of service, degrees held, tenure status, organizational memberships, and scholarly activities was solicited. Finally, respondents were asked about their plans for staying with or leaving the college. A total of 542 questionnaires (78 percent of those distributed) were completed and returned.

The second set of data was collected from professors on twelve campuses of the California State University and Colleges System (including the campus studied in 1965) in the spring of 1981. By this time the organizational context had changed dramatically from what it had been in 1965. Enrollments were no longer increasing as they once had. On most campuses the enrollments had stabilized, and on a few they were actually declining as the college age population shifted from the baby boom to the baby bust generation. Faculty recruiting was at a standstill except in business administration and a few other areas where enrollments were still expanding. In general, however, faculties had reached what was characterized as a "steady state." As a matter of fact, on some campuses professors were being laid off in departments that were perceived to be overstaffed. There were also isolated incidences of majors being discontinued for lack of sufficient enrollments. Budgets were very tight. Very little building was going on and, although faculty members did receive salary raises periodically, they were not large enough to offset the effects of inflation.

Another significant change that occurred between the time of the first study and the second was the advent of collective bargaining in higher education. Unionism and collective bargaining began to catch on in higher education in the late 1960s, and by 1972 some 160 colleges and universities across the country were covered by collective bargaining contracts (Bunzel, 1974: 158). At the time of the 1981 study, the State of California had enacted a collective bargaining law to cover public higher education, but the election to select an agent had not taken place. The election was, however, just a matter of months off.

In the spring of 1981, a massive study of student needs and priorities was being conducted on twelve campuses in the system by the Social Systems Research Center of California State University, Dominguez Hills. In conjunction with that study, a random sample of the full-time faculty members on those same twelve campuses was drawn and questionnaires were sent to 1000 of them. These questionnaires included a few questions that were also included on the student questionnaires for the needs and priorities survey, but they also included many of the same questions that were asked in the 1965 survey of faculty. Occasionally, question wording had to be changed to suit the changed situation in 1981, and wording was improved on a few questions, but the information solicited was very much like that solicited in 1965. In all, 376 of the questionnaires were returned completed. Obviously, these 376 questionnaires do not constitute a representative sample of the faculty of the twelve campuses surveyed, but they do provide enough data to make comparisons with the 1965 data. Wherever possible, such comparisons were made.

THE FINDINGS

The heart of the analysis of the data was the classification of faculty members into the four role types: cosmopolitans, local-cosmopolitans, locals, and indifferents. In the 1965 study, a ten-item scale dealing with commitment to the college was combined with an item on the future of the college to produce a measure of each respondent's orientation toward the college.

Items dealing with publications, research grants, and other forms of scholarly activity were combined to produce a measure of each respondent's orientation to his/her discipline. In the 1981 study, a six-item scale combined with the item on the future of the campus was used to measure the respondent's orientation toward the campus. Orientation toward the discipline was measured by the same items dealing with scholarly activities as were used in the 1965 study. These measures of orientation toward the campus and orientation toward the discipline were combined to produce the four role types as follows:

(1) The Cosmopolitan: measured low on orientation toward the campus (low commitment to the campus and pessimism about its future) and high on orientation toward the discipline (a high level of scholarly activity).

(2) The Local-Cosmopolitan: measured high on orientation toward the campus (high commitment to the campus and optimism about its future) and high on orientation toward the discipline.

(3) The Local: measured high on orientation toward the campus and low on orientation toward the discipline (a low level of scholarly activity).

(4) The Indifferent: measured low on orientation toward the campus and low on orientation toward the discipline.

Comparative distribution of role types. The 542 faculty members who were respondents in the 1965 study distributed themselves among the four role types as follows: 16 percent were cosmopolitans, 26 percent were local-cosmopolitans, 43 percent were locals, and 15 percent were indifferents. Among the 376 respondents in the 1981 study, 41 percent were cosmopolitans, 22 percent were local-cosmopolitans, 12 percent were locals, and 25 percent were indifferents.

Obviously, a dramatic shift took place in the distributions of the four role types between 1965 and 1981. The percentage of cosmopolitans among the respondents increased from 16 percent to 41 percent. At the same time, the percentage of locals dropped from 43 percent to 12 percent. The percentage of local-cosmopolitans dropped slightly from 26 to 22 percent; and the percentage of indifferents increased by 10 percent.

Role types and personal characteristics. The distributions of the four role types differed from the earlier to the later study on such personal characteristics as possession of the doctorate, years of service on campus, and age. Table 7.1 presents the percentage distributions of those who had doctorates in 1965 and 1981. Note that the percentages having doctorates in each of the four role types went up, but the locals were still least likely to have

TABLE 7.1   Role Types and Percentage Distribution of Possession
of Doctorate: 1965 and 1981

Role Type	1965 Percentage	1981 Percentage
Cosmopolitans	79	84
Local-Cosmopolitans	70	86
Locals	32	58
Indifferents	50	65
	N = 542	N = 376

TABLE 7.2   Role Types and Percentage Distribution of Ten or More
Years of Service: 1965 and 1981

Role Type	1965 Percentage	1981 Percentage
Cosmopolitans	28	67
Local-Cosmopolitans	32	55
Locals	14	69
Indifferents	17	70
	N = 542	N = 376

doctorates and the cosmopolitans and local-cosmopolitans were most likely
to have them. While the cosmopolitans had a higher proportion of doctorates
than the local-cosmopolitans in 1965, the percentage of local-cosmopolitans
with doctorates was slightly higher than the percentage for cosmopolitans in
1981.

Table 7.2 presents the percentage distributions for those with ten or more
years of service to the campus by role type for both the earlier and the later
study. The percentages of those with ten or more years of service were higher
for all four role types in 1981 than they were for 1965. There were
interesting shifts, however, among the four role types. The locals and indifferents who had the lowest percentages in the earlier time period had the highest
percentages in the later time period. The local-cosmopolitans, who had the
highest percentage in the earlier time period, had the lowest percentage in the
later time period.

In keeping with the shift to more years of service to the campus in 1981 as
compared to 1965 there was a corresponding shift in the ages of the
respondents. There were larger percentages of older faculty members in 1981
than there were in 1965. This is dramatically illustrated by the fact that in
1965, 45 percent of the cosmpolitans were under the age of 30, while in 1981
only 2 percent were under the age of 30, and 73 percent were over the age of

TABLE 7.3   Role Types and Percentage Distribution of Tenured
             Faculty: 1965 and 1981

Role Type	1965 Percentage	1981 Percentage
Cosmopolitans	79	93
Local-Cosmopolitans	81	88
Locals	46	84
Indifferents	47	84
	N = 542	N = 376

40. In 1981, only 3 of the 376 subjects in the study were under the age of 30! In 1965, the local-cosmopolitans had the highest percentage of older faculty members and the indifferents had the highest percentage of younger faculty members; but in 1981, the local-cosmopolitans had the highest percentage of younger faculty members and the locals had the highest percentage of older faculty members.

Role types and rewards. Campus rewards for meritorious service take the form of tenure and promotion. It is instructive to examine the distributions of these rewards for faculty members in the four role types, comparing the 1965 with the 1981 data. These distributions are presented in tables 7.3 and 7.4. Examination of table 7.3 reveals that the percentages of faculty members in all four types who were tenured increased between 1965 and 1981. In 1965, local-cosmopolitans and cosmopolitans had much higher percentages of tenured faculty members than did locals or indifferents. In 1981, the local-cosmopolitans and the cosmopolitans still had an advantage over the locals and indifferents, but the gap was narrowed greatly so that the locals and the indifferents were only four percentage points lower than the local-cosmopolitans in percentages tenured.

Table 7.4 presents the percentage distributions of faculty members in the four types who held higher ranks (associate or full professors), both in 1965 and 1981. Again, it can be seen from an examination of the table that all four types gained significantly in rank between the earlier and the later period. In both periods, however, the local-cosmopolitans and the cosmopolitans enjoyed an advantage over the locals and the indifferents. The gap between these types decreased in 1981 over what it had been in 1965, but this gap was not as narrow as it was for tenure.

Attitudinal reactions to organizational contexts. In order to test their reactions to the organizational contexts in which they found themselves, respondents were asked a series of questions in both studies designed to tap their feelings about their positions. They were asked (1) Would you recommend your campus to a friend who is seeking an academic position? (2) If

TABLE 7.4   Role Types and Percentage Distributions of
Higher-Rank Faculty: 1965 and 1981

Role Type	1965 Percentage	1981 Percentage
Cosmopolitans	63	92
Local-Cosmopolitans	71	90
Locals	39	73
Indifferents	35	76
	N = 542	N = 376

you were starting all over again, knowing what you do now, would you still accept a position on your campus? and (3) a question about whether they were seeking another position or whether they would accept another position if it were offered them.

In 1965, cosmopolitans and indifferents were least likely to say that they would recommend their campus to a friend seeking a position. The percentages who would make such a recommendation were 17 percent for cosmopolitans, 19 percent for indifferents, 75 percent for locals, and 83 percent for local-cosmopolitans. In 1981, all four role types were more likely to recommend their campus to a friend, but cosmopolitans and indifferents were still less likely to make such recommendations than were the two other types. The percentages of those who said that they would recommend their campus to a friend in 1981 were as follows: 62 percent for cosmopolitans, 59 percent for indifferents, 96 percent for local-cosmopolitans, and 96 percent for locals.

In both 1965 and 1981, cosmopolitans and indifferents were those least likely to say that, if they were starting again, they would accept their present positions. However, they tended to be much more negative about their positions in 1965 than they were in 1981. Local-cosmopolitans and locals were likely to say that they would accept their present positions both in 1965 and 1981, but they were only slightly more positive in 1981 than they were in 1965. The percentages saying that they would still accept their present positions were as follows for 1965: 21 percent of the cosmopolitans, 31 percent of the indifferents, 82 percent of the local-cosmopolitans, and 82 percent of the locals. The percentages for 1981 were as follows: 56 percent of the cosmopolitans, 57 percent of the indifferents, 87 percent of the local-cosmopolitans, and 87 percent of the locals. Thus, the percentage increases between 1965 and 1981 for local-cosmopolitans and locals who said that they would accept their present positions were only 5 percent for both. The percentage increases, on the other hand, were 35 percent for cosmopolitans and for indifferents, 26 percent.

TABLE 7.5   Role Types and Intentions to Leave Position: Percentage
Distributions for 1965 and 1981

	1965			1981		
Role Type	Not Leaving	Consider Leaving	Yes Leaving	Not Leaving	Consider Leaving	Yes Leaving
Cosmopolitans	16	29	55	42	45	13
Local-Cosmos	62	23	15	78	20	1
Locals	41	41	18	80	18	2
Indifferents	8	46	46	54	42	4
	N = 542			N = 376		

The question dealing with the possibility of respondents seeking another
position or taking another position also revealed some interesting differences
between 1965 and 1981. Table 7.5 summarizes the 1965 and 1981 percentage distributions of responses to this particular question. Note that the
percentages of faculty members in all four types who said that they were
leaving dropped dramatically between 1965 and 1981. Conversely, the percentages of all four types who said that they were not planning on leaving
increased dramatically. The most striking changes in responses between 1965
and 1981 were for the indifferents and the cosmopolitans. The percentage of
indifferents who said that they were not considering leaving increased from 8
percent in 1965 to 54 percent in 1981, and the percentage who said that they
were seeking to leave dropped from 46 percent in 1965 to 4 percent in 1981.

The percentage of cosmopolitans who said that they were not considering
leaving increased from 16 percent in 1965 to 42 percent in 1981, and the
percentage who said that they were seeking to leave dropped from 55 percent
to 13 percent. The cosmopolitans were still most likely to leave during both
periods.

Role types and collective bargaining. Because an election to select a
collective-bargaining agent was imminent in 1981, respondents to that questionnaire were asked whether they favored collective bargaining. Although
the same question was not asked on the 1965 questionnaire, respondents to
that survey were asked, "Do you feel that the current standing of the faculty
could be improved by coordinated group effort by the faculty?" The questions are not the same, but they do touch upon the same general areas of
concern. Therefore, responses to the 1965 question were compared with
responses to the 1981 question. Table 7.6 compares the responses to the
1965 question with the responses to the 1981 question for all subjects in
both studies. It is interesting to note that there was more support for a
concerted faculty effort in 1965 than there was for collective bargaining in
1981.

TABLE 7.6   Comparison of 1965 Responses on Coordinated Faculty
Effort with 1981 Responses on Collective Bargaining,
for all Respondents

Responses	1965 Percentages	1981 Percentages
In favor of	59	53
Undecided	28	23
Not in favor of	10	24
	N = 542	N = 376

When the responses to the 1981 question on collective bargaining were
broken down by role types, significant differences in degree of support for
collective bargaining appeared. The greatest support came from the indifferents (63 percent) and the cosmopolitans (58 percent). Only 37 percent of the
local-cosmopolitans and 45 percent of the locals supported collective bargaining.

The 1965 responses were not broken down by the four role types;
therefore, it is not possible to make a direct comparison with the 1981 data
by role types. However, in the 1965 study, responses to the faculty group
effort question were tabulated separately for those faculty with high scholarly output and those with highly positive feelings about their campus. For
both of these categories of faculty members, 62 percent were in favor of a
coordinated group effort by faculty.

INTERPRETATIONS AND CONCLUSIONS

The contrast between the organizational context in 1965 and that of 1981
comes through rather clearly and consistently in the data. While 1965 was a
period of expansion in enrollments, active recruitment of faculty, and a fluid
academic labor market, 1981 was a time of stable enrollments and steady
state faculty. No longer were faculty members in a position to improve their
lot by moving to new positions. The predominant sentiment seemed to be
that if one had a tenure track position, one had better hang on to it. In truth,
though, there was no assurance that even a tenured position was secure. When
the results of the comparisons of the two studies are examined from the
perspective of these two contrasting organizational contexts, the findings are
logical.

The shift in the distributions of the four role types between 1965 and
1981 may be interpreted as being a direct result of the much tighter academic
labor market in the latter period. The percentage of cosmopolitans increased

from 16 percent to 41 percent, while the percentage of locals decreased from 43 percent to 12 percent. This could be because the faculty members had been in their positions for a longer time and had had a chance to establish their professional reputations, whereas in 1965 they were relatively new in the academic world and fell into the local type because they had not had sufficient opportunity to establish records for scholarly activity. It could also be that the tight academic labor market improved the competitive positions of the campuses studied in 1981 and made it possible for them to retain a larger proportion of cosmopolitans than would have been possible if academic mobility had been greater.

The findings with respect to possession of the doctorate, years of service, and age distributions tend to support the interpretation that the tight labor market constricted faculty members' mobility. They had little choice, because few other academic positions were available; therefore, they grew older, accumulated more years of service to the campus, and had sufficient time to complete their doctorates. Still, the differential between cosmopolitans and local-cosmopolitans versus locals and indifferents persisted. The doctorate was more common among the cosmopolitans and the local-cosmopolitans than it was among the locals and indifferents, but the locals and indifferents were more likely to have over ten years of service to the campus. Apparently, the locals and indifferents who were appointed to their positions early enough were able to retain them, even though they did not complete the terminal degree. The finding that 84 percent of the locals and 84 percent of the indifferents were tenured in 1981 seems to be consistent with this interpretation.

Although the percentages of locals and indifferents in higher ranks were greater in 1981 than in 1965, those percentages were not as high as the percentages of locals and indifferents who were tenured. This seems to indicate that they were able to reach the relative security of a tenured position, but without the terminal degree and the expected scholarly activity, they were less likely to reap the rewards of promotion.

Responses to the three questions dealing with recommending a campus position to a friend, with accepting a campus position again if one were starting over, and with intention to seek another position are also consistent with the changes in organizational contexts between 1965 and 1981. Although local-cosmopolitans and locals were most likely to recommend a campus position to a friend, were most likely to accept their own positions again, and were least likely to be seeking another position during both time periods studied, all four types were more likely to give those responses in 1981 than they were in 1965. Obviously, if one doesn't have alternative positions to turn to, one makes the best of what one has. The fact that 13 percent of the cosmopolitans said that they were seeking another position or were leaving in 1981 reflects their feeling that they still retained some mobility, even in a tight labor market.

The final questions on coordinated group effort by the faculty in 1965 and collective bargaining in 1981 also elicited answers responsive to the changed organizational context. While majorities of respondents were in favor of a concerted effort by the faculty in 1965 and collective bargaining in 1981, the percentage in favor in 1981 was lower than the percentage in favor in 1965. When the 1981 data were broken down by role types, collective bargaining was favored by majorities of cosmopolitans and indifferents, but not by majorities of local-cosmopolitans or locals.

It appears that the timing of the collective bargaining legislation in California was not optimal from the faculty standpoint. Faculty members had more leverage in 1965 than they did in 1981, because in the earlier period the academic labor market was in their favor. They were in demand and were able to find other positions if they were unhappy with their present ones. In 1981, their security in their positions was jeopardized by shrinking enrollments and tight budgets. They had finally won the legal right to bargain collectively, but their bargaining position was considerably weaker than it had been during the earlier period. The fact that the percentage of faculty members in favor of a group effort such as collective bargaining was smaller in 1981 than it had been in 1965 may indicate that they had mixed feelings about the effects that bargaining would have on their positions as professionals. By entering into collective bargaining, they would be accepting an employee-employer relationship with their administrators. While they stood to gain something in terms of working conditions within the bureaucratic structure, they risked the loss of some of the autonomy and decision-making power characteristic of the professional.

Overall, both the institutions of higher education and their faculties lost something with the changes in organizational contexts which occurred between 1965 and 1981. On balance, however, the faculty lost more than the institutions because the tight labor market of 1981 gave the institutions leverage over faculty positions and put pressures on faculty members to surrender some of their professional prerogatives in the name of security.

CHAPTER EIGHT

POWER AND ENTREPRENEURSHIP IN ACTION
Corporate Middle Managers

Rosabeth Moss Kanter

POWER ACQUISITION HAS always been a salient issue in determining how well people do their jobs in management, but in new kinds of organizations, with new structures and facing new environmental issues, it is starting to dominate. In the more traditional mechanistic or bureaucratic organizations, jobs are generally rather clearly delineated, tasks bounded, and authority defined by formal position in a more-or-less unitary chain of command. But in the new organizations (e.g., matrixes, fast-growth companies, QWL-based work units), authority has loosened, the unitary chain of command notion has been violated, and tasks have grown interdependent. Much of a manager's focus has shifted from the ongoing management of routine activities to the handling of issues, the introduction of changes, or the development of projects. Without clear singular authority for engaging in the tasks included by the shift of focus, managers have to rely on a set of skills related to power acquisition: securing high-level backing for ideas; selling projects to others; building a team of supporters; acquiring information and resources not automatically given by the formal position; handling potential opposition; doling out the "spoils of victory" to supporters, and so forth.

In short, the "cutting edge" of new skills for managers may be *political* rather than strictly managerial, and the acquisition of power for its own sake may be replaced increasingly by the acquisition of power primarily as a *tool* for accomplishments. The new view of power suggested by this analysis is transactional: that the key to becoming powerful is the effective *investment* of power in activities and other people, not just the acquisition of power.

This chapter focuses on issues surrounding the skills, tactics, and strategies of effective middle-level managers in the new style settings. These settings are defined as "entrepreneurial" and the managers as "entrepreneurs," to distinguish them from their more bureaucratic counterparts. Even though such managers are not the prime organization decision-makers, they show the same kind of spirit of risk, initiative, and enterprise within the middle layers of a corporation that are usually associated with the more classic definition of entrepreneur.

The conclusions, speculations, and findings reported here are the result of pilot interviews with 26 managers with a reputation for effectiveness, representing 18 different companies. Of these, 20 were "entrepreneurial" and 6 were "bureaucratic." These interviews were carried out in preparation for a larger study of 160 middle managers in five companies, which is still underway but which has also informed this analysis. The interviews are designed to uncover the skills-in-use that managers employ as they move a concept through their organization: how they develop a strategy and acquire the power to carry it out without mobilizing incapacitating opposition or resistance. The interviews ask for an in-depth history of a major recent accomplishment, interrupted by structured questions, and followed by description of the job and the organization (1-2 hours total time). This combination of structured and unstructured interviewing and the focus on events and process proves to be very information-rich.

THE LARGER PICTURE: CHANGING CONTEXTS
FOR MIDDLE MANAGEMENT

For middle managers and their equivalent in staff professionals, changing times and environments are making issues of power and influence even more salient on a daily basis. One source is direct career pressures, because of trends in the labor market, on both the demand side and the supply side. On the labor market demand side, declining productivity and foreign competition have helped increase career insecurity and reduce the meaningfulness of formal (university and civil service) tenure or informal (corporate) tenure. On the labor market supply side, relevant changes include the dramatic increase in jobholding women, increasing the competition for some kinds of jobs, and the almost-equally-as-dramatic increase in years of schooling, which tends to be associated with increased ambition as well as a larger pool of competitors (Kanter, 1978a).

Another source of the increased salience of power issues in the middle level ties career anxiety to organizational functioning. In this second power arena, it is interdepartmental power rather than merely individual power that is at stake. While peers in the same work unit may be direct competitors for better jobs, they are also collaborators in the larger struggle to improve the entire unit's bargaining position in the organization. Resource scarcities increase internal bargaining for resources, which affect daily quality of life as well as ability to produce accomplishments that net career advantages. Turbulent environments keep shifting the focus of relevance (see Kanter, 1977b, ch. 6) and make whole functions or departments relatively essential or inessential, depending on their control over critical contingencies (Hinings et al., 1974), as those contingencies themselves shift. Thus, the critical issues being managed at the top—from changing market conditions to regulatory pressures—shift the ways functions and units line up with respect to one another. They affect both the opportunity structure (which career paths are likely to be significant, which fields will be included in dominant coalitions) and the power structure (who has access to resources, information, and support, as manifested in discretion, visibility, and relevance in job activities (Kanter, 1977b, 1979).

Thus, the classic struggle for power in the middle ranks of the organization concerned individuals vis-à-vis each other and sets of tasks. For managers, it took the form of career competition: succeeding in winning over their peers in the competition to take on ever-more-important sets of responsibilities. For professionals, it took the form of struggles over job control: succeeding in gaining desired degrees of autonomy and control over the conditions and standards for their work. But now the terms of the power struggle have shifted away from individuals to departments, a focus that is barely realized in the organizational literature (with a few exceptions: Hinings et al., 1974; Pettigrew, 1973; and Mintzberg, 1979). Just as adversity can bind together the members of a collectivity as they struggle for joint survival, while prosperity may drive them to compete (Kanter, 1972), and a "lean" environment cause organizations to form resource-sharing networks (Aldrich, 1979), so can the new environment for middle-echelon employees drive them to jointly seek to elevate and protect their own unit of the organization. It has long been well-known that subunits suboptimize, and that differentiation creates dramatically different outlooks as well as conflicts that organizations must manage (e.g., Lawrence and Lorsch, 1967). But the heightening of interunit conflict and competition, overlaid on career anxieties and competition, may make power struggles *the* most central issue in the behavior of the middle ranks, rather than one of several.

Furthermore, the new terms on which organizations meet their environments add a new possibility for interdepartmental power struggles. As new players enter organizational fields, they add new territories for power battles. Management of an active, turbulent, changing environment poses a continuing series of new issues for organizations, issues that must be located in the structure. The middle-level power struggle is in part over "ownership" of new issues, which by definition cannot be fit into existing functional boxes without throwing the meaning of functional distinctions up in the air to be renegotiated.

For example, who should handle new issues in government relations— existing staff or a new department? At what level should productivity improvement programs be designed and managed, and who should be included in their managements? Where should the EEO function be put? If the latter decision seems obvious, just consider this finding from research-in-progress: all the legal mandate entails is that an EEO Officer be identified. In 32 corporations, our research found five different departments in which the EEO office was located: Legal, Administration, Personnel, Labor and Industrial Relations, and Operations. In many cases, the EEO office had moved several times. In one not untypical case, the formal EEO Officer was in the Industrial Relations function, but the primary "champion" of the issue reported to the Vice President of Personnel, who had a working charter from the top to "do something" about EEO; there was, as must be obvious, a great deal of political maneuvering around who "owned" EEO and how credit or blame would be distributed. The "blame" part whould not be ignored, either. While some new issues seem highly desirable and therefore are candidates for power plays, others may seem risky, and those who are assigned to them may engage in a series of self-protective political maneuverings. We see this too in the case of EEO.

The "garbage can" model of organizational choice (Cohen et al., 1972) is certainly relevant, but it tends to underplay the patterned nature of the struggles for issue control. New kinds of political analyses are needed for this as well as other aspects of change in organizations. Recent research on adoption of innovations, for example, has shown that one of the key factors is political: the presence of a well-placed "champion" who will put up a fight on the issue (Freeman, 1974; Kantrow, 1980).

Finally, new organizational structures also make power issues salient. In these turbulent times, and particularly for fast-growing high technology industries (as well as for those that are following "fashion" by adopting new structures whether or not they are optimal—see Mintzberg, 1979), the new forms of organization structure have been designed to maximize responsiveness, including "matrix" (Davis and Lawrence, 1977), "parallel" (Stein and Kanter, 1980), and "ad-hoc" (Mintzberg, 1979) structures. In adding responsiveness and minimizing traditional line authority, they can also maximize conflict, thus ensuring that power struggles dominate much of the life of the middle of the organization.

In matrix organizations, employees or managers may combine two or more dimensions in their jobs: a functional specialty (such as sales) and a responsibility to a particular product line or market area. Thus, they also report to two or more bosses, e.g., one for the function, and one or more for the product areas (see Davis and Lawrence, 1977). Unlike the classic unitary chain-of-command in which authority could be directly and relatively easily exercised, in the matrix influence, down-the-line has to substitute for formal authority, since neither boss has complete control over the employee. The employee is expected to be the resolver of conflict, integrating the demands of these two dimensions of the organization. Conflict is thus built into the matrix, and power struggles ensue. Depending on the design of the particular job and the coalitions that form, the balance of power may be held by the employee who plays bosses off against one another or by one or another of the managers (see Kanter, 1977b, ch. 7, for concrete examples.)

Other new forms of organization also make influence—or informal power struggles—more prominent than traditional line authority. Parallel structures (Stein and Kanter, 1980) add a series of temporary, rotating task forces managed by a steering committee to the conventional line organization. "Ad-hocracies" (Mintzberg, 1979) may encompass similar fluid nonhierarchical structures, including project teams and other professional or quasi-professional self-managed work teams.

Thus, for middle managers in all of these forms of organization, authority is no longer relatively guaranteed, and the struggle for power moves from the sidelines to center stage.

THE GUIDING QUESTIONS

Entrepreneurial middle managers accomplish a great deal of value to their organizations as well as their own careers. They develop new products, introduce new departments, help reduce the workforce without conflict, consolidate inventory, design more streamlined systems aiding transactions across departments, and invent new procedures that change fundamental characteristics of the organization. Table 8.1 illustrates some of these accomplishments.

How do they do it? Under these new conditions, how do middle managers go about getting things done? How do "entrepreneurial" managers in such "new style" settings differ from their "bureaucratic" brothers and sisters? And how are their accomplishments linked to the kinds of settings in which they are performed? Under what circumstances, and using what tools, can people in middle-level jobs have a significant impact on their organizations, redirecting its energies, reorienting its activities, or developing new procedures?

The answers to these questions can help us understand several things. First, they shed light on the process by which organizations change. The role of mid-level personnel is almost entirely neglected in the examination of orga-

TABLE 8.1　Illustrative Accomplishments

Accomplishment	Job	Type of Company
Identified quantity of gold used in the manufacture of components and developed plan to reduce costs by reducing gold use	Manager of Critical Materials and Long-range Planning for Corporate Purchasing	Computer
Development of a data base management system product (hardware and software)	Manager of Systems Development	Data Communication
Developed the company's first sales incentive program and increased sales	Business Unit Manager for Product Area	Manufacturer of identification equipment
Designed, developed and implemented a new corporate recruiting department	Manager of Corporate Recruiting	Aerospace
Developed a system for optimizing training time in Japan by developing network of relationships with brokers and bankers in Japan, U.S. and London	Manager of Securities Operations	Financial Services
Developed an adjustable field accounting system reducing administrative detail for agents	Director of Systems Development	Insurance
Started up a new plant location, transferring 100 employees and saving an equivalent number of jobs	Employee and Community Relations Manager	Electrical Manufacturing
Changed nine regional inventories to three area warehouses	North American Logistics Manager	Computer
Influenced manufacturing to simplify the flow of goods through the company	Assistant to Vice President of Manufacturing	Computer
Led special project team recommending specific reductions in the size of the management force	District Manager for Emerging Issues	Communication Services
Developed viable international distributor program used worldwide	District Sales Manager for Latin America	Computer

nizational change. Yet they are critical actors, almost regardless of the origins of change. First, those changes that are authorized by the top still need to be translated into the operations of those at middle ranks who guide the ongoing business of the organization. There is a large gap, for example, between the decision to implement a new program or undergo a new strategic thrust and the working out of all of the details of that initiative in ongoing operations. At the same time, there are also a large number of changes in organizations that take place because of the initiative and enterprise of people at middle levels who themselves design new ways of carrying out their routine operations that may quickly or eventually add up to an altered state for the organization. Indeed, without sufficient flexibility to permit random creativity in unexpected places in the organization, many companies would not have developed new programs, new products, or new systems that were eventually adopted as organization-wide initiatives to the great benefit of the whole. Thus, the issue is not simply how middle managers get things done—a mechanical question that could be embedded in a procedural manual—but rather how they manage to get anything *significant* done, operating through the organization to change it in some small respect—a question of creativity and, occasionally, politics.

The skills involved also shed light on how power is actually used in organizations. Most analyses of power in organizations tend to concentrate on its bases or sources rather than on its uses. They concentrate on the acquisition rather than the investment side of power, thus leaving several major gaps. To identify bases of power may not tell us whether and how the power is actually used, or whether the sources that are available are tapped and by whom. A common complaint of upper-level managers in organizations is that their people do not take advantage of all of the power available to them. While we may view this comment with considerable skepticism, there may also be a grain of truth in it: while we can certainly characterize broad chunks of the organization as possessing more power than others, there are still enough ambiguities about the existence of power such that not everyone in a position to have access to power actually seizes it.

Furthermore, many of those who possess ample bases of power may not actually do anything with their potential power—in effect, hoarding it to acquire organizational prestige rather than investing it in new initiatives. But unused power may decline in value over time. Thus, the study of organizational accomplishments by middle managers also informs us about the more dynamic side of power: how power is acquired in the service of tasks, and how available power sources are systematically tapped in the interests of investing that power in getting something done. (Of course, as I have already indicated, this issue has meaning only when the nature of the process of getting things done is creative rather than mechanical; the full implications of this will become clear later.)

"BUREAUCRATIC" VERSUS "ENTREPRENEURIAL" SETTINGS

In those organizations generally termed mechanistic or "bureaucratic," a large proportion of all activities carried out by middle managers are *specifically authorized:* that is, they are clearly assigned, to a high degree of specificity, as part of the responsibilities of the job. They are also clearly bounded. Not only are the limits of authority specified, but these limits are carefully delineated so as to avoid overlapping with anyone else's territory. The organization thus pays a great deal of attention to issuing specific mandates. This in turn makes middle managers unlikely to exceed the bounds of what has been formally authorized. The combination means that practically all activities can be traced to specific charters. (Note that this provides a more dynamic definition of bureaucracy, one dependent not on structural characteristics but rather on the dynamic properties of the kinds of processes likely to be set in motion by degrees of specification of authorities.)

More "entrepreneurial" and less bureaucratic organizations, then, are ones in which *authority is loosened or ambiguous.* Sets of activities may be only generally authorized, or the authorizations themselves may be vague. Job assignments or territories for activities may be shared or overlapping, or the individual manager may not by himself or herself possess the resources necessary to carry out the activities that are authorized; i.e., managers' activities may thus indeed be authorized, embodying legitimacy assigned, with others acknowledging the legitimacy, but the authorization to *do* XYZ may not include jurisdiction over all of the tools necessary to carry out the task.

Therefore, a large proportion of activities in more entrepreneurial settings are self-propelled rather than specifically authorized. They are invented or customized rather than assigned. There is a high component of uncertainty in both the definition of the task and the provision of the means to carry it out. Accomplishments are often change-oriented and nonroutine—even though, ironically they may also be "expected" in that authorities had the outcome in mind when generally authorizing the manager to be active in that area.

TRADITIONAL BUREAUCRATIC MIDDLE MANAGERS

Among the characteristics of the "bureaucratic" managers in "traditional settings" is that they have difficulty even identifying accomplishments or achievements for which they can take credit. They are just "doing their jobs." When they do identify accomplishments, often after considerable effort, these generally involve beating their own record or adding incrementally to an ongoing process rather than introducing anything, changing anything, or redirecting or reorienting their area. There is little specific goal orientation, only an ongoing stream of organizational events in which they have a clearly delineated territory and rather unchangeable activities. It is also for this reason that they lack the excitement about their work characteristic of the other sets of managers. "Just a job" is rather dull, lacking the spark which is characteristic of defining and carrying out a specific project.

The experience of one sales manager is typical of those in heavily bureau-cratized settings. The "accomplishment" he identified, after considerable prodding, involved developing a new sales training program for the company which is now in use nation-wide. From initiation to final achievement, this accomplishment was fully under the control of the manager, who was mandated to carry out efforts of these kinds, specifically related to what he was authorized to do. He identified an improvement in ongoing operations that increased profits. From the start, this was a fully authorized solo effort:

> I realized my job had to take a different focus. I started to focus on changing from a product-selling orientation to a solution-selling orienta-tion. I started in my division to develop a training program. I thought of it and it worked. My profits grew.

Neither resources, nor information, nor support were problematic.

> I didn't need any resources to proceed with the idea. I was in command in my division. I just wrote out the ideas in a training process. I came out with six main financial problems for people and a process for salesmen to provide solutions. (What about information?) I don't know what you mean. I had an idea and I talked to others and we developed the training. (Whose support did you need?) No one's from my division. When I was asked to join a company-wide planning committee, I had to give that committee support. I convinced them I knew what I was doing and I had the profits. That's all.

There were no roadblocks or opponents in this case because the division manager was in a position to immediately implement any program that he designed that did not go beyond the grounds of his authority. There were no reasons that his subordinates would not go ahead with it, nor were there any conflicting territories or overlapping jurisdictions that would prevent implementation. Whatever politics were involved in the situation did not emerge until the point at which the division manager had already been so successful in his area that his proven results could outweigh the tendency on the part of other committee members to favor their own pet projects. The fact that he could act virtually alone within his own territory made it difficult for him to identify even this as a victory. And the achievement that was officially recognized by the company was a standard one, improvement in sales volume, for which he received the usual plaques and recognition certificates to hang in his office.

There were also few problems with instant implementation on a company-wide basis, because the program was straightforward and did not change any basic operating procedures of the system. It simply provided another set of tools by which ongoing operations could be rendered even more effective. It is intelligent but straightforward, lacking either uncertainty or drama.

In general, the bureaucratic managers say they have an easy time handling opposition, mostly because they ignore it, as this interview indicates:

Question: Was anyone opposed or critical?

Answer: The manager of a neighboring department.

Question: How did you handle this criticism or opposition?

Answer: I told that manager that this was not his business.

Question: Did you win over the "critics"?

Answer: No.

Question: Did you hit any roadblocks or low points when it looked like the whole thing would flop?

Answer: I never thought about a flop.

Thus, the more traditional managers in the more bureaucratized settings tend to define only a narrow range of accomplishments: those closely identified with the specific mandate in their job, such as incremental improvements in performance, or importing and implementing a well-known practice. They are rather likely to possess already nearly everything they need to carry out the related activities. Hence, they tend to act alone. Their ability to act unilaterally is, of course, a function of the first two features, which makes the accomplishments low-risk as well as low-gain. Being low-risk, they are also not particularly threatening to others, arousing little opposition. What opposition does occur can often be handled merely by avoidance.

ENTREPRENEURIAL MIDDLE MANAGERS

The accomplishment process for the entrepreneurial managers, in contrast, is long, complicated, and involves much more collaboration and communication. It generally consists of three phases. There were obvious differences in detail stemming from the nature of the task, the organization, and so forth, but the accomplishments also tended to embody a number of skills that recurred throughout the interviews.

During phase 1, *Initiation,* entrepreneurial managers tend to:

- Define, or be assigned, a critical problem, opportunity, or unmet need.

- Look closely at the matter from a variety of different viewpoints, perspectives or frameworks.

- Choose a definition of the project most closely related to legitimate, relevant organizational or area goals.

- Gather as much hard data as possible about the area involved; know more than "anyone" about the issue or problem.

- Use intuition or imaginative leaps into unknown territory; assume the uncertain is possible.

- Define an approach to the problem that embodies a "vision" of eventual results.

During phase 2, *Coalition-building,* they tend to:

- Assess the political climate carefully; understand current pressures on the organization.

- Understand how relationships between functions and between people work.

- Determine who in the immediate area has (a) power and (b) a stake in the issue.

- Determine who at a top executive level has power.

- Negotiate for the support of these people by showing them how important the issue is and by convincing them that the approach chosen will work.

- Make sure the approach meshes with the politics; redesign if necessary.

- Secure promises of supplies of resources (time, budget, space).

During phase 3, *Action,* they tend to:

- Form committees or task forces, trying to hand pick members or mobilize subordinates for action.
- Meet with appropriate groups and individuals to discuss activities and plans; be well-prepared and present issues and solutions clearly.
- Be willing to take sensible risks.
- Be persistent but *discrete,* backing off where necessary.
- Manage information to create favorable and up-to-date impressions in the minds of key supporters.
- Remind people continually what *they* stand to gain from the manager's plan (and at the end, be sure they get it).

In practice, of course, the phases are overlapping and some actions recurrent. Furthermore, retrospective accounts, particularly those prodded by questions, tend to make action sound more strategic than it was at the time. But even with these reservations in mind, the common features of many accomplishments provide a striking set of insights into the investigatory, political, and collaborative nature of achievements in new-style entrepreneurial settings.

Specific issues for each phase follow:

Initiation

There are two sources of legitimacy for middle-manager activities in entrepreneurial settings. One derives from authorities who assign general territories and make tools available. The other derives from individual skill at envisioning a not-specifically-authorized-but-plausible project and acquiring the resources, information, and support to carry it out. In various combinations, these two sources of legitimacy are behind the accomplishments of successful middle managers in these settings.

In the first instance, the manager is given a general assignment, but initial authorization for any *particular* activity is vague. The manager is handed by his or her boss or higher official a charter for the job that involves problem-solving or development. In those cases, any accomplishments are in a sense planned or "expected," but organizational authorities could never specify in advance the means by which the person would actually manage to tackle the assignment. In retrospect, the outcome seems more certain or predictable than it did when the activity began. "They expected this in the sense that they knew I was the kind of person who could carry out an accomplishment like this," one manager said. Others equivocated on the issue of whether such an achievement was expected or unexpected for someone in a position like theirs, and preferred to answer "some of both." It is striking that a large number of job titles of the managers identified to us as effective contain a hint of a broad entrepreneurial focus.

Because of the high uncertainty and thus the risk built in, such broadly mandated, high discretion assignments at middle levels tend to be hemmed in with a number of formal and informal safeguards and constraints. One safeguard is careful selection of people (Kanter, 1977b: ch. 3). Another is to make sure that such assignments are staff rather than line in nature, so that the problem-solvers or developers are not in a position to implement what they develop but must convince others of the appropriateness of their plans. (Will we find cases where accomplishments or achievements under this broad developmental mandate are viewed as *unexpected* by the company? Perhaps in those situations, the company either had no real hopes for the function or put somebody in the job that they were not expecting to be able to pull it off.)

A second source of initial authorization comes out of group discussions that identify areas not clearly handled by any existing staff or procedures. Such discussions might bring together people across organizational territories and make clear to the entrepreneurial manager what kinds of new situations are developing in other areas that have implications for his or her own activities. The *idea* thus comes out of a group process, but the decision to pursue the idea and develop a project around it comes from the entrepreneurial manager. Most often the activity can be plausibly tied to the manager's mandate. But in some cases it requires an extension of his or her territory to encompass this new activity. In this instance, entrepreneurial managers demonstrate their enterprise by plucking a possible course of action out of ongoing discussions about the organization's operations and needs. Out of the multiple issues that are under constant discussion, the enterprising manager decides which constitute opportunities and thus should be pursued.

Unlike the first kind of authorization, the origins of enterprise here do not lie in a job assignment or in the more formal aspects of organization and job design, but rather in the conjunction of two sets of circumstances: constant communication about emerging issues and problems, generally involving people from more than one area, coupled with a manager who has an eye out for worthwhile projects that involve a degree of inventiveness. (In the pilot research, only one of the examples of effective managerial accomplishments involved importing a system from another company—all the manager really did was implement something he had used before—rather than designing and building it from scratch.)

There are two kinds of projects initiated in this way, which can be seen as examples of minimal and maximum enterprise. Those involving minimum enterprise are cases in which the manager simply decides to rearrange or reorient his or her own territory or activities in response to information about changes occurring elsewhere, especially where the managers' territory intersects with or is interdependent with other areas undergoing change. Very little skill is needed beyond this point, because the manager's authorization downward is clear by organization design, and outwardly the manager is doing things that are designed to be responsive to other areas and therefore should be pleasing to them.

The maximum enterprise case is, of course, the one in which the project intersects other territories and where the enterprising manager does not alone possess all of the tools necessary to carry it out. The latter case is highly significant. It represents the source of unplanned organizational creativity that gives some companies their adaptive capacity.

After initiation, the effective managers seek additional bases for legitimacy which will aid them in gaining support and gathering resources in the coalition-building stage that follows. They do this by spending a great deal of time working on problem/project definition and gathering data—sometimes weeks or months. They carefully shape the definition of the task to fit organizational and political realities, choosing an approach that meshes with critical current concerns. And they add expertise to their authority by learning as much as they can about all angles of the subject in question, and, in particular, its impact for and on the organization.

This early research and careful consideration of the political climate stands the effective managers in good stead later, when they have to answer the questions of potential critics and convince others to join them. And it is a key factor in the ability of the entrepreneurial managers to get sponsorship from higher authorities.

Coalition-Building

The issue of sponsors or champions serves as the bridge between Phase 1 and Phase 2. It is only after a rather extensive preparation that the effective managers look for higher-level backing, and then they choose the backer most suitable for the issue under consideration. They thus identify the appropriate "bellwethers," whose positive comments about a project will draw others in, and they also identify the possessors of necessary resources.

The nature of the bargain struck with sponsors minimizes their risk. First, they are asked for a very specific kind of supply or support rather than for generalized backing. This issue-specificity is important; power is "loaned" for a specific project and the sponsor remains free to commit other resources elsewhere. The act of sponsorship itself does not implicate the sponsors in the success or failure of the project, and the careful preparation and presentation of a case to sponsors gives them something "tangible" to point to as a reason for taking any risk at all. If it sways or impresses some sponsors, it provides a rationalization for others.

Sponsorship is the first step in coalition-building, since higher-level support encourages others to join the team and contribute time, energy, or resources. In very few cases are the entrepreneurs out there alone plugging away in isolation. The image of the solo inventor single-mindedly pursuing a project through to completion is highly unlikely to occur in a corporate setting, although there may be occasions where the model fits technological inventions. Even in those circumstances where the accomplishment seems most isolated (such as an engineering development manager who proved he could develop a new product in an isolated location far from corporate headquarters), there are strong communication links built into key authorities who would then be using the results of the product development efforts. The accomplishments of entrepreneurial middle managers are thus more likely to be collaborative or group efforts than would be those of the more traditional bureaucrat. They involve the contributions of a number of peers and subordinates, whose active involvement is sought in this middle phase.

An important part of coalition-building involves what one company calls "managing the press," or managing information. Effective managers are frequent communicators. They spread information about project activities in such a way that opposition is effectively neutralized and key supporters are in a position to do more than broadly legitimate or initially authorize, but can also "run interference" during low moments in the project itself—e.g., answering a critic in a meeting the middle manager does not attend. They work to create an image of their activities that put them in the most favorable light—perhaps by exaggerating the number of risks successfully pulled off. They keep the project alive in the imaginations of those around, especially the investors of power who now have an equity position in the accomplishment. Frequent and politically savvy reports are a good way of keeping members of the coalition from wondering whether their involvement or investment is still wise, a question most likely to arise in those accomplishments taking many months to realize (as truly *significant* accomplishments often do).

Action

The action phase is straightforward. It consists of applying the acquired resources to carry out the task, which has now been reshaped by the interactions of the coalition-building phase. This may involve forming committees to develop concrete plans, or it may involve implementing a pilot project. Here the critical tasks are to fend off potential opposition—more likely to arise now that the project looks as though it may actually happen—and to sustain momentum.

It is striking how little overt political opposition is encountered by managers in the pilot interviews. Opposition or resistance seems to take a more passive form: criticism of specific details of the plan, foot-dragging, low response to requests, unavailability, or arguments for preferential allocation of scarce time and resources to other pet projects. (In the latter case, it is not so much that the enterprising manager's project is argued *against* as that arguments are mounted *for* other activities.) Perhaps the lack of overt opposition comes from the strength of the initial authorization, as well as the political skill of the enterprising manager; but another explanation might lie in the extent to which overt conflict is dangerous to those engaging in it, for just as the enterprising manager needs their support in this instance, so might they need his or his advocate's support in the future.

Early opposition is likely to take the form of skepticism and therefore reluctance to commit time or resources. Later opposition is likely to take the form of direct challenge to specific details of the plan that is unfolding. The nature of the opposition becomes clearer at later points in the accomplishment's history, in part because the impending development or change has become more concrete, and in part because the very act of contacting others in the course of bringing an accomplishment into being may mobilize what would otherwise have been latent or unorganized opposition. Each action designed to develop a broad base of support or solicit suggestions also bears the risk of arousing opponents or eliciting criticisms. Ironically, the very way that the effective enterprising managers handled later-stage criticism—by open discussion in which they provided a carefully thought-through answer to each criticism—can also potentially run the risk of publicizing the arguments against their plan. The managers who deal with this most easily, of course, are those who have authorization to implement as well as develop, because as long as they can keep their opposition from interfering with their activities, they can eventually counter all arguments with proof of results.

In addition to continual discussion and communication, the effective managers disarm opposition by deescalating the issues involved. Whereas critics will operate by escalating the issues, enterprising managers reassure potential opponents by minimizing the amount of required change on the part of other people.

Raw power politics seem much more common in heavily bureaucratic than in the more entrepreneurial settings. The specific, delimited authorizations characteristic of more bureaucratized organizations not only create an incentive for territorial protection and fighting across groups (as in my arguments about powerlessness corrupting) but also create the illusion that managers can indeed act alone, maximizing the value to their own area without having to take the needs and concerns of others into account. In the more entrepreneurial settings, the very ambiguity surrounding the managers' areas and the absence of clear possession of all of the resources, coupled with the nature of the issues that are being tackled, means that managers are impelled to behave more cooperatively in order to survive. Thus, even though the system is more politicized in one sense—with managers having to capture power that they are not directly given in order to get anything done—it is also more civil, at least on the surface. The picture that emerges across a large number and variety of companies shows opponents being won over by persistent, persuasive arguments. Perhaps the very publicness and openness of the battlegrounds—if that word even seems appropriate—make "reason" prevail. It is hard for back room bargaining or displays of unilateral power to occur when issues are debated in group settings. Public meetings require that concerns be translated into *specific* criticisms, each of which can then be countered with data or well-mounted arguments.

Foot-dragging is in many ways a more potent form of opposition; both the enterprising managers and the people they are trying to engage in their projects complain constantly about limited time. The biggest problem for many of them is the tendency for day-to-day activities to take precedence over special projects. In addition, it is easier to whip up excitement over a vision at start-up than to keep it in mind when facing the practical tedium of work. In these cases, sustaining enthusiasm over the long haul is a matter both of the personal persistence of the managers and the strength of their authorization—when a key authority or set of authorities is clearly waiting for the results, the impetus for persistence exists.

Here is one area in which staff managers have an advantage over line managers. Whereas line managers can more generally command resources and people's time, their attention tends to be focused on ongoing operations. But staff are often free to single-mindedly pursue a vision, because (a) this is a larger part of the definition of their job; and (b) there are few other tangible results on which they can be measured, providing a career incentive to see a project through to completion. Staff need to work through the line, but they can operate very effectively as prime movers or pushers. One staff manager, whose accomplishments involved the development and support of a number of work improvement programs in manufacturing facilities, commented:

> One of the things that I see here is that staff functions are the real managers of the bureaucracy and are key people to have involved in any ongoing project ... What I tried to do was set boundaries in requirements for the project but had those owned by the participants. This

does not always mean having decisions made on a local level. One of the things that I found was that my assumptions that decisions made on a local level would be the best were totally wrong. A more effective strategy was developing what I thought would be reasonable solutions to problems and getting people to own those and follow through on them on the local level.

FINAL THOUGHTS

We had initially intended to ask each middle manager to describe two completed accomplishments and two failed accomplishments—or "disappointments." Traditional bureaucratic managers had little trouble responding within a 90-minute interview. We soon discovered, however, that the intricacies of getting something done in the new-style settings were such that a full elaboration of just one accomplishment process for entrepreneurial managers took a good hour and sometimes as much as two hours.

We also discovered that the effective entrepreneurial managers found it difficult to identify *any* "disappointments"—paralleling, but in greater magnitude, the problems the bureaucratic managers had defining accomplishments. Some of this is self-serving, of course. But the other reasons lie partly in the person and partly in the surrounding organizational structure and process. First, nearly all accomplishments seem to have a point at which they look like a disappointment—if the action stops. The difference between success and failure often lies simply in the persistence of the manager, in his or her continuation of a single-minded pursuit of a clearly articulated vision, even when the line of least effort or resistance would make it easy to give up. At the same time, these managers also know when to back off and stop pushing, how to wait for a more favorable moment or to choose a better source for needed tools. Their skills involve a cross between persistence and discretion. Of course, it is easier to show both when time is not an issue for the project.

Second, the organizational context and political processes surrounding the activities of entrepreneurial middle managers also act to eliminate failures early. The very looseness of authority that gives enterprising managers both the incentive and the freedom to act entrepreneurially also serves as a control on their actions. The necessity of seeking legitimation, forming coalitions, generating persuasive information, counting on other people for resources, and so forth—all this means that few projects that could fail will go very far, and it also means that many others along the way develop a stake in successful completion. Of course, there *are* bad initial ideas and dead-end tracks, especially in more technical areas. But these will, via persistence and politics, be converted into a more success-prone direction. (This is one reason we are defining the unit activity set by its end result—the "accomplishment"—rather than by the initial definition of the project, since part of the process involves shifting definitions of what the project is in order to channel it toward success.)

Thus, in an ironic sense, freedom and control in organizations are roughly equilibrated. As new organizational conditions and circumstances create opportunities for enterprising managers to act boldly and creatively—to the great benefit of their organizations—the process through which they act and acquire the power to act also serves as a check on their actions.

PART IV

OCCUPATIONAL CONTEXT

TWO MAIN AREAS in which the occupation can control its autonomy are in the tasks performed and the way the occupation is organized. In this chapter, both types of control are examined. Certain occupations have more or less autonomy at both the role and group levels, according to the nature of the tasks performed. The obvious example is the mass production worker who has little control over his work because the tasks are defined by the organization. Only through sabotage and work slow-down can a worker on the line have any control at the role level. At the group level, the organization of the occupation itself becomes important. Unions can and often do work for greater control over the work situation for their members, though this is not necessarily their main function.

ORGANIZATION OF OCCUPATIONS

The power and autonomy of workers in America is related to how (and if) they organize. In the United States there are two common types of workers' organization: the professional association and the labor union. Both types are outgrowths of nineteenth-century industrialization. The union is the result of those forces which centralized production in factories, and the professional association is the result of having a class of free professionals who practiced independently of the workplace (Freidson, 1970a; Larson, 1977). Although the union and professional association were originally opposite in philosophy and orientation, as the work of both professionals and industrial workers converge, so do the philosophies of the organizations. Today's professional workers are not as likely to be the independent practitioners they were in the nineteenth century but rather are salaried employees. Many industrial workers have also become professionalized as they acquired technological skills.

Professional associations. Historically, the purpose of the professional association was to protect its members from encroachment by the state and to secure status and economic privilege for its members. Essentially, the professional association's purpose was and is to create a monopoly over the skills and knowledge of the profession. The prototype of this kind of association is the American Medical Association. The foundation on which a profession must base its authority and strength is in its relation to the state. In the case of medicine, some, if not most, of its strength is based on legally supported monopoly over practices, a monopoly operating through a system of licensing bearing on the privilege to hospitalize patients and prescribe drugs and other procedures virtually inaccessible in most other professions. In the United States, physicians, through their national and state associations, have largely been given the right to determine how political and legal power bearing on medicine is exercised (Freidson, 1970a: 83). Medical associations have the power to set standards for training, socializing, and recruiting members to the profession. Through state associations, physicians also essentially control the licensing procedures for new members and the other aspects of medical practice. Through these practices, the number of potential physicians admitted to medical schools can be limited. In this way, both the practice of medicine can be controlled and the high fees for its members assured through scarcity.

Industrial unions. An ideal union has an opposite philosophy. Rather than organizing those who can meet credentialed qualifications, an industrial union organizes members of an industry or craft to bargain collectively at the point of production—usually the workplace. Implicit in the idea of a union is the ideology that sees workers and management (or capital) in an exploitative relationship. The purpose of the union is to be the mediator between the worker and the owners/managers of the means of production. Under this procedure, collective bargaining committees negotiate issues relating to the content and conditions of work, such as salary and wages. When negotiations fail, workers withhold their labor (their power) through the mechanism of the strike. It is the ability to strike which enables unions to disrupt the economy in some instances and in all instances to keep business enterprises from making a profit. Ideally, professionals are not supposed to strike, their power resting in monopolizing skills and training.

American craft unions, including some which can be considered professional, such as Actors' Equity Association, have had a long history. The American Federation of Labor, essentially a federation of craft unions, was formed in 1881, but it was not until the Great Depression that large numbers of industrial workers were able to organize.

That struggle was over the right to unionize at all. Industrial unions were still considered illegal during the thirties when workers began to organize, and the increasing numbers of workers attracted by the union movement were considered a threat by management, who often reacted with violent resistance. Union organizers were fired and sometimes jailed (a recent example is the film, *Norma Rae*), and union meetings broken up by police and hired ruffians. Workers were locked out of their jobs, and some strikes were broken through the use of military troops (Piven and Cloward, 1977).

Political power rested with management (capital), not with the workers, but the Great Depression changed the relationship. By the 1930s, industrial workers comprised 40 percent of the labor force, with most located in large centralized industries (e.g., steel, automobile). Therefore, the strikes that occurred (legal or not) were massive, and no sector of the economy was immune. It became increasingly clear to the Roosevelt Administration that a stable workforce was necessary to economic recovery, or else the political stability of the country would be threatened.

For these reasons, Congress passed the Wagner Act of 1935, which was declared constitutional in 1937. In addition to giving workers the right to organize and recognizing unions as legitimate collective bargaining agents, the Act contained enforcement provisions through the National Labor Relations Board (U.S. Department of Labor, 1976; Piven and Cloward, 1977). Since that time, several additional Acts have been passed which prescribe how unions are to act as organizations.

Between 1935 and 1947, when union membership had jumped from 3 to 15 million, Congress passed the Taft-Hartley Act (over the veto of President Truman), whose purpose was to reduce the bargaining rights and power of the workers. Taft-Hartley contains a section allowing individual states to pass laws outlawing union shops, thus, along with several other laws, weakening the Wagner Act.

Industrial unions ideally include all workers within a plant or industry rather than organizing along craft lines, but in reality particular groups of workers are often excluded—blacks, for example.

White collar, craft unions, and employee associations. The strength or weakness of unions not only depends on the law but on the nature of work available. The success of the union movement in the United States in part depended on the growing number of workers engaged in industrial work, but with the growth of the service sector and white collar work, there has been a decrease in the proportion of workers belonging to the large industrial unions. Although these unions are still very big and powerful, the number of people belonging to the craft-like employee associations, professional associations which bargain collectively for their members, and white collar unions has generally increased. In 1956, just 2,500,000 white collar workers belonged to unions, a figure representing 13.6 percent of total union membership. By 1978, the percentage had doubled to 28.2 percent. White collar unions are usually less militant than industrial unions and when strikes do occur, they usually involve an occupational group striking against a smaller industry and do not have the power to disrupt the larger economy. In contrast, the largest number of new union members are public employees, such as mail carriers, policemen, school teachers, and others who do have the power to disrupt daily operations of social life.

Professional associations as unions. In recent years the distinction between professional associations and the unions has become blurred, because many professionals now work for organizations, and most professional organizations also act as collective bargaining agents for their members. Medicine, law, and dentistry have maintained purely professional associations, but many doctors, lawyers, and dentists also work in organizations with employees' unions, meaning that they could also bargain collectively at their workplace, as many have.

The profession providing the best example of changing ideology about professional status and its ideal of appropriate behavior for a profession is teaching. Some teachers and college professors belong to the American Federation of Teachers (the AFT), a craft union affiliated with the American Federation of Labor/Congress of Industrial Organizations (AFL/CIO). Still other teachers belong to the National Education Association (NEA), which was originally organized as a professional association with the purpose of professionalizing its members. After World War II, when it became evident that teachers would not be able to limit their membership or protect their income through scarcity, many teachers began to join unions. To keep their members, the NEA was forced to change its philosophy, and in some jurisdictions the NEA even acts as a collective bargaining agent; in others, the AFT does the bargaining. Because Taft-Hartley allows employees to decide who will represent them, teachers in various school districts also vote for an organization of their own choice. Before World War II, it was unlikely that teachers would go out on strike, but since then, and especially since 1965, there have been many strikes with school districts closed for long periods of time (U.S. Department of Labor, 1976).

No matter how powerful and strong a union is, the tasks performed are important mechanisms of work control. In this chapter, the work tasks of the various occupations will be the major unit of analysis. Our main thesis is that for all occupations, each of the controls (societal and cultural, organizational, occupational and client control) interacts in various degrees. The result of this interaction is greater or lesser autonomy for an occupational group and for occupational roles. This has been demonstrated in the chapters on societal and organizational control. The work task is often neglected by sociologists who put more emphasis on outside controls such as status, prestige, and organizational context. On the other hand, those interested in job satisfaction, the professional status of an occupation, and alienation have considered the task, possibly even over-emphasizing the task, in relationship to other forms of control. Part of our purpose is to put the task in perspective with these other concepts.

TRUCK DRIVERS AND CABBIES

These workers do routine tasks; they deliver goods, people, services, and so forth to a variety of places. While Peterson et al. do not elaborate on what these workers do, everyone has some notion of what is involved in this type of transport work. Limited skills are required, and the complexity and range of tasks is not broad. Non-union workers work long hours, often by themselves, for relatively low pay.

This comparative study of transport operators supports the argument that worker autonomy is important to these workers. For some, it is so important that ownership of the means of production is essential. The autonomy resides in being able to pace and control one's work when one owns the truck or cab. The potential to increase one's income was not the crucial factor which influenced owners to buy their own vehicle. The reward was autonomy at the role level.

Several types of autonomy were derived from this study: (1) freedom from direct control by a machine; (2) freedom from direct managerial supervision; (3) freedom from the unilateral action of management; (4) freedom from control by clients; (5) freedom to define conditions of work; and (6) the opportunity to combine life on the job with other roles.

This study reinforces the kinds of worker autonomy found in the poultry processing industry. Autonomy in the workplace is defined as freedom to determine *how* the worker will do his job and to some extent *when.* The nature of the work, whether pleasant or unpleasant, does influence to some degree the structure of work. Then the structure of the work compliments the structure of nonwork; the specific "dirty" and "unpleasant" work component loses importance for these workers.

While these workers experience autonomy at the role level, they have less autonomy at the group level. While some operators are union members, union concerns have been focused more on economic benefits for workers rather than autonomy in the workplace. This may be an important finding, because there are many views on the success and failure of particular unions to satisfy the members and retain membership. If workers value autonomy at the role level more than other conditions of work, they will accept unpleasant tasks in order to obtain the freedom to define how the work will be done. These workers, however, are limited in work alternatives because of their level of skills.

THE POULTRY WORKER

The tasks of the poultry processor are to: (1) snatch live birds from cages; (2) hang these birds; (3) slaughter the birds by cutting their throats; (4) remove feathers and dress the birds; (5) disembowel the birds; (6) inspect and grade the birds; (7) cut, boil, and trim birds into pieces; (7) package the dressed pieces; (8) store and ship the poultry. Some of these tasks are completed by machine and some by hand. But however these are completed, it is in uncomfortable working conditions. Foul odors, varying degrees of dampness, and dirty conditions resulting from the nature of the work. In addition, this work is not without potential hazard, even to the point of skin problems from the poultry body fluids.

Clifton Bryant and Kenneth Perkins found the workers in this environment to be satisfied with the job, despite the nature of the work. A most common favorable comment was that the workers got along with each other. The workplace was to some degree an extension of the community of residence, and the bonds of solidarity were confirmed in the workplace. The workers lived, worked, and played together.

Some of the tasks in these jobs required a machine line processor. Workers on the line were able to some degree to regulate the pace of their work. These were generally the male workers. The sexual division of labor resulted in the males doing the work that required physical strength; the women's activities on the processing line included tasks which women would be doing as housekeepers. The division of labor and corresponding structure of the workplace was accepted as appropriate by these workers and as complimentary to their community roles and positions.

Bryant and Perkins's study of the rural industrial workers suggests that worker autonomy is related to job satisfaction. The structure of the workplace provided workers the opportunity to pace their work to some degree, the opportunity to socially interact while working, the opportunity to see a product to the end, and the opportunity to purchase the product of their work at a discount. These features of the workplace were perceived by the workers to make up for the unpleasant nature of the work. Autonomy at the role level was important to these workers.

NURSES

The tasks that nurses perform are both complex and differentiated. Basically, the nurse is concerned with multiple aspects of patient care. Not only can a nurse perform a number of different tasks, but there are a number of different kinds of nurses: licensed practical nurses, registered nurses, graduate nurses, nurse clinicians, nurse practitioners, and the like. The basic feature of differentiation is the number of years in school. Also, nurses are usually women. Here, Bullough and Bullough examine the interactions of these factors and the impact on nursing.

Several of their findings are important in explaining the limited autonomy of this occupation at the group level. A sex-segregated system, especially one with a feminine image, does not provide much opportunity for upward mobility. What does a nurse move to after she has assumed a leadership role in nursing? Her knowledge and skills are limited to one industry.

Also, the authority relationship between nurses and physicians has essentially remained the same, even though nurses have acquired considerable knowledge that may be useful to doctors in their decisions about patients.

Because the nature of the nurse's work is to observe the patients all day, the nurse is able to gather from observations important information relative to a patient's changing condition. Whether this information is used by physicians in their decisions about their patients has been a source of conflict for nurses for some time. Nurses value the autonomy to make important decisions about patient care, especially at critical points.

A recent examination of cardial intensive care units has shown higher-than-usual nursing staff turnover. One important reason offered by nurses was that doctors did not listen to them or accept their evaluation of changing patient conditions. The nurses argued that they needed the autonomy to act quickly on the basis of their judgment, based on knowledge and first-hand experience.

Nursing as an occupation continues to change in its structure and knowledge base. One fact still remains: there is a shortage of available trained nurses who are willing to work as nurses. Hospitals are closing wards because of nursing staff shortages, and are also having to increase nurses' salaries. This still does not seem to be adequate for solving the nursing shortage. Autonomy at the role level seems to be an important concern that nurses are determined to obtain.

CONSTRUCTION WORKERS

Construction workers have been studied from a perspective that assumes nonbureaucratic organization and occupational autonomy (see Silver for a review). This model assumes autonomy at the group and role levels, based on the complex nature of the work and precision skills developed through apprenticeship, and is described by Riemer in his discussion of license and mandate.

But not all construction workers are skilled. Silver notes a wide range of jobs for unskilled, semi-skilled, and skilled workers. Thus, it is likely that a wide range of autonomy will be found among these workers. This may take various forms: degree of freedom from supervision; discretion to make decisions with consultation with management; and freedom to plan and carry out projects.

Both Riemer and Silver note the changing patterns of discontent and alienation characteristic of this occupational group. Why such discontent is occurring is approached by them using different data collection techniques and theoretical approaches. Their arguments and their findings are not necessarily similar, but there is one point on which they agree: management does exercise considerable control over these workers, and autonomy at the group and role levels is not present to the degree expected.

CHAPTER NINE

ENTREPRENEURSHIP OR AUTONOMY?

Truckers and Cabbies

Richard A. Peterson
John T. Schmidman
Kirk W. Elifson

THIS CHAPTER REPORTS the results of two studies. The first focuses on dump truck drivers hauling earth from major construction sites around Madison, Wisconsin. The second deals with cabdrivers plying their craft on the streets of Nashville, Tennessee.

The project began when we learned that some of the drivers hauling earth from the site of a new campus building adjacent to the sociology offices at the University of Wisconsin owned their own trucks, while others who worked side-by-side with them, doing exactly the same work, were employees of the building contractor. The only apparent difference in the jobs of these two groups of drivers was their relationship to the means of production—ownership on the one hand, and employee status on the other. This seemed an ideal locus to seek answers to the question: What impells some persons, but not others, to become self-employed?

Borrowing the view held widely among economists and psychologists, our study began with the idea that ownership is sought by persons with a strong entrepreneurial drive (Schumpeter, 1934, 1965) or, as the psychologist McClelland (1961) calls it, "a high need for achievement." The wide-ranging literature on entrepreneurship has been reviewed by Kilby (1971), Wilken (1979), and Peterson (1981).

We formulated and pretested a 45-item interview schedule to test four specific hypotheses relating to entrepreneurship which have been noted frequently in the literature.

(1) Compared to employee-drivers, owner-drivers will more often espouse the values of, and beliefs in, entrepreneurship. Specifically, owner-drivers will more often stress self-determination, risk-taking, pride in ownership, and a need to achieve success.
(2) Owner-drivers will more often come from middle-class, rather than working-class backgrounds.
(3) Owners will express more conservative economic and political attitudes.
(4) And finally, owners will exhibit a more middle-class way of life than their working-class employee-driver co-workers.

In our first formulation, no thought was given to the possibility that job autonomy, as distinct from entrepreneurship, might influence the actions of our two groups of respondents. The results of this study, however, led us to assert that a quest for job autonomy, and not entrepreneurship per se, led our respondents to follow the careers they have.

THE TRUCK DRIVER STUDY

Method

A list of potential respondents was drawn from the membership of Locals 200 and 695 of the International Brotherhood of Teamsters. All dump truck drivers engaged in general hauling, whether employees or owners, must be members of these locals to gain entrance to building and highway construction sites in the Madison, Wisconsin area. A sample of men drawn from these union lists was contacted and recontacted by Schmidman until 30 usable interviews, including 15 owner-drivers and 15 employee-drivers were obtained. One driver, an owner, refused to take part in the study, and several other drivers were too busy to be interviewed during the time interviewing was taking place. Once they found time to talk, the respondents were quite interested and helpful in answering our questions. For a further discussion of methodological considerations, see the Methodological Appendix at the end of the chapter.

General Results

All respondents were white and male; they ranged in age from 25 to 58. The data reveal differences between the owner- and employee-drivers. However, these differences are at variance with those predicted in the four hypotheses. We had expected that owner-drivers would come from middle-class backgrounds more often than their employee-driver counterparts, exhibit middle-class behavior and beliefs more often, express an entrepreneurial ideology more often. These predictions were based on the assumption that the one group desired ownership and bought a truck when they had finally succeeded in saving enough money to buy one. But the primary deterrent to truck purchase does not seem to be financial. We learned from truck dealers that used dump trucks, which cost many thousands of dollars, can be financed readily through a bank loan with a down payment of no more than $500, using the truck itself as collateral.[1]

In the pretest, we found that the drivers, especially the owner-drivers, were very sensitive about income questions. Therefore, we asked the question in relative terms: "Who is able to make more money, the owner-operators or employee-drivers?" Both groups were almost evenly divided on the question. However, all but two of the owners who asserted that they earned more put this on a highly conditional basis. "Owners can make more money," they said, "if they do all of their own repair work, if their truck loan interest charges are not too great, if they push themselves to work longer hours, and the like."

The number of hours worked per week does, in fact, condition the relative income of the two groups. While all of the men are members of the Teamsters Union, the work week of the employee is strictly limited, while that of the owners is clearly open. Employees reported working an average of 45 hours per week, while owners reported working 60 hours per week on the average. Thus, if owners do earn more money, it is only because they work almost three hours for every two hours that employees work.

We asked interviewees which working arrangement, in their opinion, was better. Not *one* of the employees clearly favored owning. The most often mentioned reasons for preferring employee status were the lack of financial risk and the shorter hours worked by employees. Three of the owners favored employee-driving, and the rest gave conditional answers which accented the economic hazards of self-employment.

Just over half of the owners answered "yes" to the question, "Have you ever considered getting out of truck driving?" yet only one is actually trying to sell his truck. In answer to the question, "Would it be easy to change jobs?" most answered "No." In explanation of this and in answer to the question, "Why do you work at this rather than some other sort of work?" they mentioned lack of education, advancing age, poor health, lack of other skills, and the preference for truck driving—in that order. These findings clearly suggest that owners feel trapped in their current line of work. As noted earlier, none of the employee-drivers reported wishing to become owner-drivers. Why then did the owners buy their trucks?

Entrepreneurship?

When asked, "What do you like most about truck driving?" three-fifths of the owners mentioned "being my own boss." However, in answer to an earlier question asking why they had purchased the truck, only four men gave reasons which even remotely related to a desire for entrepreneurship. Over two-thirds of the owners said they liked their work because they were able to be outside, it allowed them freedom of movement, and lacked continuous close supervision, as compared with factory work. For these blue collar owners, "being one's own boss" seemed to mean freedom from the direct supervisory control experienced by most blue collar workers.

Most of the owner-drivers *had* worked in factories earlier in their job careers, and almost to a man, they volunteered hatred and contempt for factory work. When asked how they would rank their work relative to other occupations, the owners did not take as a point of reference their status as owners. Rather, they compared truck driving with factory work and accentuated their own job autonomy and craft-status as expressed in expert driving. Thus, the aspects of their work which these owners reported liking had to do with the job autonomy experienced by *all* dump truck drivers and not with ownership per se.

The employee-drivers, for their part, often referred to a dislike of close supervision and reported feeling that, as drivers, they enjoyed a high degree of job autonomy. Several of the employees volunteered that as employee-drivers, they felt as if they were their own boss but without having the worries associated with truck ownership.

Although in hindsight it seems like an obvious question, we did not probe in detail for why owners bought their rigs, but an answer begins to emerge when the 30 interview protocols are viewed jointly. From them, we infer that with but two exceptions, the men had bought their first trucks in order to maintain their status as truck drivers when they had been laid off as employee-drivers. Seen in this light, these truck purchases represent a special case of a process taking place widely in which workers buy the factory, mine, or shop in which they work in order to keep it from being closed or relocated in another part of the country. (See Conte and Tannenbaum, 1978; Zwerdling, 1978; and Carnoy and Shearer, 1980 for numerous examples of this process.)

Social Class Differences?

Now we turn to a consideration of the data relevant to the second, third, and fourth hypotheses.

Based on the assertion that the desire for entrepreneurship is learned early in life (Schumpeter, 1934, 1965; McClelland, 1961), it was hypothesized that our owner-drivers would more often come from middle-class rather than working-class families. The interviews reveal absolutely no differences between the family backgrounds of employee- and owner-drivers. The two groups are the sons of farmers, skilled craftsmen, shopkeepers, and laborers in equal proportions.

Answers to questions relating to the third hypothesis show the same pattern. Two-thirds of each group identified themselves as "working class," and the other third of each identified itself as "middle class." Their attitudes toward specific labor unions are also similar. The political party identification of the two groups showed the same distribution, and their preferences for candidates in the most recent presidential election were quite similar. In responding to the open-ended question, "What is the major problem the United States faces?" both groups focused on problems of the economy, communism, and civil rights with no clear differences between the two groups. Again, when asked, "What groups in America have too much power?" both groups mentioned "business" and "extremist organizations" in equal proportion. In all these instances, there was no clear difference in the response patterns which might distinguish owners from employee-drivers. This finding, that the attitudes of owners and employees do not differ, adds weight to our assertion that the decision to buy a truck is not rooted, to any important extent, in values and beliefs relating to entrepreneurship.

There are, however, some clear differences between owners and employees on the questions relevant to the final hypothesis having to do with lifestyle differences. While both groups report leisure activities which include hunting, fishing, watching television, and playing cards, the employee-drivers more often report drinking and dating, while owners more often bowl, work on their homes, or work in their gardens. These differences are reflected in the fact that the owner-drivers are more likely to be married and own their own homes, while the employees are more often single and renters.

Such differences might suggest that owners have a somewhat more middle-class life-style, but another interpretation is possible. The factor which most clearly differentiates the two groups is their age. The median age of the owners is 44 years, and that of the employees is just 29. What is more, the median age for truck purchase is 39 years of age—10 years beyond the current median age of employee-drivers.

In view of the finding that owners were not, as we had predicted, more desirous of taking financial risks, more often from affluent backgrounds, or middle-class in their attitudes, it may well be that the lifestyle differences found between the owners and employees can be accounted for by differences in their ages rather than by a greater entrepreneurial drive among owner-drivers. Our second study of cabdrivers was designed to further explore this possibility.

THE CABDRIVER STUDY

Moving to Nashville, the first author found a study site with close parallels to the one in Wisconsin. Two cab companies controlled two-thirds of the licensed cabs on Nashville Streets. The largest company employed Teamsters Union drivers; its chief rival employed owner-drivers. To drive for this latter company, a person simply had his own auto painted in the appropriate colors, and the company installed a meter and a radio telephone. He then paid a weekly fee for the radio dispatching service. As in the case of the truck driver study, the only significant difference between the two sorts of cabbies was their relationship to the means of production: owner versus employee. This provided the opportunity to replicate the earlier study and add items to address the questions it had raised.

Method

Based on the experience of the first study, a 44-item questionnaire was constructed by Peterson and Elifson. A number of questions relating directly to the Wisconsin situation and dump truck driving were cut, and questions were added to get a clearer picture of the job history of each respondent and to probe more deeply into why respondents had, or had not, chosen to buy a cab. Interviewing was conducted by Elifson over a three-month period.

Samples were drawn from the list of 125 cabbies working regularly for the two companies. We had intended to interview 25 from each group, but while the employees were quite cooperative, some of the owners, for reasons discussed below, were reluctant to be interviewed within the time frame available for data gathering, so the cabbie study is based on completed interviews with 25 employee-drivers and 20 owner-drivers. For a fuller discussion of methodological considerations, see the Methodological Appendix at the end of the chapter.

General Results

All the cabbie respondents were white and male, as were the truck drivers.[2] In one vital way, however, the cabbie samples differed from those in the earlier study. While the employee truck drivers had been considerably younger, on the average, than their truck owner counterparts, the owner and employee cabbie samples were found to have the same age range (from the late 20s to the mid 60s), have the same median age (40), and differ in the mean age by only two-and-one-half years (40 and 42.5 years, respectively). Thus, age, the variable which had confounded the interpretation of results in the earlier study, seemed to be irrelevant in this sample of cabbies.

Both employees and owners typically asserted that their own group was able to make more money than the other. However, cab owner-drivers tended to hedge this statement, saying that they can make more money *if* they are able to meet their fixed costs on the car, including insurance, depreciation on the car, and the fee for the dispatcher service. These costs can be met if: (1) owners stay in good enough health to work regularly; (2) their car does not break down often; and (3) they can get a reliable relief driver so that the car can be earning money at least two shifts per day.

While it was possible to get income data for the employee-drivers from their employer, it proved entirely impossible to get such data from the self-employed drivers. Persons knowledgeable about the conditions of drivers in Nashville estimated that cab owners and employees make about the same amount of money after expenses are paid if owners work considerably longer hours. This latter is in line with our findings. Our sample of employees worked 52 hours a week, while the owners drove an average of 63 hours per week. These findings on wages and working hours parallel those of the Wisconsin study.

The Four Hypotheses Reevaluated

It was hypothesized first that the owners would more often express an entrepreneurial orientation to their work. While owners did express a pride in being their own bosses, so did employees. What both groups seemed to refer to was not ownership, but rather the freedom which *all* cabdrivers enjoy from close supervision and the confining routines associated with factory work. This finding parallels the Wisconsin study.

Second, it was hypothesized that owner-cabbies would come from middle-class backgrounds more often than their employee counterparts. In fact, the occupations of these men's fathers showed exactly the same ranges and distribution. Again, these findings replicate those of the Wisconsin study.

The third hypothesis was that owners would hold more middle-class attitudes and beliefs than the employee-drivers. In fact, there was no difference between these two groups in terms of their voting behavior, attitudes toward labor unions, estimates of those groups in America which hold too much power, or their subjective social class position. Both groups predominantly defined themselves as working-class, rather than middle-class.

The occupational prestige ranking completed by Hodge et al. (1964) shows taxi drivers to be ranked near the low end of the prestige scale. Cabdrivers clearly concurred in this evaluation. For example, one driver said, "Cabbies are only one notch above the scum of the earth, police." Our cab owners showed no falsely elevated notion of the reputation of cabbies. The owners of cabs believed that people in society rank cabbies even lower than do employee-drivers we interviewed, and more often tended to say that there is no occupation that is lower than the cabbie. Clearly, these data reveal no great pride in cab ownership and suggest no reason why the owners bought their cabs.

The cabbie data do not support the fourth hypothesis of the earlier study, that owners would exhibit a more middle-class life-style. Measures of home ownership, organizational activities, and leisure time pursuits showed no differences between owner-drivers and employees. Of equal importance, these two groups gave the same range of answers when asked, "What kinds of jobs would you advise a son of yours to get into?" The younger respondents in both groups advised the professions, while the older men in both groups tended to mention crafts and technical jobs most often.

Turning from wishes to real-life attainments, our data show that none of the sons of respondents in either group had achieved more than a year of college. Likewise, the employed sons in both groups held jobs in the same range of skill and income. None of the sons of owner-cabbies held anything above the level of blue collar jobs. Of course, the children of the younger cab owners were still in school, but it is quite clear that the sons of older cab owners had not achieved intergenerational social class mobility, and the jobs they held tended to preclude future mobility. Thus, nothing in the data we collected suggests that owner-drivers have a more middle-class orientation than their employee-driver counterparts.

Career Lines

All of the findings discussed so far replicate the results of the first study and cast further doubt on the hypotheses we derived from the writings on entrepreneurship. The results discussed so far, however, do not provide a clear answer for our primary question: Why have some of these men bought cabs while others work as employee drivers?

To pursue this question, we collected detailed job histories of all our respondents, in each case asking them to recall, as best they could, why they left each job and took the next. From these data, it was possible to construct a career line for each of our respondents. Since some of these job changes had taken place over a quarter of a century earlier, and others had taken place under circumstances which the respondent might not want to publicly acknowledge, the reasons given were sometimes vague or superficial. The interviewer pursued the question as far as he could without causing the respondent to break off the interview.

Putting together all this job history information, it is possible to create a composite diagram which begins with what we call "first jobs"—one or more jobs taken in their teen-age years before they began their stable careers. The composite flowchart ends with the current job status as cab owner or employee. A number of conclusions become apparent at once.

First, none of the drivers have returned to other types of work for more than a few months once they began cab-driving. What is more, none of the employee-drivers had ever bought a cab, but, with two exceptions to be detailed below, all of the owners had been employee-cabbies for from 18 months to 28 years before they purchased a cab. Thus, for our interviewees, cab-driving became the occupation of choice once it was tried, and once drivers buy, they don't return to employee status.

Second, all of the men had held other sorts of jobs before they became cabbies, and the range of these jobs was just the same for employee- and owner-drivers. Most of our respondents had been in the armed forces, more than half in each group had worked in factories, and nearly half of each group had had experience driving trucks, heavy machinery, buses, or light delivery vans. Thus, nothing in the early job histories of these two groups suggests why the one group bought cabs while the others remained employee-drivers.

Third, entrepreneurship is evident in the job histories of two of the owner-drivers. Their career lines are distinctly different from those of the other 33 interviewees. Neither of these men had been a cabby before he bought. Rather, in both cases, cab ownership was an adjunct to their principal self-employed line of business. One owned an auto repair shop, owned three cabs, and drove only when one of his regular drivers was out sick. A pilot and Civitan Club member, he is the only respondent who fits the middle-class entrepreneurial mold. The other respondent who did not drive before he bought a cab provides a contrasting example of entrepreneurship. He told us that he drove a cab in order to have an excuse to cruise the neighborhoods where his 20 illegal pinball machines were located, and that he had to buy the cab in order to be able to control where and when he drove.

Reasons Given for Buying

Based on the questions raised by the results of the Wisconsin study, we designed several questions to find out why some men, but not others, buy the cabs they drive. The results are revealing for our speculations about the importance of entrepreneurship versus autonomy.

The largest single group of buyers, seven in all, were older men who became owners when the cab company for which they had been driving went out of business. They chose to buy their cabs and remain affiliated with the reorganized cab dispatching service. They were not happy about buying. One said, "I don't like nothing about it, I had to." Others said, "It was this or nothing"; "With my bad back, there was no alternative"; and "Driving a cab is what I know. Who else would hire me?"

Another seven men bought a cab after they quarreled and quit or were fired from the other large local cab company. Another experienced cabdriver was fired by the police department and then became a cab owner. These eight argumentative, independent, younger owners reported buying in order to sustain their job freedom and to avoid the close supervision and control by machinery characteristic of factory work.

There is a related factor which most respondents were reluctant to mention, however. As has been noted widely in the literature on cabdriving (Morris, 1951; Miles, 1953; Vaz, 1955; Davis, 1959; U.S. News and World Report, 1964; Henslin, 1967, 1974; Backes, 1969; Stannard, 1971; Christiansen, 1977; and Hirshey, 1980), cabdriving allows the mobility and potential contacts necessary for providing a wide range of illegal services: illegal liquor, prostitutes, homosexuals, drugs, gambling, and so forth. One of these respondents said candidly that he left the other cab company because the management objected to his taking too much time out to engage in illegal activity.

Arrest Records

The case of the man just described leads us to suspect that for some cabbies, ownership may be a necessary part of what might be called entrepreneurship in deviance. We were able to pursue the question through the generous assistance of several city officials who made available to us the complete police records of all our respondents.[3] Neither cab owners nor employee-drivers showed any arrests for the sorts of illegal services that many cabbies are said to provide. Thus, the emerging conjecture concerning entrepreneurship in deviance did not seem to account for why some people buy cabs and others do not.

The arrest records were very revealing nonetheless. Of the employee-drivers, 62 percent had arrests for nothing other than traffic violations. The other 38 percent had arrests for misdemeanors such as public drunkenness, disorderly conduct, and resisting arrest. In marked contrast, only 40 percent of the owners had records with nothing more than traffic arrests. A total of 25 percent had arrests for misdemeanors such as drunk and disorderly conduct. The remainder of the owner-drivers, fully 35 percent of the sample, had numerous arrests for serious crimes ranging from repeated larceny, criminal assault, and robbery, to murder. While these are only records of arrests, and hence do not show whether the men were found guilty, they do, however, show that a goodly proportion of the owner-drivers had been publicly accused of being violent, untrustworthy, and dangerous persons.

Whether or not they use their cabdriving to facilitate illegal activity, their arrest records may well account for their quitting or being fired as employee-cabdrivers. Such a record would also make it difficult for them to find alternative employment even if they wished to leave cabdriving. This conjecture gains weight when the dates of arrest for major crimes are seen in conjunction with the job histories. In six instances, arrest for a major crime, considered with cab purchase and the accumulation of arrests for minor crimes, may have been contributing factors in several other cases. The arrest records add further weight to the evidence that most drivers are pushed by negative circumstances to buy their cabs, rather than being pulled by a positive desire for entrepreneurship.

THE DRIVE FOR AUTONOMY

The data from our two studies lend little support to the assertion of Schumpeter (1934, 1965) and others that individuals seek self-employment from a strong desire for entrepreneurship. Rather, our findings are in line with a wide range of studies reviewed by Kilby (1971) and Peterson (1981) suggesting that self-employment is most often chosen at that point in a person's career when other options are blocked, and that self-employment offers the best chance to utilize the skills and experience gained as an employee.

As a recent investigation by Bulkeley (1981) suggests, this rule—buy when blocked—even holds true for those who have already established their own successful businesses. Bulkeley found that many self-employed business people become frustrated with the growing size, complexity, and routine of the businesses they have founded. A goodly number of these people leave their own firms in order to start new ones.

We did not specifically ask dump truck drivers why they bought their rigs. Nevertheless, several of them volunteered that they had bought their first rig to remain drivers after having been laid off from their driving jobs in the highly seasonal construction business, or when they had lost their driving jobs due to an injury.

These findings are corroborated by the more systematic probing of owners in our study of cabdrivers. Most bought their cabs when they could no longer remain employee-cabdrivers because the firms for which they worked went broke, or for reasons relating to their job and criminal records.

As noted above, some of the older drivers in both our studies said that they remained drivers because it was the only line of work they knew. Most of our respondents, however, remained drivers because they liked driving relative to the other blue collar jobs open to them. The general term which describes what all drivers liked about their work is "autonomy."

Dimensions of Autonomy

Autonomy has a number of dimensions, and as the editors of this anthology note, autonomy of one sort may restrict autonomy of another. Six sorts of autonomy seem to be important to the drivers we interviewed.

First, autonomy means freedom from direct control by a machine-paced work process. Comparing themselves to assembly line factory workers, numerous respondents said in effect, "I drive the machine, not vice versa." Such a control over machines (Larson, 1981) and freedom from control by machines (Thurow, 1981) is highly prized by contemporary American blue collar workers.

Even though they recognize that, relative to most other jobs, cabdriving is dangerous, poorly paid, and held in low repute by the general public, owner and employee cabby respondents alike expressed a high degree of job satisfaction (Elifson, 1968). The high levels of job satisfaction are explained, we believe, by the relatively high level of job autonomy experienced by all drivers.

Second, autonomy means freedom from direct managerial supervision. Truckers and cabbies alike mentioned the great freedom they felt in being able to do their jobs "without a foreman breathing down your neck." This autonomy is exemplified in the frequently reported arguments between bemused cabbies and exasperated dispatchers who can't locate or direct their activity. This driver-dispatcher tension is often mentioned in the literature on cabdriving (see especially Backes, 1969; Henslin, 1974; and Hirshey, 1980).

Recent studies of contemporary cowboys (Blundell, 1981), high-rise building steel-workers (Harris, 1981), and game wardens (Slocum, 1981) all note that freedom from bureaucratic routine or close supervision is the prime compensation in these dangerous, demanding, and relatively poorly paid pursuits (Rothschild-Whitt, 1979).

Third, autonomy means protection from the unilateral action of management. In the United States, the most important means of gaining this sort of protection is collective action through a labor union (Schmidman, 1979). The employee truck and cab drivers in our study are members of the International Brotherhood of Teamsters, which has done a great deal to improve wages, hours, and working conditions for drivers, but the union's record on individual worker grievances is mixed. Many of the cabdrivers complained that the union didn't actively press their grievances against management except just before election time. The rest of the time, union officials seemed to accommodate the interests of management at the expense of the interests of drivers. Henslin (1974) reached this same conclusion in his study of St. Louis cabbies.

While our sample of truck owner-drivers are members of the Teamsters Union, they find themselves in an ironic situation. Through agreements with the construction companies, the Teamsters Union requires all owner-drivers to be members of the Teamsters Union. But, at the same time, the law enjoins the union from representing the interests of the owner-drivers.[4] Cab owners have no union or other form of occupational association to protect their collective interests. They do not participate in any group accident insurance, retirement plan, or unemployment compensation.[5] Thus, the owner-drivers enjoy, or as is more often the case, agonize over the freedom of the competitive marketplace.

Fourth, autonomy means freedom from control by clients. Accommodating to the often conflicting demands of the employing organization and the clients it serves has long been recognized as a major problem for service workers (Hughes, 1958; Blau, 1960; Ryan and Peterson, 1982). The problem has recently received a good deal of attention under the rubric of "burn-out" (see especially Bishop, 1980; Cherniss, 1980; and Edelwich and Brodsky, 1980). Unlike many kinds of drivers, dump truck drivers do not have to accommodate the needs and interests of passengers and persons other than their employers.

Cabbies, on the other hand, must deal with a series of different customers each day. Like waiters and others whose income depends in part on tips (Butler and Skipper, 1981), cabbies must develop strategies which facilitate tips while at the same time allowing them to restrict the demands made by customers. The strains and hazards of these fleeting relationships have been a major focus of the academic research on cabbies (see especially Davis, 1959; Henslin, 1967; Stannard, 1971; and Hirshey, 1980). Although our interview schedule did not include questions about clients, many of the respondents regaled Elifson with stories about the demands and foibles of their "fares." As predicted by Bensman and Lilienfield (1973), a great deal of the pride in the craft of cabdriving and the driver's definition of self is tied to the means of gaining and maintaining autonomy from customer demands.

Fifth, autonomy means the freedom of an occupation to define the conditions within which it works. Such a "mandate" of autonomy, as Everett Hughes (1958) calls it, is most likely to be granted when an occupation is socially defined as engaged in a task which is vital, demands personal sacrifice, and requires special skill or knowledge. The established professions such as law and medicine provide cases in point.

All occupational groups proclaim their own skill, self-sacrifice, and worth to society, but most blue collar occupations receive very little societal support for these claims. Both truckers and cabbies are distinctive in this regard.

The freedom of the road has given truck drivers a special aura, like that of the cowboy or railroader. The heroic aspects of driving are regularly celebrated in movies, TV programs, and popular songs. In addition, the association with major construction projects heightens the heroic dimension of dump truck driving. The only challenge to this autonomy comes from traffic police and truck safety inspectors.

The cabby's definition of self-worth, however, is continually open to challenge. Cabbies perform a service for persons in a hurry; the rates they charge and the routes they drive are often open to question; they are asked to engage in activities which are illegal; and they are required to go at night into "undesirable" parts of town. They must continually be wary of traffic police, the vice squad, and several sorts of inspectors. Some of our respondents seemed to take great pride in surviving by offering a range of services in what they define as a jaded world. Others gained self-worth by disassociating themselves from the other cabbies whom they consider contemptible. Further corroboration for the existence of these two quite different ways of viewing the occupation of cabbie is found in Henslin's (1967) account of cabdrivers in St. Louis, and from the observations recounted to us by Dan Bednarz, an informant who has worked as a cabby in a working-class suburb of Detroit.

Finally, autonomy means successfully accommodating life on the job with the other life roles that workers play (Staines and O'Connor, 1980). Our dump truck drivers seemed to be stereotypical, working-class types. The only unusual tension between the demands of the job and those imposed by other roles occurs when drivers are employed at a work site too far from home to commute home each night. They have reacted to this by pressing the union to bargain for keeping their weekends free to spend at home. The owner-drivers, as we noted earlier, often work many more hours than their employee counterparts. They say they compensate by spending a great deal of time at home during the winter when earth-moving work comes to a halt.

As their seniority grows, employee-cabdrivers can insist on day shifts, but their owner-driver counterparts must work most evenings and many weekends in order to keep ahead on the payments for their cabs. The long hours would be a burden to most blue collar workers, but many of our respondents have driven cabs for years and don't seek other types of work. Some of the drivers do seem to have families, while others have adapted their lifestyles to the legal and illegal opportunities afforded by cabdriving at the expense of an ongoing marital relationship and family life.

CONCLUSION: NOT ENTREPRENEURSHIP BUT AUTONOMY

Rather than report these two studies in the neatest way with the clear vision of hindsight, we have taken the reader on an intellectual odyssey through some ideas and a surfeit of data. What began as hypotheses about entrepreneurship has ended with conclusions about autonomy. The reader may wish to disagree, but what we have learned on this journey can be put in three sentences: (1) Our respondents chose driving as a way of gaining job autonomy relative to the other blue collar options which were open to them. (2) With but a few exceptions, our respondents bought a truck or cab in order to remain employed at the type of work with which they were familiar. (3) With but a few exceptions, our respondents acted as they did more out of a desire for autonomy than out of a desire for entrepreneurship.

A good deal more research needs to be done to extend these findings, but this research project contributes to the increasing mass of evidence that blue collar workers are not interested in owning the means of production for the sake of ownership per se, a point made several decades ago by Chinoy (1955) in a study of restive auto workers, many of whom wanted to leave factory work and set up their own businesses. Rather, blue collar workers wish to obtain or maintain a secure job, and to have a greater degree of control over the means of production (see especially Rogers and Berg, 1961; Peterson and Berger, 1971; Conte and Tannenbaum, 1978; Perry, 1978; Zwerdling, 1978; Schmidman, 1979; Bernstein, 1980; Carnoy and Shearer, 1980; Westin and Salisbury, 1980; and Greenberg, 1980, 1981). In brief, they desire autonomy, not entrepreneurship.

NOTES

1. Two knowledgeable persons told us that several of the local used truck dealers make a good deal of their profits from these small, individual down payments. Their practice is to sell, repossess, and resell trucks when each new buyer is in turn not able to meet the necessarily high monthly payments. This suggests why down payments are so low, and why there seems to be no great concern with buyer credit worthiness.

2. At the time the data were collected, no women were licensed to drive cabs in Nashville (Christiansen, 1977), and no blacks drove for the two major companies from which our respondents were drawn. All of the black cabbies worked for several smaller companies primarily servicing the black community. For a discussion of race relations between cabbies and their customers, see Henslin (1967) and Stannard (1971).

3. The arrest record of a person is supposed to be checked before a license to drive a cab is issued or renewed. These records are not routinely open to the public, but we were able to obtain access for research purposes on condition that the information be kept confidential, and that the files not be taken from the office. In our files, the information on arrests was linked to the respondent's interview code number and never linked with their names. We agreed not to tell the respondents that we had access to their arrest records, which sometimes noted the disposition of the case. Thus, we could not check the conflicts between several records of incarceration and the job history data that showed certain respondents to be out of prison and working at the time. Because of understandable increasing public concern about the privacy of individual files, arrest records would not now be made available to social science researchers.

4. The National Labor Relations Act excludes "independent contractors" from the right to organize and bargain collectively afforded those with employee status (Kottkamp, 1957). In identifying an independent contractor, the National Labor Relations Board and the courts apply the common law right of control test.

> If the recipient of the services in question has a right to control not only the end to be achieved but also the means to be used in reaching such result, an employer relationship exists as a matter of law; otherwise, there exists an independent contractor relationship. The application of this principle is not a mechanical one in any case, but requires a careful balancing of all factors bearing on the relationship [National Freight, Inc. 146 NLRB 144, 145-146, 55 LRRM 1259, 1964].

In addition to losing the protection of the NLRA, the owner-drivers and their union run the risk of antitrust prosecution if they collectively attempt to better their economic condition (Sears, 1951). Unions are exempt from prosecution under the antitrust laws while collectively pursuing their members' self-interest; but self-employed, independent contractors are not. See Allen Bradley Company versus Local Union No. 3, IBEW, 325 U.S. 797, 16 LRRM 798 (1945).

5. While construction contractors and cab companies give up some degree of control when they engage owner-drivers, there are numerous economic advantages. First, the companies do not have capital tied up in the trucks or cabs, and don't have to be concerned with their depreciation and repair. Second, the owner-operators don't have to be treated like other employees. The companies do not have to pay the usual sorts of fringe benefits such as health insurance, retirement benefits, extra pay for over-time work, and the like. What is more, the companies are not required to make social security and unemployment insurance payments for owner-drivers they engage.

METHODOLOGICAL APPENDIX

If the results of a study are not published in two or three years after the data are collected, they are ordinarily buried forever, so this project stands as a great exception. The dump truck driver study was conceived by Peterson and Schmidman in 1964, while the former held a grant from the Russell Sage Foundation in the Law and Society Program at the University of Wisconsin. The field work was completed by Schmidman while he was a research assistant on the Russell Sage grant in the summer of 1965. The cabbie study was formulated by Peterson and Schmidman (1966), Peterson and Elifson (1967), Elifson (1968), and Peterson (1973: 87-88). The first author bears the full responsibility for not bringing this final report to publication in a more timely fashion.

Conditions at the two research sites have changed greatly in the 15 years since the data were collected. There is much less building and highway construction in Wisconsin now than there was in the mid 1960s, but if our respondents are like others in the industry, the oldest drivers will have retired, while the younger employees and owners alike will have moved to the Sunbelt in search of jobs for truckers there.

The Nashville cab company that employed drivers has gone bankrupt in the years since the study was made and, like its rival, its drivers now own their own cabs. Nonetheless, conditions of ownership versus employee status have not changed for truck drivers, according to *Business Week* (1980a, 1980b) nor for cabdrivers, according to Backes (1969), Henslin (1974), Christiansen (1977), Hirshey (1980), and Garino (1981). It is hazardous to conjecture, but perhaps the greatest difference we would find if the study were replicated in the early 1980s would be that because of rising levels of education generally, and because of the tighter job market, most drivers today are better educated, but cabdriving in Nashville still attracts persons with impressive criminal records. According to a news item broadcast on January 25, 1979, "over half of all Nashville cabdrivers have felony convictions."

One of the reasons for publishing findings as soon as possible is the possibility that other researchers may report discoveries first. Two studies are notable in this regard. First, Greenberg (1980, 1981) compares workers who have joined producer cooperatives with others who have not. He focuses on the social attitudes and job satisfaction differences between the two groups, but does not trace the career lines of respondents to find why one group has bought shares in the cooperative while the other has not. Second, Brown and Atkinson (1981) note that farm land is worked in a number of different ways, ranging from cases of owners hiring labor at a fixed rate and taking all the risks, through sharecropping to land renting, in which case the owner takes a fixed rent, and the renter takes all the risks. They did not, however, interview farm workers to find out what has induced some to take more risks while others play it safe. Insofar as we are aware, no one has reported a study which duplicates our research or contradicts our findings. We invite inquiries and citations.

CHAPTER TEN

CONTAINING WORK DISAFFECTION

The Poultry Processing Worker

Clifton D. Bryant
Kenneth B. Perkins

THE SOCIOLOGY OF WORK and occupations has been relatively silent on the subject of rural industries and nonagricultural work systems. Industry, however, has located in rural areas, and some of these enterprises have distinctively rural characteristics and are largely integral to the rural context. Poultry processing plants are particularly notable examples. The work forces of such plants are frequently rural and agricultural in origin. Agricultural work is largely self-paced and self-directed, affording a large measure of job autonomy, whereas industrial processing work activities are usually directed by the speed of the line, severely restricting the parameters of job autonomy for the workers. Poultry processing plants have the mechanical characteristics of urban industry, but also have a malodorous atmosphere, uncomfortable temperatures and humidity, and involve aesthetically offensive work. Beyond this, poultry processing employment carries an element of social stigma and is sometimes the butt of humor, as witness the ubiquitous "chicken plucker" jokes and comedy sketches.

Given the marked departure in job autonomy from agricultural to industrial work and the added disagreeable working conditions attendant upon industrial contexts such as poultry processing, there was reason to believe that workers in poultry plants would exhibit especially severe manifestations of frustration, discontentment, and work dissatisfaction in reaction to what were seemingly extraordinarily disaffective working and job conditions. A rural industry with assembly line work, employing a labor force of agricultural origin, and one that incorporates an inordinate degree of "dirty work" (i.e., work that is culturally defined as aesthetically distasteful, physically uncomfortable, or psychologically repugnant), poultry processing represents an unusual work situation with seemingly constituent unsatisfactory working conditions, disaffection, and worker morale problems.[1] This study was an attempt to explore such disagreeable work and the means by which poultry processing employees accommodate themselves to the intrinsic dimensions of their job and to the constituent working conditions, as well as to examine the processes of morale maintenance and the mechanisms used in coping with such work.

Surprisingly, the study revealed that poultry processing employees managed to identify effective means of accommodating themselves to their employment, demonstrating a relatively high degree of satisfaction with their work, and sustaining morale through a widespread network of social interaction both on and off the job. To appropriately understand this phenomenon, some familiarization with rural industry in general, and the nature of poultry processing work in particular, is indicated. The subsequent discussion will address the industrial components of poultry processing and the attendant work role of employees before turning to an examination of the individuals who work in these plants, their careers, and the means by which they socially adjust to such disaffective work.

THE POULTRY INDUSTRY IN THE UNITED STATES

Food processing represents one of the major sectors of the manufacturing industry within the United States. Approximately 15 percent of the value of all manufactured or processed products is as food products, and approximately 9 percent of all employees in manufacturing are directly involved in food processing industries and receive a similar percentage of all manufacturing wages. Within the food processing industry, 26 percent of all food products is meat and 19 percent of its employees are engaged in work related to meat processing, while 27 percent are engaged in poultry processing activities. The poultry industry in the United States is responsible for bringing over *10 billion pounds* of edible birds per year to the marketplace.

With the advent of widespread refrigeration, air conditioning, modern packaging techniques, and supermarket merchandising arrangements, mass production poultry slaughtering and dressing has become economically and technologically feasible. In the first two decades after World War II, poultry processing plants were very labor intensive, and there was only a minimal mechanized component to the process. Subsequently, however, poultry processing plants have become increasingly automated as new techniques have been developed. This has resulted in fewer but larger and more highly mechanized poultry processing plants, some of which are capable of slaughtering and processing as many as 50,000 turkeys or 150,000 chickens in a single day. In 1972, for example, there were a total of 522 poultry dressing plants in the United States, but by 1975, this number had been reduced to 441. This decrease in the number of plants appears to be due to the closing down of the smaller, less mechanized plants, so that today greater production outputs are coming from fewer, but more modernized, plants. Just under one-half of the nation's poultry dressing plants are located in the South. Approximately one-quarter are located in the north-central or midwestern states, with the rest just about equally divided between the Northeast and the West. The preponderance of these plants are located in small towns and rural areas.

The poultry processing industry is composed of two basic sectors. The first, poultry and egg production, is primarily involved in growing poultry and egg-gathering. The second sector of poultry processing begins with the live bird, slaughters it, then dresses and prepares it for marketing. Poultry processing establishments may also engage in what is called "further processing"—cooking, canning, smoking, freezing, and dehydrating. (The present study is concerned exclusively with the poultry processing sector of the industry.)

POULTRY PROCESSING AS RURAL INDUSTRY

The poultry processing industry would appear to qualify as an authentic rural industry. Rural industries are technologically advanced production systems originating and subsequently located in rural areas. They are also frequently compatible with the ethos and routine of the local community and its citizens. Although many corporations locate their subsidiary plants in small towns or even in open country, they generally continue to reflect the urban industry model. Much of the work force may be imported or transferred from urban areas. Suppliers and raw materials may well be obtained from urban industrial sources. Thus, raw materials, work force, process, product, and even the culture of the plant itself may well have an urban progenesis. The true rural industry, such as poultry processing, is largely integral to the rural context and therefore differs substantially in these respects.

Since the mid-twentieth century, when technology and science combined with agriculture to create the modern mass-produced chicken, the poultry industry has, in most instances, effected as an industrial model a "six-stage, vertically coordinated operation, with the family farmer as only one link in the chain" (Talbot, 1978). The various components of the industry are systematically linked and are generally located in rural areas or small towns, and the industry is, accordingly, integrated with the farm. The work force is generally local and thus rural, often even into the supervisory levels. Poultry processing, although it is highly mechanized, basically derives from a rural process, originally involving all handwork. In contrast to urban industries, poultry processing can claim raw materials, work force, process, product, predominate value system, and plant culture as being of rural origin and orientation. The rurality of poultry processing has significant social import for both the assimilation of the work role as well as for the manner in which the dissaffective nature of such work is addressed.

THE RESEARCH SITE AND THE DATA BASE

Data for this research were obtained from the work force of two poultry processing plants located in the Shenandoah area of Virginia.[2] The first of the plants, for purposes of anonymity, is labeled "Valley Farm Plant," largely processes chickens, and is located just outside a small town in a rural area of the state. The plant employs a total of 490 workers, all of whom work one daytime shift. The workers at this plant come from a rather wide area of the rural countryside surrounding the plant location.

The second plant, given the pseudonym "Central Town Plant," is located just outside the major population center of the area in a bordering small town and draws its employees from this circumscribed area. This plant employs a total of 1200 workers on two shifts. (To control for this difference, only workers from the daytime shift were included in the sample.) The characteristics of the workers in this plant, however, did not appear to differ from those at the Valley Farm Plant. The management at Central Town Plant takes a somewhat more distant and impersonal attitude toward its employees than is the case at Valley Farm and this, coupled with its location and larger size, makes it appear much more removed from its rural base than is actually the case. The plants included in this study were two of the 100 largest such operations in the nation. Central Town Plant is the largest turkey dressing plant in the nation.

In addition to extensive observation of the work process in the two plants, and a number of probing interviews with plant officials, in-depth interviews were conducted with a random sample of 60 production workers from each of the two plants. Most of these interviews were conducted in the homes of the workers. The overall study focused on five job parameters of the poultry processing industry: the organization of the work force in the work setting; the personal and background characteristics of the work force; career patterns of the work force; job satisfaction; and the individual and social effects of work in the plant on the workers.

"FOWL WORK AND OFFAL ACTIVITY:"
POULTRY PROCESSING AS DIRTY DISASSEMBLY

Poultry processing is a highly rationalized industrial technique that involves a series of well-defined tasks. It is an extremely efficient and productive process. As one of the interviewed workers characterized it, "You don't throw nothing away but the cackle." Poultry processing differs from most manufacturing work, however, in that it does not incorporate an assembly effort but rather involves an inherently dirty disassembly process. In contrast to a certain neatness of solidity of auto parts, fowl bleed, excrete, and otherwise emit odorous fluids and semi-solids. A poultry processing factory can, in effect, be conceptualized as an assembly plant running in reverse, accomplishing to disassemble dead, feathery, bleeding chicken and turkey carcasses.

Poultry must be handled, initially, as live birds. Workers (almost inevitably male because of the weight handled) must snatch live birds from cages unloaded from tractor trailer trucks and hang them, upside down, on shackles attached to moving conveyor lines. The "hanging" job may even involve 30-40 pound turkeys. The "hangers" are subjected to wing battering by the dirty, squawking birds who not infrequently urinate and/or defecate on the workers handling them. As the flopping, noisy birds move down the line, they undergo an electric shock intended to relax all muscles for a thorough bleeding after the throat is cut. This step also results in additional execretory discharges from the birds. All five senses of the workers are assaulted. One "hanger" who was interviewed revealed that, on weekends, he took six to eight showers trying to rid himself of the stench.

After being shocked, the birds are slaughtered by having their throats cut, either by hand with a knife or by a machine with a worker standing by to kill birds where the machine fails to do so. As with all workers who are involved in "dirty work," there is the incipient problem of social stigma and low self-esteem resulting from such an identity. Poultry processing workers are aware of the potential social image of their "dirty work," but attempt to ignore it. One female from the "killing room" explained it this way:

> You go out there and tell a lady in a store that you back up a killing machine and she will say, "Oh, what's that," and tenses her face up. But that don't bother me none.

After killing, the carcasses move along the line and are dipped in scalding water, then taken through a device with rubber fingers to remove the feathers, after which a "pinner" removes any remaining feathers. In the next phase of the dressing process, the birds move along the line into the eviscerating department, where another set of activities occurs. Here, through successive steps, the employees disembowel the birds, removing their viscera. The eviscerating department employs the largest number of workers.

Within the third department, cooling and chilling, the carcass is dipped into ice-chilled water to reduce the temperature. Workers in this department are responsible for keeping the cooling tanks supplied with ice. In the next department, workers are employed who separate the poultry products according to gross size and/or inspect the carcasses for grading purposes. After sizing and grading, the carcass moves to the department employing the second largest number of workers, where the cutting, boiling, and trimming is accomplished. Here the bird is prepared for packaging, either as a whole bird or as clusters of pieces. The employees in the packaging department then package the dressed poultry. From here, the product moves to be weighed and either stored or routed and loaded for shipping. Further processing, the final department, converts meat into quick food dinners, pies, sandwich meat, and the like.

Poultry processing of necessity involves the commodious use of water, and thus there is an inevitably high degree of dampness and frequency of standing water constituent to this industrial process. The water used may have to be scalding, to remove feathers, or near-freezing, in order to cool the carcasses of the birds. Extreme temperatures are, accordingly, encountered. Thus, employees may have to work in damp, cold, or hot rooms, literally standing in water (and sometimes blood, such as in the "killing room"), handle blood, gore, offal, and visceral organs and materials. In short, the sights, sounds, smells, and tactile sensations associated with their work appear to be aesthetically distasteful, if not repugnant.

Poultry processing work is not without hazard as well. Working with boning knives and equipment such as the "lung gun," that sucks the air sacs and lungs out of the scalded carcasses, the employees sometimes experience minor injuries, and also complain about dermatological problems from the water and poultry body fluids.

THE SOCIAL PROFILE AND CAREER

Unlike poultry dressing plants in other parts of the country, the two plants in this study employed a labor force that was almost exclusively white. The production line work force at both plants was made up of approximately 75 percent females. The predominantly female force apparently resulted from the fact that the plants were located in rural areas, and traditionally the male population has been heavily involved in agriculturally related work. Also, the salary level in the poultry processing industry is relatively low and men, having greater opportunities in the job market, presumably seek higher paying jobs. In addition, it appeared that because of the traditional pattern of female employment and because of the nature of the work, preparing poultry for eventual consumption, work in poultry dressing plants had come to be defined primarily (though not exclusively) as "women's work."

Although the workers were distributed throughout all age ranges, there are relatively fewer workers between the ages of 31 and 40 than there are under 30 or between the ages of 41 and 50. This pattern holds for both the male and female employees. Presumably, the females feel the need to contribute to the family finances in the early years of marriage, drop out of the work force during their husbands' more economically productive years, and go back to work after their children have left home.

Of the total sample, 57 percent never received a high school degree, and a sizable proportion of this group (one-third) never went beyond the eighth grade. The educational achievements of the women surpassed those of the men, in that almost two-thirds of the men had never received a high school degree as compared to only slightly more than one-half of the women. Upwards of one-third of the men never went beyond the eighth grade, as compared with only 15% of the women. The workers who did not complete high school indicated that they had dropped out to go to work or because they didn't like school. Women, in addition, mentioned that they had dropped out of school to get married. Some of the workers had dropped out of school in order to help out their families. Given their educational back-grounds, their occupational horizons had been definitely limited—something the workers clearly perceived themselves. The workers, with their substandard educational background, were following the tradition of their parents. Of those respondents who were able to report on their parents' educational level, 85 percent reported that their mothers, and 92 percent their fathers, had less than a high school degree.

Of particular interest is the fact that a fairly substantial number of the parents had also had occupations in the poultry dressing industry. In all, 19 percent of the fathers and 43 percent of the working mothers (13% of all mothers) had worked in poultry dressing plants. Poultry dressing, then, represents a two-generational work pattern for a good number of these workers. For those workers from families where farming was the basic means of livelihood, work in a poultry dressing plant would seem to represent the first step away from farming. Given the nature of the work, this step may represent one much more amenable than, say, work in other types of industrial enterprises. For women from farming backgrounds, work in poultry dressing may be perceived as essentially the same type of work done by their mothers. And for those whose parents worked in poultry dressing, this type of industrial work represented something about which they had some knowledge and, perhaps, that they could feel comfortable going into. For the rest of the workers, whose parents were primarily in semi-skilled and skilled occupations, poultry processing work represented a continuation, for the most part, of the occupational level of their parents.

A rather large number of the spouses (32 percent) also worked in the poultry dressing industry (42 percent of the male workers' wives and 29 percent of the female workers' husbands). Work in the poultry plant appears not infrequently to be a family affair. Husbands, wives, parents, in-laws, and children often work in the same plant, as do many of the respondents' friends. As will be indicated later, such an arrangement appears to have a positive influence upon work satisfaction, and tends to extend the rural ambience into the work place.

CAREER

The workers studied had enjoyed only minimal work ambitions. When asked about their particular work ambition when younger, 25 percent of the males and 37 percent of the females responded that they had had no particular occupational aspirations. Of the males, not a single one had held professional aspirations when younger, and only one mentioned a white collar occupation. One-quarter of the males specified that they had hoped to be mechanics. The rest of the males (38 percent) mentioned a variety of vocational pursuits that could only appropriately be categorized as "Other" (these included pursuits ranging from professional baseball to contracting). The females had apparently held higher ambitions. Almost one-half had entertained professional, semi-professional (including nursing and teaching), and white collar occupational aspirations. Only 8 percent had planned to be a housewife and the others, in general, had hoped for various kinds of service occupations such as being an airline stewardess or beautician.

When asked why they originally came to work at the poultry dressing plants, approximately half of the workers interviewed could give no reason other than they needed a job or the money, or that there were, simply, no other job choices. Approximately one-quarter of the respondents said they came to work because of friends or relatives working there, and another 16 percent mentioned convenience or location as leading them to come to work at the plants. Only 19 percent mentioned a positive feature about the job (the fact that it was full-time, paid better, or was preferable to what they were doing before) as being important to their coming to work at the plants. When asked outright if they had had a choice in coming to work at the plant, almost 40 percent of the total sample said no. Some 46 percent of the females, as compared to 18 percent of the males, indicated that they had had no choice. When asked if they felt they would still be working at the poultry dressing plants in the future, 75 percent indicated that they thought they would be. However, only slightly over 40 percent indicated that this would be because of free choice.

In general, the workers were realistic about their job qualifications and their prospects in the labor market, and were also quite fatalistic (that abiding characteristic of all rural persons) in their assessment of employment possibilities. The inevitable can be more pleasant, however, if meaningful social interaction is available. As this one female employee succinctly expressed it:

> Well, I guess in a way it is about as good as you gonna find for the education because the one thing about it is its mostly women there working. I'd say it's a pretty good place. There is a lot of women who work there and you are bound to find someone you can be friends with, and you have time to be sociable and get to know (them). Some other place you might not have time.

The largest percentage category of number of years worked in the plants for the total sample was 5 to 10 years, with the median for males being 5 years and that for females 7 years. The range of years worked was 1 to 35 years, with 3 to 5 years and over 15 representing the second largest percentage categories. The findings also indicated a good deal of movement out of and back into the plant work forces. Some 13 percent of the workers stated they had left work and then come back. Of the total sample, 8 percent had left and come back two or more times.

Job Autonomy and Containment of Disaffection

The discussion thus far has pointed to the unmistakable problematic character of poultry processing work. From the lack of alternative job opportunities and the low educational level of the workers to the messy nature of the work, poultry processing presents itself as a difficult job to which to accommodate oneself. The point to be developed in this final section is that poultry workers did, in fact, express positive aspects about the work: 60 percent of the respondents said they were either "generally satisfied" or "completely satisfied" with their job; 63 percent reported that they would choose that same job again; and, when comparing their job to the worst and best of all possible jobs they could think of, *81% gave a rank of 5 or better on a scale of 0 to 10* (with 10 symbolic of the "ideal" job).

When probed about the rationale for their expressions of work satisfaction, the interviewees were inclined to mention factors such as "co-worker relations," "management relations," "treatment by management," or "liking that kind of work or activities" as the major reasons. Human relations concerns appear to be generally more important thatn other kinds of considerations in terms of job satisfaction. As one worker, for example, phrased it when asked what she particularly liked about her job:

> The people, I think, more than anything—that I work with. That really helps out. I mean if you are working with somebody that you like. I just—I just like that kind of work.

Yet another replied to the same question:

> It's the company I work for I guess. They have always treated me good and everything.

When the workers were further queried about the things that they particularly liked about their job, approximately 40 percent of all the respondents listed "people" or "co-worker relations" as the thing they liked most about the job.

Additional insights concerning work satisfaction were gained from examining the workers' approach to job autonomy via the traditional sex role division of labor, and their sense of occupational community, which functioned to insulate them from the harsher and more disagreeable parameters of their work role.

THE SEXUAL DIVISION OF LABOR

There was a very pronounced, implicit, sexual division of labor evident in the plants. In the departments requiring a considerable degree of physical strength, such as in the hanging and killing rooms, and in the shipping and storage rooms where the processed birds had to be stacked and loaded, men frequently had the jobs. Males also had most of the foreman and supervisory positions. Although some males were scattered along the processing line, these were activities that were for the most part carried out by females. Of these line activities, four were identified as "women's jobs": eviscerating, cutting and trimming, boning, and packaging. The employees explained the segregation of activities into "men's jobs" and "women's jobs" by offering several different reasons. In regard to the "men's jobs," it was stated that men were required to do them because of strength requirements. In addition, respondents, both male and female, noted that it wasn't the place of women to be doing these jobs because, simply, they were "men's jobs." In discussing the "women's jobs" the major response given was that men could do these jobs, but should be doing, and were needed to do, other things—presumably picking and hanging, and weighing and shipping. Another reason given was that these were "women's jobs" because they involved something women normally knew how to do and would ordinarily be doing in their roles as housekeepers—the preparation of meats for cooking and consumption.

From the standpoint of the male employees, the sexual segregation of work activities seems to be a compensating factor in facilitating their toleration for disaffective work. Sexual differentiation in work assignments serves as a major mechanism by which the male employees can maintain their sense of masculinity. Positioned in jobs that are primarily closed to females and of a higher status serves to offset the ego threats and anxieties, and to compensate males. For the most part, having specific jobs in the plant that are sex-classified as masculine work makes it possible for the male workers to accommodate themselves to low status, low paid, and uncomfortable work. Importantly, the men are able to perform their "male" jobs in such a way that they are able to structure a considerable degree of job autonomy into their work role. In some departments, for example, men who are not as tied to the pace of the line as the women workers will stand and wait until a fairly large number of packages are finished and then route them for weighing or box them. In this way they retain a degree of individual control over the actual way in which they perform their jobs.

Although some of the women workers did complain about the inequitability of work roles that grew out of the sexual stereotyping of certain jobs in the plant, the sexual division of labor seems also to operate to make the female employees more content with their work. While many see themselves as doing the messier and more difficult jobs, as compared to the men, they are able to accept that because of the fact that it is "women's work." Just as a housewife might see her own responsibilities as being perhaps more demanding and exhausting than those of her spouse, but accepting such a division of labor as natural, so too do the female workers reconcile themselves to the more demanding, difficult, and seemingly more disagreeable types of work. In one sense, there is a kind of pride in the fact that "women's work" is often more difficult and that female workers are more stoic than males in performing the harder jobs. As one female worker put it in describing the plant jobs that women tend to get:

Take a man, he won't stick to some of those harder jobs like craw pullin'. A man will stick his finger in there and gets a sore finger and walks the floor all night long—he will quit that job, he won't stick to it.

OCCUPATIONAL COMMUNITY

The study vividly demonstrated that the physical activity of the job was secondary to interactional dimensions. Poultry processing workers know each other, go to church together, and visit in each other's homes, from time to time date and marry one another, and are seldom other than friends. The working relationship is the mainstay of their social existence as employees.

The most intriguing finding was that, in the plants studied, there was the presence of an occupational community. Workers participated in an occupational community which functioned not only to insulate them in a "cloak of mechanical solidarity," as it were, but also provided margins for a gregarious and sympathetic curiosity and concern about one another. One worker described this sympathetic concern:

> Last year I had cobalt. I had about 70 meters [sic] of radiation. I was off my job from the first of March to the very last day of May. I was able to talk to my nurse at the plant. She was very encouraging. April Fools' Day I went to take my cobalt and I come back home. My friends down there called me and asked me to come down. If you've ever had a call on April Fools' Day, you wonder what it's all about. And I got down there and they said, "Good Morning," and there sat a huge table of the most delicious lookin' cakes there are. Those girls raffled those cakes off and made me pretty near four-hundred dollars in money to help me plus give me a beautiful cake. The thoughts of that beautiful cake . . .

The literature on occupational communities contains various overlapping definitions of the concept. It has been suggested, primarily by Blauner (1964), and later Salaman (1974), that occupational communities are characterized by a "convergence of work and self," the presence of an occupationally based reference group, and off-hour socialization among workers, along with the emergence of positive social sentiments. The poultry processors' occupational community exhibited these characteristics to a significant degree, even the convergence of work and identity. The emergence of their occupational community was a case of an already existing network of relationships moving into the workplace, but their cohesiveness, to a great extent, could be understood as an effort to protect themselves from the imposition of stigma due to the dirty-work component of their labor. This protection was accomplished by banding together as a group, which could translate objective disaffection into a "collective representation" in the Durkheimian sense; that is, poultry processing employment as a requirement for group membership and the attendant gratifying social interaction.

Within any occupational community there is a degree of mechanical solidarity. There is a pressure to be like everyone else, at least to some tolerable degree defined by the group. In this case, the typification of being a poultry processing worker, along with a few other basic themes (e.g., religious preference and community of residence), was the benchmark for social interaction. In more Durkheimian terms, the "social resemblances" facilitated social interaction, dating, and marriage among the workers, and largely precluded interaction with outsiders and strangers. This attraction and concern for one another exemplified by the April Fools' Day cake raffle would seem to be a vivid operationalization of Durkheim's original conception of mechanical solidarity. The interface of work and friendship is indicated in the following comment from an employee:

> Nobody else likes that job [cutting the oil sac on the tail of the carcass]. I don't know why. They have a hard time gettin' anybody to stay at it. I like it though. I like it because I get to work with Donnie . . . she is my best friend. We double up and let each other go out whenever we want to.

CONCLUSIONS

Aesthetic concerns or physical annoyances such as odors, heat, dampness, and the like were apparently only minimally disaffective. Workers frequently expressed the belief that cutting chickens or using knives was something women would do at home, and therefore there was no reason to dislike such activities in a job. Where job dissatisfaction was evident, it seemed to stem largely from the pressure of speed and tempo on the line, in the case of women, and from managerial pressure in the case of male workers. Workers seemed particularly sensitive to such things as the speed of the line and the managerial posture toward workers. Some workers complained of their "nerves," or their jobs "getting to them" if the work tempo was too fast or if they sensed undue pressure from their supervisors.

One might anticipate that killing, plucking, and eviscerating poultry carcasses all week long would be at least sufficiently disaffective as to spoil the workers' appetite for chicken. Not so! The plants give the workers a discount price on dressed chicken, once a week, and on Friday afternoon (discount price day) they literally line up to take advantage of the offer. The workers are even able to structure both a craftsmanship and religious rationalization into their work, which lets them accept it as both challenging and fulfilling. As one female employee who worked as a killer detailed it:

> It is just as I said a while ago—you stop and look at that bird. It's such a simple little thing to make that little cut. You don't have to stand there and think about I'm killing this man or I'm burning this man or something like that. You're helping—you're doing like I just said . . . You are preparing a piece of delicious meat. I've been there so long—I know how to do it to the best of my ability and I try to do it to the best of my ability. I believe He puts the food here for us to eat, and I believe He meant for us to process it and eat it.

She went on to say with pride:

> No, I kinda look to my work as a thrill. I want to go to work.

This research was a pilot study and thus the beginning of a larger inquiry into work satisfaction and dissatisfaction. The findings so far, however, would seem to suggest that even in the instance of the seemingly most unpleasant work situations, there are compensatory circumstances and mechanisms. In the instance of these poultry processing employees, the male workers hold jobs that are appropriate to their sex role, enjoy relatively good salary levels, occupy work statuses higher than the female workers, and see their jobs as both secure and a mark of work attainment in excess of their educational capability.

The women enjoy the sociability of interaction with fellow workers, view their job as activities which were not unlike what they might naturally perform as part of household duties, enjoy the advantages of additional family income, see working as preferable to staying home alone, and conceivably, given the fact of their husband's low educational-aspirational level, may well see work in the plant with its opportunity for interaction as a satisfactory means of compensation for a relatively mundane marital relationship.

From an urban perspective, work in a poultry dressing plant is viewed as basically unappealing and disaffective work. This is apparently not the case, however, inasmuch as there are a number of ameliorating circumstances and operative conditions in the work setting which tend to compensate for the seemingly disagreeable nature of the job. Poultry work is a traditional type of work in the area, and in some cases workers have parents, friends, and relatives who work in the industry. The social-interactional opportunities, among other factors, are a sufficient tradeoff for the messy work, and a means of containing the attendant work disaffection. In view of this, and the rural context, such work is apparently not viewed as especially unpleasant. As one worker summed it up, "I like to work with chickens."

NOTES

1. The literature on industrial morale problems and work disaffection is voluminous, but for one classic statement see Chinoy, *Automobile Workers and the American Dream* (New York: Doubleday, 1955). See also Swados "The Myth of the Happy Worker," in *A Radical's America* (New York: Atlantic-Little Brown, 1957). For more recent overviews of industrial ennui see Kahn, "The Meaning of Work," in *The Worker in the New Industrial Environment* (Ann Arbor: Foundation for Research on Human Behavior, 1967); also Sheppard and Herrick, *Where Have All the Robots Gone? Worker Dissatisfaction in the '70's* (New York: The Free Press, 1972).

2. For a detailed report on this research process, see Bryant et al., *Work and Career in Poultry Processing: A Pilot Study of Morale and Disaffection in a Rural Industry* (Blacksburg, VA: Virginia Polytechnic Institute and State University, 1980).

CHAPTER ELEVEN

NURSING AS A PROFESSION

Bonnie Bullough
Vern Bullough

NURSING AS AN occupation has been strongly influenced by two structural variables. First, it has been dominated by women, and second, it exists as part of a very complex hierarchy. The interaction and implication of these two variables are the subject of this chapter.

Since it developed as an occupational grouping in the nineteenth century, nursing has been defined in what might be called feminine terms: nurturing, supportive, caring, extending tenderness, and so on. Objectively, nursing could also be defined in masculine terms, since it is scientific, physically demanding, emotionally draining, and ego-satisfying. The fact that women filled the role gave it its feminine image.

Nursing historically was not the only female-dominated profession, but others such as social work, elementary school teaching, and library work avoided falling quite so deep into the "feminine trap" by their ability either to attract a sufficient number of men into their ranks (usually into executive positions, as in the case of social workers and librarians) or as allies (secondary teachers allying with elementary teachers). Nurses, however, like secretaries, were caught with the female role prescriptions, and they stayed female. The reason for this male exclusion in nursing is due in part to the historical development of modern nursing. Until almost the mid-1900s, the education for nursing was dominated by the hospital training school, where the student nurses were required to live in dormitories and where the rigid sex exclusion in the dormitories worked to exclude men who might otherwise have entered. The major exception was the all-male schools in the mental hospitals. The hospital schools were also dominated by staff physicians who

TABLE 11.1   Sex Segregation: Women in Medicine and Men in Nursing

Year	Percentage of Women in Medicine	Percentage of Men in Nursing (R.N.s)
1870	0.8	N.A.
1880	2.8	N.A.
1890	4.4	N.A.
1900	5.6	N.A.
1910	6.0	7.0*
1920	5.0	3.7*
1930	4.4	2.0*
1940	4.6	1.0
1950	6.1	1.0
1960	6.0	0.9
1970	7.2	0.9
1976	8.0	1.4

*Data for registered nurses in 1910, 1920, and 1930 are derived from census data which included both graduates and students; after 1940 the data are for graduates only.

SOURCES: 1. Walsh, M. R., Yale University Press, 1977, p. 186
            2. American Nurses Association, 1941, p. 7; 1967, p. 17, 1971-72, p. 17,19
            3. National League for Nursing, 1980, p. 49
            4. U.S. Department of Health, 1978, p. 80
            5. American Nurses Association, pre-publication data.

consciously or unconsciously wanted to exclude male nurses (Bullough and Bullough, 1978). Women in effect became nurses while men became physicians. Table 11.1 shows the historical pattern of this sex segregation.

STRATIFICATION

The second structural aspect of nursing that is remarkable is the complexity of its hierarchy. The whole health care industry is highly stratified, and within this complex stratification pattern, nursing is also highly stratified.

In 1977 (the latest date for which we have accurate statistics as of this writing), a total of 5.1 million persons were employed in the health professions and occupations (National Center for Health Statistics, 1977, 5, 165), up from 3.7 million in 1970 (U.S. Public Health Service, 1970a: 8-10). Similarly, the complexity of the health occupations has increased. In 1970, the Public Health Service listed 33 categories of workers and a total of 74 occupational roles. In 1977, 717 primary and alternate job titles were listed, and the report explained that the inventory was still incomplete since some types of health workers might have been inadvertently omitted. The health care industry is a major industry, and far more complex than its other traditional rival, the educational system, although included in the health category are various types of educational employees, from professor to school nurse. Nursing and nursing-related services comprise the largest category of health workers, with nearly half of the total group (2,481,600) classified as nursing-related. Registered nurses comprise approximately 35 percent of this group, while licensed practical nurses make up 20 percent, and orderlies, nurses' aides, and attendants 45 percent of the nursing work force. Not included in these statistics are ward clerks, sometimes called floor clerks, who act as receptionists and who also relieve the nurses of much of the paperwork in the patient care units of an institution. These workers are prepared for their jobs in a wide variety of settings and for varying lengths of time. Since aides (who are usually female) and orderlies (who are male) are not licensed, the quality and quantity of their educational experience is usually determined by their employers. They may be given short preemployment courses or be trained on the job. The other health workers, by law, are usually better trained. Courses for licensed practical nurses usually last one year, while registered nurses may have graduated from a two-year Junior College Associate of Arts program, a three-year hospital training school, or a four-year baccalaureate program. Nursing specialists usually have master's degrees.

All of these jobs listed under nursing were once held by registered nurses or by students training to be registered nurses. Most of this complex role differentiation within nursing has taken place since World War II. Until that time, graduate nurses were employed primarily as private duty nurses caring for only one patient at a time. Hospitals were run by nursing students, a plan that had existed since the first Nightingale training schools had been set up in this country after the Civil War. Nurses were not unaware of the exploitative characteristics of this system, and most worked to improve educational standards, particularly as the depression of the early 1930s created severe unemployment among their ranks. Eventually, they were able to get some of the least adequate schools closed, to cut the on-duty time of students to approximately 40 hours a week, and to increase the amount of classroom time for student nurses (Bullough and Bullough, 1978).

These educational reforms, modest as they were, coincided with several other trends and events which increased the need for nursing, so that within a decade the problem of an oversupply of nurses changed to one of acute shortage, and this has been more or less the same picture that has prevailed for the past 40 years. The shortage first appeared in World War II, when the need for nurses to work in base hospitals and overseas created what was believed to be a temporary shortage, but in the post-war period changed to a permanent shortage. This was primarily due to the changing nature of the hospitals, which switched from institutions of last resort to being the locus of scientific health care. Aiding this change was the growth of prepaid hospital insurance, federal monies for hospital building, and ultimately federal intervention into the health care delivery system.

During World War II the gap in nursing services had been "temporarily" filled by volunteer aides who were trained by the Red Cross and the Office of Civilian Defense. At first these aides were allowed to perform only those tasks not directly related to patient care; they ran errands, cleaned equipment, and carried food to patients. Eventually, however, the shortage of help forced nurses to turn over some of the less complicated aspects of patient care to the aides. Their entry into the hospital was the beginning of the nursing team as a replacement for the nurse, since it soon became obvious that much of the work performed by nurses could be delegated to less expensive workers. On the other hand, as nursing duties were sloughed off or delegated, the nurses picked up many of the tasks previously performed by the physicians, and in the process nursing education was upgraded and lengthened. The delegation of the nursing duties to lower paid nursing personnel was, however, usually much more obvious than the assumption of other duties from the physician.

Hospital management quickly endorsed the idea of using workers with less training whenever it was possible. They were in effect seeking a replacement for the unpaid student nurses, and while they were never again able to find such a bargain in help, the utilization of auxiliary nursing personnel kept costs down. Nurses themselves encouraged the delegation, and the American Nurses Association sponsored a series of studies and reports which recommended that the nursing role be further broken up. The most influential of these was done by Esther Lucile Brown (1948), who surveyed the work nurses were doing in various settings and recommended the development of "non professional" trained nurses who would carry out the routine procedures and leave the registered nurse more time to concentrate on complex procedures, preventive medicine, and administration. The result was the rapid growth of practical or vocational nursing.

Not all of the role differentiation among nurses was as well planned as the move for practical nurses appeared to be. Some of it was also a consequence of an educational system that had been in transition for the last 40 years. As nursing education became more adequate, it also became more expensive. Hospitals found that operating nursing schools was no longer a profitable enterprise, particularly when federal regulations prevented them from writing off such training onto patient bills. As a result, the number of hospital training schools has declined from about 1200 in 1930 to about 330 now, and most of the remaining ones exist on the borderline of educational respectability. The void left by the closure of the hospital schools was filled by the development of baccalaureate and associate degree programs, the first of which started in 1909.

As nursing has become more sophisticated, higher degree programs have also expanded rapidly, in part because they were given a strong impetus by federal financing. In 1955 there were only 526 master's degrees granted in nursing; by 1969 that number had tripled, and by 1979 the number had reached 4621 (NLN Data Book, 1981). At the same time, the number of doctorates in nursing has increased, but these are more difficult to measure since many of them are in fields such as sociology or education rather than in nursing itself where the number is still limited.

The biggest increase has been in the master's level preparation for jobs such as nurse anesthetists, nurse widwives, nurse practitioners, and various clinical specialists. The nurse practitioners were originally conceived of as physician extenders, but since have been effectively integrated into the nursing role. Inevitably, the term "nurse" is confusing since it covers everything from an aide to a Ph.D.

The situation is most confusing in the hospital setting where the hospital training school graduate intermingles with the associate degree and the baccalaureate-trained nurses. All start as bedside nurses with little differentiation in the tasks they perform. All of them are eligible to become team leaders and are expected to supervise other registered nurses, practical nurses, aides, and orderlies. However, the nurse with the baccalaureate degree is likely to move up faster in the administrative hierarchy or to leave the hospital for work in community health agencies, where she may be allowed to better use her broader behavioral science background. The better educated nurses have also pushed for primary care nursing where hospital nurses are given full 24-hour responsibility for the care of selected patients. The difficulty is that there are not enough nurses with adequate training to do primary care, and any further extension is dependent upon more baccalaureate graduates.

Further complicating the situation is the new influx of nurses with master's degrees. Although many of them become administrators, an increasing number are becoming clinical specialists interested in finding employment as skilled bedside practitioners. The job market for clinical specialists is best in critical care situations, but the emotional toll of working in such situations is heavy.

CONSEQUENCES

The consequences of the sex segregation and the highly stratified pattern of the health occupations have not all been negative, although probably the negative consequences of these two characteristics of the profession outweigh the positive. The chief advantage for nurses has been the opportunity for leadership within the profession. Historically, many influential female activists of the twentieth century were nurses, including Lillian Wald, Margaret

Sanger, Emma Goldman, and Edith Cavell. Many other nurses have achieved managerial positions as directors of nursing and as deans of nursing schools. The segregated stratification system furnished many levels for advancement.

The disadvantage of the segregated system with its feminine image of the helpful "girl Friday" is that upward mobility beyond the segregated ceiling was blocked, and that the system masked the real abilities of nurses. Nurses appear to outsiders to lack decision-making power, and to display a seeming unwillingness to take responsibility. The words apparent and seeming are used in these two categories because nurses in fact do make decisions and do take responsibility, although they may appear not to do so by playing the doctor/nurse game, a long-running variant of male and female role playing.

This traditional game was most effectively and unconsciously described by the anti-ERA Helen Andelin in her book, *Fascinating Womanhood* (1980). Mrs. Andelin (the name she prefers to use) urges women to never confront a man directly, never denigrate his masculinity, and never contradict him. Instead, she is to use feminine wiles, even to acting the role of a little girl, stamping her feet, shaking her curls, and if necessary breaking into tears when she is frustrated. Fortunately, nurses were never quite the ideal woman of Mrs. Andelin's book, but they did play their own version of the male/female game.

The physician ordinarily sees the hospitalized patient for only a short time each day, and this means he depends on the nurse for information about the patient. But the nurses who assess the patient 24 hours a day often act as if they had not made any diagnosis. Instead, over the years women in nursing have constructed a fantasy that the doctor is and should be omniscient and omnipotent, that it would be rude for a nurse to speak to him openly and honestly or even to offer suggestions about the care of the patient.

Obviously, this indoctrination is at odds with reality. Nurses have many more opportunities throughout the day to observe the patient's condition and to hear what he has to say; their observations are crucial and in fact do constitute diagnoses. To care for the patient adequately, they must act on these observations and make recommendations to the physicians; under the rules of the old doctor/nurse game, however, nurses had to pretend that they never diagnosed or made recommendations.

The game was well described by the psychiatrist Leonard Stein (1967), who was fascinated by the strange way in which nurses made suggestions to physicians so that both the physician and the nurse could pretend recommendations had not been made. He called the pattern a transactional neurosis.

A good example has often been observed by one of the authors of this chapter in supervising students on a medical floor. Many of the patients on the ward, seriously ill cardiac patients, were receiving digitalis or related synthetic drugs. The dosage for these drugs must be adjusted to the individual patient, and since the therapeutic dose is fairly close to the toxic dose, the patient must be observed carefully for symptoms of toxicity, particularly when such drugs are first being administered. The conscientious and knowledgeable nurses on the wards observed the patients for symptoms of toxicity such as a slow pulse rate, nausea, or depression. They could read the monitors and readily identify the characteristic cardiac arrhythmias that suggested this type of toxicity. When they noted symptoms of a developing toxicity, they would immediately withhold the drug and notify the physician—not of their actions, but of their observations. In fact, they would not say they had noted symptoms suggesting toxicity, they would simply report the discrete symptoms as if they did not understand the implications. The doctor would then tell them to withhold or lessen the digitalis dosage, and they would thank him for the "order."

If, however, the doctor were a new resident or for other reasons did not appear to understand the implications of what the nurse was reporting, they would "accidentally" later drop the information about the symptoms in a conversation with a third-year resident or an attending physician, and the hapless young physician would be in trouble for not acting on the nurses' observations. Thus, even though the nurse had made a decision and acted, she avoided at all costs the responsibility for her decision.

The complex stratification pattern and sex segregation of the health occupations have also fostered sharp differences in income. Table 11.2 shows these differences, calculated using 1970 census data. In this table, the first two columns show income as a percentage of the amount paid male physicians. As can be noted, there are dramatic differences related to both the position in the hierarchy and to the sex of the worker. Moreover, although education level is clearly a variable in these calculations, it is insufficient to explain all of the differences. While the differences related to sex are sharpest at the higher salary levels, the most tragic differences are at the level of the nurses' aide. Since there were 600,000 aides in 1970, their economic deprivation is not insignificant. Their salary fell $700 below the poverty line of $3,743 for a family of four established by the Social Security Administration in 1969 (U.S. Census, 1970c). Thus, if the nurses aide had children, she would be better off if she quit work and applied for welfare. It is interesting to note that one of the strategies proposed for helping people escape the welfare trap is to train them for low-level jobs in the health and service fields (Riessman, 1969; Conway, 1965). This was not in 1970 and is still no way to escape from poverty.

A more recent demonstration of the consequences of sex segregation of nursing was brought out in the case of Lemons et al. versus the City and County of Denver, which reached the U.S. Supreme Court in 1980. The

TABLE 11.2 Income and Education Distribution in the Health Occupations, 1970

Occupation	Median Income (Dollars)		Percentage of Male Physician's Salary Earned by Other Male Workers	Percentage of Male Physician's Salary Earned by Other Female Workers (using $25,000 as base)	Percentage of Men's Salary Paid to Women	Median School Years Completed	
	Men	Women				Men	Women
Physicians	$25,000+	$9,788	—	39%	39%	17+	17+
Dentists	21,687	6,351	87%	25%	29%	17+	15.8
Optometrists	17,398	6,455	70%	26%	37%	17+	16.8
Veterinarians	16,503	5,641	66%	23%	34%	17+	17+
Chiropractors	11,957	3,985	48%	16%	33%	16.8	16.1
Health Administrators	12,087	7,149	48%	29%	59%	16.1	13.5
Laboratory Technicians	7,242	5,560	30%	22%	77%	14.7	14.6
Radiologic Technicians	8,185	5,017	20%	20%	61%	13.0	12.7
Dental Hygienists	14,291	5,074	57%	20%	40%	12.7	14.9
Health Record Technicians	5,852	5,687	23%	22%	97%	14.5	14.0
Other Technicians	6,976	4,473	28%	18%	64%	14.6	12.8
Therapists	7,851	5,384	31%	22%	69%	16.0	16.3
Registered Nurses	7,013	5,603	28%	22%	80%	13.5	13.3
Dieticians	6,037	4,462	24%	18%	61%	12.7	12.9
Practical Nurses	5,745	4,205	23%	17%	73%	12.4	12.4
Non-nursing Health Aides	4,354	3,460	17%	14%	79%	12.3	12.3
Dental Assistants	4,094	3,405	16%	14%	83%	12.6	12.5
Nurses' Aides/Orderlies	4,401	2,969	17%	12%	67%	12.2	11.8

+Table does not go beyond $25,000, which was well below actual income of physicians in 1970. This makes the discrepancies even more significant.

SOURCE: U.S. Census Bureau, 1973: 1, 3, 10

TABLE 11.3   Sex Segregation: Inequalities in Income in the City
and County of Denver

Job Classification	Monthly Starting Salary		Dollar Difference	
	1977	1979	Month	Year
Graduate Nurse I (Beginning)	$ 929	$1064		
100% Male Jobs Classifications				
Sign Painter	$1245	$1361	$297	$3564
Painter	1088	1191	127	1524
Tree Trimmer	1040	1164	100	1200
Tire Serviceman	1017	1113	49	588
Parking Meter Repairman	994	1113	49	588

SOURCES: 1.   American Nurses Association and NURSE, Inc., 1979.
2.   C. Barnes, in B. Bullough, 1980, pp. 125-137.

lawsuit brought by a group of Denver nurses and carried by the Denver attorney Craig S. Barnes proved serious economic discrimination against nurses. Using jobs held primarily by males and comparing them to nurses, it was demonstrated in every case that male occupations, regardless of the educational training required, paid more (Bullough, 1978). The 100% male classification jobs, for example, averaged $1,593 per month while the 100% female classes averaged only $1,091. Some examples of these groups are indicated in Table 11.3. Starting salaries for male dominated jobs were found to be consistently higher, even though the male-dominated jobs required comparable or lower qualifications in the areas of education, experience, and supervisory responsibility. In one comparison of 35 exclusively male jobs, all of which required fewer years of education and experience and the same or less supervisory responsibility as a floor nurse, the male classes were paid more than both the floor nurse and the head nurse.

For the trial, a professional evaluation of traditional job worth was done. This technique computed factors such as physical effort, job complexity, responsibility, accountability, supervision exercise, and working conditions. At the same level of job worth it was determined that as the number of males in a specific classification increased, the salary also increased. Further, the sex of the incumbent was uniformly determined to be the significant factor in salary differences (Barnes, 1980).

Judge Fred Winner of the 10th Circuit Federal District Court, in ruling against the nurses, acknowledged that the evidence did indicate that nursing as an occupation had been discriminated against, but he stated that if he had ruled in favor of nurses there was the potential of "disrupting the entire economic system of the United States of America" (Bullough, 1978). The Supreme Court chose not to rehear the case, but they did rule in a case reaching the court about the same time and dealing with women prison guards. In this second case, the court ruled that not only had inequality between the sexes been demonstrated but the state was ordered to make redress.

Simply being a woman has traditionally had a significant effect. Complicating the inequalities of nursing salaries is the historical fact that nurses have not participated vigorously in collective bargaining. In 1947 the National Labor Relations Act (Taft-Hartley) specifically excluded nonprofit health care institutions from its provisions (Bullough and Bullough, 1978; Miller, 1971; Miller and Shortell, 1969). The result was that hospitals were under no obligation to negotiate with their workers. As a result, only 15 percent of the health care workers were organized by the end of 1974 when the National Labor Relations Act was revised. Nurses therefore have to overcome the fact not only that they are women but that they have been discriminated against by official policy. However, the development of the barriers is partly due to a lack of militance shown by nurses, which is also tied to a feminine identity.

Perhaps the best illustration of this attitude is the 1955 Model Practice Act adopted in 1955 by the Board of Directors of the American Nurses Association, which seriously handicapped the expansion of nursing when it was accepted by legislators in 21 states. Professional nursing practice was defined as follows:

> The term "practice of professional" nursing means the performance, for compensation, of any acts in the observation, care and counsel of the ill, injured or infirm or in the maintenance of health or prevention of illness of others, or in the supervision and teaching of other personnel or the administration of medications and treatments as prescribed by a licensed physician or a licensed dentist; requiring substantial specialized judgment and skill and based on knowledge and application of principles of biological, physical and social science. The foregoing shall *not be deemed to include any acts of diagnosis or prescription of therapeutic or corrective measures* (Bullough, 1980).

The fascinating thing about the underlined disclaimer is that it was not made by the American Medical Association but by the American Nurses Association. Although it might be a reasonable assumption that the nurses felt the disclaimer necessary to avoid medical opposition to the new practice acts of that period, there is little evidence of overt pressure by medical people. Being good women, the nurses surrendered before any battle over boundaries could occur.

Even before the disclaimer was adopted, some nurses, particularly those in university positions, were evolving an ideological position trying to separate the function of nurses from that of physicians. What these nurses did was emphasize the social and psychological components of nursing, often at the expense of the physical, and then claim jurisdiction over the social and psychological. Ultimately, however, the major reason for the disclaimer, at least in our opinion, was alienation, or what might be called anticipatory self-discriminatory behavior of nurses. Rather than risk a rebuff or a possible boundary dispute with medicine, nurses almost unconsciously decided to avoid admitting their role in the patient care decision-making process. Similar patterns of anticipatory self-discrimination are a fairly common phenomenon among minority groups; the ghetto walls are often as well policed from the inside as from the outside, and in the past feelings of powerlessness and fear have often prevented people from challenging discriminatory practices.

Men interested in becoming nurses, then, not only had to face the low salaries but also overcome the stereotypical feminine image and the very real feminine action pattern in dealing with the world. In addition, many had to confront publicly the issue of sex preference long before being "gay" was widely accepted. Since nursing was so strongly identified in ideal and in action with women, men who went into it were usually categorized as homosexual whether or not they were gay. Thus it took a strong-willed individual willing to accept his own sexuality to deal with the biases and prejudices so endemic to being a male nurse. Those men who did, however, often emerged into leadership positions fairly rapidly because they had not been acclimatized to playing the subordinate role.

CURRENT TRENDS

Probably the most important and significant movement affecting change in nursing was the women's movement of the 1970s. Whatever else the movement might have accomplished, it gave permission to women to challenge some of the age-old discrimination, and nurses were in the forefront of doing this. It also made it easier for men to enter nursing, if only because the male and female role models became less rigid than they were in the past. Of the students now in nursing schools, 6 percent are men (NLN, Nursing Data Book, 1980: 29). Coinciding with the new militancy of women in general were changes in the labor legislation which allowed nurses to organize, and a realization that they had to expand their turf to meet the threat of the newly emerging physician's assistant movement aimed entirely at men. Either nurses were going to be permanent "girl Fridays" or they had to meet the challenge. Reluctantly and with considerable ambiguity, they did so, aided by the rapid expansion of the medical industry. New specialties emerged or were re-established, often with the support of members of the medical profession, who in their increasingly narrow specialization were willing to delegate more and more to nurses. Among the specialties that emerged in the 1970s were nurse practitioners, midwives, anesthetists, clinical specialists, and in the process nurses found themselves forced to make decisions and take responsibility or lose out. The willingness to change was marked in most states by a new round of nurse practice acts which gave nurses both new accountability and more willingly accepted their right to intervene for the patient's welfare (Bullough, 1980). The health care delivery system is still highly stratified and sex segregated, but there are some new winds of change.

CHAPTER TWELVE

WORKER AUTONOMY IN THE SKILLED BUILDING TRADES

Jeffrey W. Riemer

HOW WORKERS GET through their workday depends on how much control they have over their work. Some have very little (assembly line workers), while others have a great deal (psychiatrists in private practice). Among the blue collar occupations, skilled building construction workers—electricians, plumbers, carpenters, bricklayers, and iron-workers—are very powerful. They can often determine what work they will do, how they will do it, when it will be done, and the compensation they will receive for it. Moreover, because of their attained skill certification and union affiliation, they often become the *only* workers allowed to do the work.

Maximizing this control is an important concern in any occupation. Autonomy is a feature that is continually cultivated and ardently protected by members of all occupations. Worker autonomy represents the level of labor control that can be successfully claimed by a worker or occupational group for services offered in the marketplace. This control can enhance earning power and political clout. Higher wages can be demanded and often achieved, and workplace control can be maximized when workers successfully manage the balance of power over their labor.

This chapter will delineate the sources of worker autonomy important to the skilled building trades and the threats to it. Emphasis will be placed on the social, structural, and organizational locations of control and dissent and the implications of worker autonomy for the industry and the larger society. The focus will be on the elite among these workers; that is, those who encourage formal apprenticeship training programs, have national union affiliation, command high wages, and regularly work on large commercial and industrial projects.

THE SOURCES OF AUTONOMY

Members of the building trades gain their power and control from two major sources—the publicly recognized skill of the individual worker (individual autonomy) and the collective support of their organized labor (group autonomy). These two sources are interdependent and provide a level of autonomy unknown in most occupations. Individual autonomy centers on the occupational control that a single craftperson can successfully claim through his or her attained skill level, whereas group autonomy represents an extended level of control achieved through collective trade organization efforts.

Everett Hughes's concepts of "license" and "mandate" apply here. According to Hughes:

> Not merely do the practitioners, by virtue of gaining admission to the charmed circle of colleagues, individually exercise the license to do things others do not do, but collectively they presume to tell society what is good and right for the individual and for society at large in some aspect of life [1958: 79].

Where individual autonomy is based upon the "license" that is successfully claimed by a skilled tradesperson to do certain tasks, group autonomy is based upon the "mandate" that successfully convinces others that the trade organization alone knows best how those tasks should be done.

Both individual and group autonomy emerges from the existing social structural and organizational features of the building industry. It will be shown that worker autonomy is a condition that is carefully managed and forcefully protected by building-trades members.

More importantly, this maximized control over one's work enables a worker to provide a quality product. When a worker is able to take the time to do an installation correctly, without the encumbrance of external pressures to produce quickly, the product will more likely be free of error and long-lasting. In essence, the product should reflect craftsmanship.

INDIVIDUAL AUTONOMY: THE LICENSE

Three areas can be singled out as salient in the creation and perpetuation of individual autonomy in the building trades. These include formal apprenticeship training, tool ownership, and the portable nature of one's skills. Collectively, these facilitate the successful claim of "license" by individual workers.

Formal Apprenticeship Training

Apprenticeship programs provide for the continuance of established trade skills and the perpetuation of the trade culture. These formal, nationalized programs bestow a publicly recognized certification on persons who successfully pass through the rigid training sequence.

These formal programs are an outgrowth of the National Apprenticeship Act of 1937 and are encouraged by the Department of Labor as the best training method for learning a skilled trade. Most states offer these programs, usually in their urban areas. Vocational training or working as a "helper" are other, less desirable methods of learning a trade.

The apprenticeship process is one of acculturation. The aspiring member learns the established skills of the trade, as well as the way in which work should and should not be done, the beliefs of the occupation, and the existing attitudes concerning how workers should behave, dress, and communicate. This process of occupational acculturation serves as the basis for establishing an individual worker's identity and facilitates the work group's solidarity and cohesiveness. A worker who successfully learns and internalizes the established ways of a trade is accepted as a member and at the same time accepts that designation (Riemer, 1979; Haas, 1974, 1977; Cherry, 1974).

Apprentices may spend as long as five years learning their trade. Plumbers and electricians serve the longest period while carpenters, painters, iron-workers, and cement finishers serve for a shorter period, usually three years. This is typically accomplished by a combination of classroom education and on-the-job training under the guidance of established workers. During this period, apprentices experience a range of installations that those in their trade would be expected to encounter as journeypersons. Apprentices are continually monitored and periodically tested, and if successful, they become the certified carriers of their mastered skill and trade culture. Worker autonomy is a by-product of this process.

Fred Katz (1968: 21) has suggested, "the greater the degree of specialized knowledge and skills required of the occupant of a position, the greater the degree of autonomy that accrues to the position." Within the skilled building trades, plumber and electrician apprentices have to master a broader set of skills over a longer prescribed period, and upon completion command a higher pay scale, more prestige, and greater control over their work than other tradespersons (Riemer, 1979).

Tool Ownership

Skilled building-trade workers are unique in that they own most, or all, of the tools needed to perform their work. They own the means of their production. Tools are extensions of the individual, and their skillful manipulation allows for the performance of complicated tasks.

When workers own the tools needed to do the work, they enhance their control over that work. This practice is a carry-over from the guilds of medieval Europe and is perpetuated by modern-day building-trade unions. Unions strengthen worker autonomy by providing contractors with skilled workers who are "standardized." That is, *all* journeypersons are viewed as being the same in the provision of their craft (Caplow, 1964). When each worker owns a standard set of tools, individual autonomy is further enhanced (Riemer, 1979).

The purchase of tools begins during the early apprenticeship years and culminates with a complete set of tools by the time journeyperson status is attained. This is not a minor economic investment. Electricians, for example, can easily spend three or four hundred dollars for their required tools, and some of these need to be replaced periodically.

Portable Skills

Certified workers become immediately mobile; their skills are portable. The historical term, journeyman, if taken literally, conveys this source of worker control. Journeypersons are not bound to their employer as are most other workers. They are bound to their trade and, as such, can and do move from contractor to contractor if work is available. If dissatisfied, they can simply pack up their tools and leave for another contractor or even another city. This is done through union referral. Independent contracting is also an option. Building-trade workers are not wed to their employing organization, they are wed to their craft (Caplow, 1964; Strauss, 1958).

Labor unions enhance mobility opportunities with their national network ties. If a particular location needs workers, a "call for workers" may be placed throughout the country. Some trade workers known as "boomers" or "travelers" are continually on the move, seeking out the better jobs, or those that pay overtime wages.

Collectively, the successful completion of a nationally recognized apprenticeship program, along with resultant certification, the ownership of the tools of one's trade, and the portable nature of one's skills enable the individual worker to have a great deal of control (individual autonomy) over his or her work.

Where the individual worker carries the "license" to do the work, the worker's trade organization promotes the "mandate" that only they know how that work should be done. This added factor serves to enhance the level of craftsmanship at which skilled building-trade workers are able to perform.

GROUP AUTONOMY: THE MANDATE

Three areas can be isolated as salient in the fostering of group autonomy in the skilled building trades. These include: recruitment control, informal work group control, and formal union control. Collectively, these facilitate the successful claiming of an organizational mandate for the sole provision of this work.

Recruitment Control

In the past, nepotism (the hiring of relatives or friends) was the primary means of recruitment in the building trades (Myers, 1946). Today, formal apprenticeship programs have largely replaced that method (Riemer, 1979). The selection of new apprentices is in the hands of joint apprenticeship and training committees composed of an equal number of representatives from labor (union) and management (contractors), and coordinatored by an appointed apprenticeship director. All interested persons are required to make application for an apprenticeship slot. These are evaluated by the committee, and a formal interview is usually conducted with the candidate, who then answers committee members' questions. The selection of new apprentices follows. For some trades, certain high school math courses are necessary, and most require a complete physical examination. Age limitations are also enforced.

At the same time, trade unions are careful to control their total membership (Caplow, 1964). Entrance and attrition figures are monitored to insure that enough, but not too many, tradespersons are available to work. Ideally, a trade union would have enough workers to supply all contractor needs while insuring that few workers would be "on the bench" (out of work) at a given time. When there is an increase in the amount of work available, a union may issue "permits" to workers from other areas of the country to work on a temporary basis during the "boom" period. Permit-holders will then be "bumped" by regular members when the work becomes slack.

New apprentices are carefully monitored throughout their training and may be terminated for unsatisfactory performance. The apprenticeship director is in charge of monitoring each apprentice's progress and administering written examinations. This procedure enables the trade to control the entry and ultimate certification of new members. Thus, skill level and loyalty to the organizational goals of the trade are maintained. Undesirables are terminated.

Those who become journeypersons will have internalized the expected values of their trade as part of the occupational socialization process. Consequently, they are inclined to perpetuate the value orientations of their fellow workers in the training and monitoring of new recruits. This control over the recruitment of new members fosters in-group solidarity and cohesiveness, and serves to strengthen collective autonomy. In turn, this serves to increase the control over one's work.

Informal Work Group Control

Working in concert with respected, like-situated others serves to create standards and practices that are acceptable to the work group members. Work groups within each building trade select the work pace and the level of quality in workmanship for a particular project. This is done informally, with an implicit set of norms being enforced by group members (Riemer, 1979; Feigelman, 1974). Persons that work too hard or not hard enough will be subtly managed through informal means, usually verbal ridicule (Riemer, 1979; Haas, 1972, 1974).

This control over worker behavior by the workers themselves exists because the nature of the work is flexible rather than consisting of routine tasks, and the immediate supervisor, the foreman, is also a trade worker, having come directly from the ranks. A foreman's primary alliance is typically to his trade, not to the employing organization. Moreover, multiple trades on the same project will usually cooperate with other trade members, thus establishing a more autonomous labor force with maximum control over their work and working conditions.

This informal control by work group members also spills over into nonwork activities. Tradesworkers are a distinctly proud class of workers who are well-satisfied with their occupation. This general feeling encourages companionship off the job and voluntary association activities among workers (Le Masters, 1975; Riemer, 1979). These contacts away from work also serve to encourage informal social control among trade workers.

Union Control

Building-trade unions are some of the strongest in the world. As Caplow notes, building-trade unions are "restrictive." They are composed of members who are not easily replaceable. According to Caplow:

Its first objective is to control admission to the occupation so that increases in wages or improvements in working conditions will not be negated by an increase in the supply of workers. In thus fixing the supply of labor, it usually assumes responsibility for its equitable distribution among employers. This, in turn, leads to a close concern with the performance of work, and to continuous efforts to standardize work output. These motives are reinforced by the union's concern with apprenticeship, and by the necessity of safeguarding the existing craft against technological change [1964: 195].

This strength is evidenced in the monopoly that unions hold over the providing of skilled workers for construction projects. Employers have little control in the selection of employees or in how a particular installation is to be done.

The relationship between employers and trade union members is based upon the contract that is periodically struck between the two (Strauss, 1958). This working agreement specifies wage rates, eligibility and seniority rules, hiring and termination procedures, safety rules, acceptable tools and methods, and grievance procedures (Hall, 1975). It is this document that protects worker autonomy and allows them to exercise control over their work.

Collectively, recruitment control, informal work group control, and formal union control creates a level of group autonomy unknown in most occupations. Stinchcombe (1959) has suggested that the building construction union is similar to a professional association, in that it provides workers with maximum control over what they do in the workplace.

This factor enables workers to do their work in the best possible fashion. When workers are allowed the time and control to complete their work as they choose, the finished product should be of quality and should reflect craftsmanship.

Even though building-trade workers have maximized their autonomy, this is never constant. Threats to this control are ever present, and these workers and their organization must continually combat them.

THREATS TO AUTONOMY

The primary threat to worker autonomy in the skilled building trades is economic. Building-trade contractors continually attempt to maximize control over their workers to further their own economic gains. This is done daily through the manipulation of individual workers by certain managerial and supervisory personnel in an attempt to increase worker production. Similar attempts are made at the organizational level. Here, building-trade contractors and their associations attempt to erode the collective autonomy of trade workers through contract negotiations with union representatives. These negotiations usually occur each year.

This is a power relationship based on mutual dependency. The faction that controls the balance of power in the relationship depends to a large extent on the amount of work that is available. When work is prevalent, the trade workers hold the balance of power. Since they have the "license" and "mandate" for the provision of the work, they can exert control in the workplace through slowdown tactics, threats to quit, and manipulations for overtime pay. If the contractor objects, the workers may rebel and go to work for other contractors desperately in need of workers. Under these conditions, being fired would be rare and inconsequential.

When there is a shortage of work, the trade contractors hold the balance of power. During this time they can make production demands on workers that directly confront the workers' autonomy and level of craftsmanship. Workers who choose not to compromise, and those whom the contractors may deem undesirable are sent back to the union hall. Older workers, troublemakers, and those who are generally slow producers are typically terminated first. These manipulations can serve to erode the level of craftsmanship in the work provided.

Additional threats to union worker autonomy occur from non-union workers and the general public. Non-union workers typically work for a lower rate of pay, have not learned their trade in a formal apprenticeship program, are less aggressive about workers' rights and safety conditions, and work for non-union contractors. These workers possess little control over their work because they lack complete formalized skill certification and have no organizational affiliation. Lacking a true "license" and "mandate," they are typically relegated to doing the "dirty work" of the industry—house construction. This type of construction work more than any other is done as "factory-like" production work. Production quotas are placed on workers, and those who are too slow are fired. "Rate busting" and worker willingness to work more quickly, or for less pay in order to keep their job is common in non-union construction work. Any craftsmanship that exists is worn away in the process.

This condition is threatening to the union-affiliated skilled trade worker because members of the general public believe that union and non-union craft workers provide the same service. That all trade workers are the same is the prevailing view. The common quality of their work is implicit, but this assumption is erroneous.

Workers who have served a formal apprenticeship process receive the best training available in the industry. Almost all of these workers are also union members, since union membership was a prerequisite for their training. Moreover, union-affiliated workers command the highest wages for their services. True craftsmen are more likely to hold this status. When workers lack control over their work and can be coerced to produce, as non-union, inferior trained workers can be, the quality of their work will suffer and craftsmanship will be eroded.

IMPLICATIONS

It is suggested that worker autonomy in the skilled building trades can be traced to the social, structural, and organizational aspects of the industry. Trade workers possess a unique power and control over their work, both as individual practitioners and as members of a collective labor organization. They hold the successfully claimed "license" and "mandate" as providers of their craft for society.

However, this skill provision is continually under threat. It was pointed out that the major threat is economic, whereby skilled workers are continually facing attempts to erode their level of craftsmanship. Related to this are the political and technological changes that continue to threaten the skilled building construction worker's autonomy. "Right to work" legislation that threatens organized labor, and technological innovations, such as prefabricated buildings (constructed by non-union, unskilled labor), threaten craft standards and can erode the skilled worker's level of autonomy. Moreover, it was suggested that consumers in society have failed to recognize the impact of this erosion of craftsmanship.

According to Riemer:

> Builders and building trade contractors are being forced to increase their prices because of rising material costs, wages and salaries. Consumers are voicing complaints about the high cost of building and many are being priced out of the market. Tradesmen are faced with rising inflation costs on the one hand and pricing themselves out of a job on the other. Trade unions are caught in this economic vice. Craftsmanship, the art of providing sound quality installations through high level skills and workmanship, is losing out in the process [1979: 163].

The implication of this argument is that the general public, the consumers, are being mislead and will ultimately pay the added cost for the resultant shoddy workmanship emerging in the building trades. When worker autonomy is eroded, the quality of workmanship will also be eroded, and the consumer and taxpayer will be burdened with the added cost for the construction and repair of its public and private buildings. For example, Tremblay et al. (1977) indicate that about one-third of the respondents in a representative sample of Washington State residents (2790) had complaints about the poor construction of their homes.

It is suggested here that society will benefit when skilled workers are able to control their work sufficiently to minimize attempts to compromise their level of craftsmanship. This condition would allow consumers and taxpayers to better realize their expectations for a quality product. The skilled building trades provide a model for this actualization.

CHAPTER THIRTEEN

THE STRUCTURE OF CRAFT WORK
The Construction Industry

Marc L. Silver

THE STRUCTURE OF PRODUCTIVE activity remains central to the interests of organization and occupation theorists, informing both concern over organizational performance and for the physical and social welfare of those directly engaged in the production process. In recent years, manifestations of broadly felt discontent and alienation among workers at various levels of the occupational structure have spurred interest in the quality of work (Miller, 1980; Kalleberg, 1977; Kalleberg and Griffen, 1978; Kohn, 1976; O'Toole et al., 1973; Blauner, 1964). Much of the focus has been on the relationships between the inherent complexity of work, the opportunities for autonomy and self-direction in work, and the consultative nature of managerial styles.

Within this recent context, craft occupations in general, and the building and construction crafts in particular, have received only cursory and somewhat ambiguous consideration. In spite of persistent sociological interest in patterned relations of production, the organization of craft production and the quality of work for those in craft occupations remain poorly understood. Notwithstanding the increasing awareness of routinization and deskilling tendencies, and the relationship between production technique and managerial control (primarily since Braverman, 1974; but also see Edwards, 1979; Montgomery, 1979; Noble, 1977), craft production is still viewed by many organizational theorists as the exemplar of nonbureaucratic organization and occupational autonomy.

"CRAFT-PROFESSIONAL" PRODUCTION

Underlying this situation is a "craft-professional" perspective which has taken the combination of craft skill and craft organization as the determinative factors in production (Riemer, 1979; Le Masters, 1975; Hall, 1975; Stinchcombe, 1959, 1965; Blauner, 1964; Caplow, 1964). Presumably, monopolistically controlled knowledge of the production process and a strong tradition of craft unionism has established control over the process and organization of work on the one hand, and the perpetuation of that control through domination of knowledge transmission and labor supply, on the other. Craft production is considered distinguishable from other types of manual labor because work practices are "occupationally controlled" (Hall, 1975).

According to Stinchcombe, the distinction between bureaucratic and craft forms of production resides in the fact that in mass production, work practices are decided upon and planned in advance by management, while "in construction all these characteristics of the work process are governed by the worker in accordance with the empirical lore that make up craft principles" (1959: 170). He notes several aspects of production about which craft professionals make administrative decisions, including location, technique, coordination, and performance evaluation. Similarly, Blauner (1964) describes craft work as inclusive of the freedom to choose the techniques of work, the tools used in production, and the sequence in which operations are performed. According to the general view, "rational" organizational imperatives refer to situations where production conditions are sufficiently uncertain and variable bureaucratic managerial control is replaced by nonbureaucratic "craft administration of work."

A second and related dimension to the craft-professional perspective is that the valued skills, knowledge, and expertise of the professionalized craft workforce directly inform the quality of authority relations. Because management must rely on craft professionals to solve technical problems as they arise during the course of production, the administration of craft work entails frequent consultational and cooperative superordinate-subordinate interactions. Rather than formalized methods of bureaucratic communication and control, craft production is hypothesized to be defined by a sense of mutual dependency, interpersonal cooperation and trust, and a generally conciliatory approach to most production issues. Hall (1975), for instance, has argued that the degree of craft influence places craft occupations closer to managerial and professional positions than to other manual occupations.

In a more recent and extreme restatement of the craft-professional perspective, Jeffery Riemer, referring specifically to production in the construction industry, contends that, "Building tradesmen know their work and are generally *free to perform it as they choose*" (1979: 161, emphasis added). Moreover, Riemer argues that craft administration gives rise to potential social problems:

> But what happens when workers gain inordinate control over their working conditions? The freedom and initiative of the construction workers to modify their work . . . suggests some of the problems that society faces when workers have this freedom" [1979: 137].

In Riemer's view, the logic of rational organization which leads to craft administration has the latent dysfunctions of low worker productivity, organizational inefficiencies, and a poorer quality product. He answers his own question by saying that builders and consumers are the ones who bear the costs when workers have inordinate control in production. Underlying his conclusion is the untested assertion that construction craftworkers uniformly lack freedom in and control over production, but that said consequences would pertain if they in fact did so.

In general, the assumption that the organization of production is fairly uniform across craft occupations and within "craft industries" has meant that little effort has been made to examine empirically craft-professional hypotheses about the structure of craft work. Much of the supportive evidence comes from comparative studies of relative interindustry differences or has been at the level of aggregated craft occupational groupings, in which there is an implicit or explicit comparison with noncraft occupations. Those studies which do look directly at craft work have tended to focus on the microsociology and anthropology of craft culture, while avoiding direct assessments of the structure of the production process itself. In consequence, the descriptive theory has never received adequate empirical appraisal.

CONTEXTUALIZING CRAFT PRODUCTION

In contrast, a framework which explicitly places craft production within its macrostructural context is better suited for uncovering the factors that determine the organization of craft work. The broader political economy defines an overarching "systemic logic" that informs the set of productive relations comprising that system. What characterizes capitalist economies most distinctively are the imperatives of maintaining control over and promoting efficiency in production. The nature of specific organizational forms of capitalist production have to be defined in relation to a dynamic political economy, comprising relations both internal and external to the organization (Zeitz, 1980; Benson, 1977; Zald, 1969) which reflect the simultaneous problematics of managerial control and effective organization. Thus, quantitative differences between craft, mass, and process forms of production notwithstanding, they are similar to the extent that ownership, managerial planning, and control continue to play significant roles in shaping the production process.

On the one hand, organizations must be effective in dealing with internal and environmental problems in order to survive. Task contingencies and environmental and market conditions thus may require a certain degree of organizational flexibility which loosens control structures and enhances the opportunities for self-direction and freedom from supervision. On the other hand, the managerial capacity for shifting organizational operations presupposes the power to control. Management strategies for coping with internal and external variabilities can be implemented only if complemented by mechanisms of organizational control.

Braverman (1974: 68) has emphasized the point that to speak of management is to speak of control. "Control is indeed the central concept of all management systems and has been recognized implicitly or explicitly by all theoreticians of management." His analysis of the relationship between labor process and management control challenges the position that formal features of occupational categories are the determining factors of the organization of work. Rather, he locates occupational attributes within the context of the imperatives of management control. The structure of the labor process reflects the confluence of organizational effectiveness and management's need to regulate organizational processes.

Kraft (1979), for instance, has shown such tendencies in computer and information management industries. As the labor process became better understood, occupations which earlier permitted workers substantial self-direction and freedom from supervision have been subdivided into simpler and more routine jobs which facilitate managerial surveillance and control.

Similarly, in their study of "affluent workers" Goldthorpe et al. (1968) found that a significant proportion of craftsmen reported a desire for changes in the organization of work, supervisory practices, and the use of tools, equipment, and machinery. The researchers point out that craftsmen expressed "strong criticism" of the closeness of supervision and the routinized organization of work:

> It could be said, then, that the main emphasis in the craftsmen's replies was, in effect, on changes which would in their view lead to greater efficiency and which would at the same time increase their own

involvement in, and control over, the work process with which they were concerned" [1968: 21].

Accordingly, the skills and knowledge required in craft occupations do not necessarily result in organizational structures reflecting either "occupational control" of work practices or "craft administration" of production. Their impacts on the structure of work, specifically on self-direction and supervision, occur in conjunction with other factors, chief among which are those affecting the efforts by management to maintain control over the production process. Therefore, in order to gain an accurate perspective on craft production, the significance of a craft's occupational characteristics must be analyzed in relation to, not in isolation from, the organization's political economy.

CRAFT PRODUCTION IN THE CONSTRUCTION INDUSTRY

A number of features of the construction industry make it ideal for a strategic assessment of the determinants of the structure of craft work. For one, it has long been taken as the exemplar of the craft form of production. As I indicated earlier, it is common for theorists to cite the construction industry as illustrative of nonbureaucratic, decentralized, and occupationally controlled organizational types. At the same time, there are also substantial organizational and occupational differences within the industry which have not received focused attention in the literature.

The building trades differ in the levels of skill and training required for journeyman status, for instance. At one end there are laborer and "helper" trades which demand little or no formal apprenticeship. At the other are the mechanical trades, such as electrician and plumber, which have extended apprenticeships to acquire the skills for complex jobs. In between are a range of intermediate occupations. Furthermore, there are variations within the industry as regards employer and union scales of operation, bureaucratization, and union-management relations. In other words, many of the factors which organizational theorists have shown to be relevant to the structuring of work in other industrial settings are also present in construction.

It is beyond the scope of this brief study to offer an elaborate description of the work process in construction. However, it is possible to specify a limited number of factors which have been shown to be relevant to the work structure: specifically, workforce size, project duration, bureaucratization, managerial position, and union-management "project concessions." It is possible to assess the impact of "craft" on the structure of construction work relative to these organizational factors.

SAMPLE AND MEASURES

The following analysis is based on a survey conducted in 1979 of craft workers in nine building construction trades and ten local unions from a northeastern metropolitan area of the United States. The crafts in the study are representative of the ranges of skill level, work organization, general conditions of work, and union-contractor relations among the building trades generally.

Individual respondents were selected through random sampling procedures from union rosters of active members. In all, 55 members of each union were mailed a questionnaire which queried various aspects of their experiences on the job, both as a union member and craft employee. Two follow-up mailings were sent to nonresponders. In addition, personal interviews were conducted with at least one full-time official—a business agent or business manager— from each of the participating local unions. Officials also completed a detailed questionnaire about labor relations practices, employment, and local union organizational characteristics.

Multiple mailings resulted in responses from 273 craftspeople: an initial response rate of 49 percent. Deleting returns which were either completed incorrectly or with too many omissions to be useful left a usable sample of 260 total respondents (47 percent return rate), of which 14 were union officials. The present analysis is based on the responses of the 246 rank-and-file craftspeople.

The relatively low return rate makes it necessary to view results with some caution. On the other hand, the sample compares favorably with national samples of unionized construction workers and with estimates of the aggregate characteristics of the individual local union organizations from which the sample was drawn.

Two measures of craft composition were used. "Craft Complexity" is indexed by the rating of occupational task characteristics by the Department of Labor, Dictionary of Occupational Titles. It is a scale of the degree of personal involvement required by the job as regards interactions with people, data, and material. "Craft Mentality" is the regularity with which a job demands dealing with written material. Respondents rated their job on a five-point scale from "never deal with written material" to "constantly deal with written material."

Work structure was assessed in terms of "Self-Direction" and "Supervision." The former is operationalized as the degree to which the worker decides "what to do" and "how to do it," self-reported on a five-point scale. Supervision is the relative frequency of having one's work evaluated by a superordinate during the workday. Respondents scored the frequency of supervision on a six-point scale.

Three clusters of antecedent variables were also included in the analysis: managerial position, organization, and job concessions. "Foremanship," "Pre-Project Consultation," and "On-Site Consultation" measure managerial position. The first is the regularity of holding an official managerial position from one project to another; the second is the regularity of being consulted by a contractor prior to the start of a project; the third is the regularity of consultations with employers during the course of a project. Each is a self-report item measured on a five-point scale.

In addition, "Size" is the number of workers from a respondent's trade on the construction site. "Duration" is the number of weeks workers from that trade will be on the site from start to completion. And "Bureaucracy" is measured by the number of supervisory positions specific to the trade on the site. Finally, "Job Concessions" refers to the regularity with which one must ignore aspects of the union contract in order to be hired or to stay on a project. As I have described elsewhere (Silver, 1981a, b), agreement by union officials and individual craftspeople to substandard working conditions is one way local unions attempt to reduce unemployment among the rank and file. The imposition of substandard circumstances as a condition of employment has a direct logical connection to control mechanisms on the construction site. Surprisingly, however, this important relationship between collective bargaining and labor relations on the one side and the organization of the labor process on the other is rarely given careful treatment.

HYPOTHESES AND ANALYSIS

Table 13.1 shows the intercorrelations among the variables, their means and standard deviations. These data from the survey were used to examine three hypotheses central to the craft-professional perspective. They concern the bureaucratization of the work organization, the degree of self-direction that craftspeople manifest in their work, and the frequency of evaluative supervision from managerial superordinates. In addition, the nature of the relationship between self-direction and supervision is examined, specifically the possibility of reciprocal effects between the two measures of work structure.

(Ia) "Craft Complexity and Mentality reduce the number of formal managerial positions in the construction site organization." This follows directly from the position that the complexity and variability of craft work lead to

TABLE 13.1 Correlations, Means, and Standard Deviations

	1	2	3	4	5	6	7	8	9	10	11
1. Size*											
2. Duration n	.34**										
3. Bureaucracy	.45**	.29**									
4. Foremanship	-.12*	.04	-.35**								
5. Prior Consultation	-.23**	-.17**	-.33**	.50**							
6. On-site Consultation	-.13*	-.16**	-.22**	.39**	.50**						
7. Job Concessions	.08	.13*	.22**	-.16**	-.34**	-.29**					
8. Craft Complexity	.04	.05	-.09	.14*	.12*	.10	-.24**				
9. Craft Mentality	.04	.09	-.05	.40**	.22**	.32**	-.08	.32**			
10. Self-direction	-.26**	-.17**	-.34**	.39**	.34**	.20**	-.15*	.03	.13*		
11. Supervision	.27**	.17**	.38*	-.29**	-.30**	-.11*	.28**	-.11*	-.10	-.47	
$\overline{X}$	1.8	6.9	1.7	2.8	3.1	2.4	2.25	12.2	3.0	3.2	3.9
SD	.94	2.6	1.2	1.4	1.4	1.4	1.2	2.7	1.9	1.2	1.6

aLogarithmic transformation

*p < .05
**p < .01

craft rather than bureaucratic administration. The construction site organization for skilled trades should be less bureaucratic, i.e., have fewer management positions, than for semi-skilled and unskilled trades.

Alternative hypotheses, based on a political economy organizational model, posit effects of Size and Duration on Bureaucracy, either in conjunction with or to the exclusion of craft effects.

(Ib) "Size increases management positions on the site."

(Ic) "Duration increases management positions on the site." Both of these hypotheses are based on the problems workforce size and duration pose for the maintenance of management surveillance and control over the labor process. Larger workforces require more supervisors and foremen than smaller ones (Ib). At the same time, establishment of a managerial hierarchy engenders certain costs for the contractor. Foremen who spend part of their time performing supervisory and coordinating functions are not directly contributing to production. It is not economically feasible to undertake additional costs if the project lasts only a brief time. A certain degree of temporal stability is necessary for bureaucratization to make economic sense.

These hypotheses were addressed by regressing Bureaucracy on the craft composition and organizational variables. The results of the analysis are shown in Table 13.2. The overall equation explains 22 percent of the variation in the number of management positions. Hypothesis Ia is not supported. The regression coefficients for Complexity and Mentality are not significantly greater than zero (Bs = .09 and .05, respectively; $p > .10$), but the signs of the coefficients are in the predicted directions. Furthermore, it is possible that the association between the two craft variables ($r = .32$, Table 13.1) suppresses their separate effects. If this were the case, their combined effect would be significant, while their individual coefficients would not be statistically greater than zero when both are in the equation.

In order to test whether the combined impact of Complexity and Mentality accounts for a significant proportional reduction in unexplained variance, a hierarchical test was performed (not shown). Adding the craft variables to an equation containing Size and Duration does not substantially decrease unexplained variation in Bureaucracy. An additional test, for non-linear effects of Craft Complexity and Mentality (not shown), also failed to yield significant effects.

In contrast, both hypotheses Ib and Ic are supported. The coefficients for Size (B = .40) and for Duration (B = .18) are significant and positive in sign. Both the size of the workforce and the temporal stability of the organizational site of production increase Bureaucracy. Larger craft components which remain on the construction site for longer periods foster the need for a larger managerial component.

(IIa) "Craft Complexity and Mentality increase Self-Direction." Work that is substantively complex and comprised of regular references to written plans

TABLE 13.2   Regression of Bureaucracy on Craft Composition and Organization

	Bureaucracy (−.18)
Craft Complexity	−.09 (−.04)[a]
Craft Mentality	−.05 (−.03)
Size[b]	.40 (.53)**
Duration	.16 (.08)**
R	.48
$\overline{R}^2$	.21

[a]Unstandardized coefficients in parentheses

[b]Natural logarithm

*p < .05

**p < .01

and instructions should allow for greater latitude in deciding procedural and technical aspects of the production process. In its most direct interpretation, craft administration signifies that the more complicated and less uniform tasks require a craftsperson to make more decisions about what tasks to perform and how to arrange the specific order of operations.

Expectations about self-direction from the political economy model stress the roles of organizational structure, management position, and labor relations outcomes:

(IIb) "Size, Duration, and Bureaucracy reduce individual levels of Self-Direction."

(IIc) "Management position (Foremanship, Prior Consultation, On-Site Consultation) increases Self-Direction."

(IId) "Job Concessions reduce the degree of Self-Direction."

Hypotheses IIb, c, and d are based on the earlier discussion of the importance of contractor control management and collective bargaining negotiations within a capitalist political economy. The greater the bureaucratic structure of the work organization, other factors equal, the greater the delimitation of the sphere of decision responsibility for the individual craftsperson; i.e., the greater the probability that job characteristics will be specified by preestablished descriptions or by a managerial superordinate (IIb). On the other hand, the nature of the administrative and supervisory functions performed by those holding managerial positions should expand decision-making autonomy (IIc). Finally, job concessions to employers may restrict self-direction. Expansion of managerial prerogative actually may be one form of concession made by the local union. Alternatively, lower self-direction may be an ancillary result of productivity concessions (IId).

TABLE 13.3   Regression of Work Autonomy on Craft Composition, Organization, Management Position and Job Concessions

	Self-Direction (5.2)	Supervision (4.3)
Craft Complexity	−.03 (−.03)[a]	−.02 (−.01)
Craft Mentality	.02 (.03)	−.04 (−.04)
Size[b]	−.12 (−.31)*	.12 (.21)*
Duration	−.08 (−.08)	.06 (.04)
Bureaucracy	−.12 (−.23)	.20 (.27)***
Foremanship	.29 (.49)***	−.16 (−.19)**
Prior Consultation	.12 (.22)	−.12 (−.15)
On-site Consultation	−.04 (−.08)	.16 (.18)**
Job Concessions	−.03 (−.07)	.19 (.26)***
R	.49	.50
$\overline{R}^2$	.21	.21

[a]Unstandardized coefficients in parentheses
[b]Natural logarithm
 *p < .10 0
***p < .05
***p < .01

Results of the tests for hypotheses II appear in Column 1 of Table 13.3. The overall effect of the equation is significant (p < .001) and explains 21 percent of the variance in Self-Direction. However, the craft-professional hypothesis (IIa) is not supported. Neither the separate nor combined effects of Complexity and Mentality are significant (again, the hierarchical test is not shown). On the other hand, there is qualified support for the other hypotheses. As predicted, Size has a modest negative impact on Self-Direction (B = −.12; p < .10) and Foremanship has a strong positive effect (B = .29; p < .001). Thus, while the size of the work organization tends to limit self-direction, other things equal, formal management position expands decision-making autonomy as regards technical and procedural aspects of the labor process.

Hypothesis IId is not confirmed by the analysis. There is no indication that work concessions made to employers in exchange for employment affect the self-directing attributes of the job. Workers who make concessions are not likely to have any less autonomy than those who do not make such tradeoffs. Overall, the amount of decision autonomy reflects the craftsperson's position in the management hierarchy and the scale of the work organization. Patterns of consultation with superordinates, apart from formal position and task characteristics, have no appreciable effect on decision autonomy.

(IIIa) "Craft composition (Complexity and Mentality) decreases the frequency of evaluative Supervision by organizational superordinates." According to the craft-professional model, the composition of the task affects the feasibility of maintaining a constant monitor on work activities. Complex and variable tasks are either so intricate and time-consuming that evaluation can occur only after the completion of all operations, or supervisory personnel do not have the craft knowledge at their disposal to make on-the-spot performance evaluations. The result is that the higher skilled construction tradespeople experience less frequent supervision throughout the course of the workday.

(IIIb) "Organization Size and Bureaucracy increase Supervision."

(IIIc) "Management position decreases Supervision."

(IIId) "Job Concessions increase Supervision."

These hypotheses follow from the same logic as IIb, c, and d. As the work organization becomes larger, indirect and informal means of surveillance are less effective. Coordination and control become increasingly problematic and require more directness and formality. This is part of the explanation for the earlier finding of the relationship between Size and Bureaucracy. The latter, in turn, facilitates the maintenance of regular supervisory contacts with the workforce. Thus, as a corollary of IIb, it may be further hypothesized that the effects of Size and Duration are indirect through the positive impact of Bureaucracy on Supervision.

Management location should reduce the experience of being supervised. At times, the foreman or supervisor is the contractor's sole representative on the construction site. When more than one foreman is on the site, there are greater opportunities for being supervised by others in the management structure, but these occurrences are more likely to be informal, possibly in the context of group consultations with the contractor.

The expectation of a positive relationship between making job concessions and the closeness of supervision bears directly on the outcomes of labor relations in which the interests of employer and worker are opposed. The contractor who succeeds in drawing additional advantages beyond those granted in the union contract is less likely to feel in a position to leave his workforce unsupervised. To the contrary, other things equal, the likelihood of an uncooperative and relatively intractable complement of craftspeople increases under such conditions, which violate the balance between inducements and contributions established by the contract. Accordingly, the contractor must rely on more regular supervision of the workforce in order to ensure compliance.

The regression of Supervision testing hypotheses III appears in Table 13.3 (column 2). The equation is significant, explaining 21 percent of the variation in Supervision. The separate regression coefficients for the independent variables indicate little support for the craft-professional, but partial support for political economy hypotheses.

Craft Complexity and Mentality both have negligible impact on Supervision. Neither is significantly greater than zero. The highly skilled construction craftspeople are supervised as frequently in their work as their lesser skilled counterparts. In other words, skill level, the composition of craft jobs, do not serve as protections against managerial surveillance. Other factors account for the variation in the supervision from organizational superordinates experienced by craft workers.

As expected, organization size and structure at the construction site have significant effects on supervision (IIIb). Size slightly increases Supervision (B = .12; $p < .10$), while Bureaucracy has a strong positive impact (B = .20; $p < .01$). Similarly, the prediction for Job Concessions is also confirmed (B = .19; $p < .01$). Craft workers who give up quality of work provisions of their union contract in exchange for employment receive greater supervisory attention. Conversely, winning concessions from workers places additional management pressure on contractors. Having gained the promise of greater economic advantage from the production process, the contractor must institute mechanisms to ensure that outcomes reflect that promise.

Hypothesis IIIc, concerning the impact of managerial position, receives only partial support from the analysis. On the one hand, holding an official foremanship on the construction site does reduce the frequency of supervision (B = -.16; $p < .05$). Craftspeople who regularly hold foreman positions generally experience greater freedom from surveillance from above. On the other hand, the coefficient for On-Site Consultations is also statistically significant, but positive (B = .16; $p < .05$). Other things equal, craftspeople who more frequently are consulted by contractors about the progress of the construction project report more frequent evaluation and supervision of their own performance. This is opposite to the expectation that direct consultations with employers would reduce supervision. One possible interpretation is that consultational interactions with superordinates inherently contain supervisory or evaluative qualities. Being consulted about a production problem implicitly entails having one's current performance subject to assessment, or at least the finding indicates that consulted craftspeople have that subjective impression.

This relationship between consultation and supervision has a significant implication for the conceptualization of the connection between managerial style and control. Without delving too deeply into the issue, it suggests that the form of the authority relationship can vary, at least in terms of its consultational aspects, without disrupting underlying mechanisms of managerial control. Consultation does not "replace" supervision in the authority relationship. Rather, it alters the way in which it is experienced by subordinates.

The final issue to be addressed concerns the relationship between self-direction and supervision. Thus far we have considered them as independent aspects of work autonomy, assessing their separate organizational dependencies without explicitly touching upon the association between them. In fact, Self-Direction and Supervision are strongly related ($r = -.47$). The inverse zero-order correlation is reduced but remains significant when organization, management, and job concession variables are controlled.

There are three possible forms of interassociation which could account for this. Considering unidirectional relationships, greater self-direction in work, deciding more often on technical and procedural aspects of the job, could reduce the frequency of evaluative contacts. In this case, greater involvement in decision processes at the production level also increases freedom in carrying out production tasks. Alternatively, supervision could influence the amount of self-direction. Craftspeople whose performance is less regularly evaluated throughout the day consequentially make more decisions about carrying out their part in production. The mechanism is the frequency of contacts with superordinates, with the latter making production decisions when contact is frequent, the craft worker making them when contact is infrequent. Third, there is the possibility of a reciprocal relationship. Self-direction may reduce supervision which, in turn, further increases the degree of self-direction, or vice versa.

In order to examine these possibilities, a least-squares test for contemporaneous reciprocal effects was applied. To make the analysis, reduced models for Supervision and Self-Direction were specified. Setting the direct effects of Bureaucracy and Job Concessions on Self-Direction and those of Foremanship and Prior Consultation on Supervision equal to zero permitted two-stage solutions for the reciprocal effects model (Table 13.4). The results show the relation between Self-Direction and Supervision to be significant ($B = -.51$; $p < .01$). The amount of decision autonomy inversely influences the frequency of supervisory contacts. The effect of Supervision on Self-Direction is also present, in the predicted direction, but only marginally significant ($B = -.23$; $.10 > p < .05$). Thus, the evidence favors the determining influence of Self-Direction over Supervision, but the likelihood of a reciprocal model cannot be dismissed.

Tangentially, the inverse effect of Self-Direction in conjunction with the positive effect of Consultation on Supervision suggests the distinction between "participation in" and "control over" production decision processes. Other factors equal, participation (i.e., Consultation) may restrict freedom on the job, possibly because it permits subtle mechanisms of managerial control. Control over production decisions (i.e., Self-Direction) may enhance freedom

TABLE 13.4   Reciprocal Effects Model: Self-Direction and Supervision

	Self-Direction (7.8)	Supervision (8.8)
Craft Complexity	−.06 (−.05)	−.03 (−.02)
Craft Mentality	−.01 (−.00)	.03 (.03)
Size	−.09 (−.22)	−.01 (−.02)
Duration	−.05 (−.04)	−.03 (−.02)
Bureaucracy	−	.05 (.06)
Foremanship	.22 (.39)**	−
Prior Consultation	.05 (.09)	−
On-site Consultation	.02 (.02)	.16 (.18)**
Job Concessions	−	.16 (.23)**
Supervision	−.23 (−.68)*	−
Self-direction	−	−.51 (−.72)***

[a]Unstandardized coefficients in parentheses

[b]Natural logarithm

 *p < .10

 **p < .05

 ***p < .01

r_{esd-es} = .85

from managerial surveillance, possibly by precluding managerial intervention in the decision-making process.

CONCLUSION

The foregoing analysis has been a modest attempt to test a limited number of hypotheses derived from craft-professional and political economy models of work organization. Overall, the evidence from the data on construction work favors the latter perspective. The composition of productive tasks shows no substantive relationship to bureaucratization of the work organization, nor to the self-direction and supervision craftspeople experience in their work activities. This held for nonlinear and hierarchical, as well as for linear additive models. The structure of work is more sensitive to a range of organizational factors, including size, temporal stability, managerial location, and labor relations outcomes.

The objection could be raised, however, that the intraindustrial data do not provide an adequate test of the craft-professional perspective. It could be argued that the variation in task composition across construction occupations is not sufficient to affect the structure of work and organization. Second, it could be the case that the research design has artificially masked the influences of task composition. Careful consideration shows that neither potential objection is tenable.

The range of skill level across the construction occupations represented in the survey sample is substantial, encompassing unskilled, semi-skilled, and skilled occupations. The range, if not the proportional distribution, of occupational characteristics in construction is not very different from that in manufacturing industries.

Second, the subcontracting structure in construction, according to which employers generally have responsibility for limited portions of the building project and hire workers specific to a single productive function (e.g., painting subcontractors hire painters; electrical subcontractors hire electricians), should mean that organizational differences are even more sensitive to task and craft characteristics than in mass production industries, where single employers have responsibility for all production functions and hire workers from many different occupations. In other words, the conditions in construction should, if anything, magnify the relationship between organizational structure and occupation. The failure to find significant effects of craft occupational properties in terms of task composition cannot be dismissed as artifacts of the research design.

At the same time, it has to be emphasized that the present findings, based on comparative data from a single industrial context, do not necessarily contradict the results of interindustry comparative research. The relative unimportance of occupational characteristics as compared to organizational factors within the construction industry does not signify that there are not important differences in the organization of the labor process across industries. The findings do bear, however, on how such interindustry differences should be interpreted.

Organization and occupation theorists have tended to attribute overarching significance to technological and task characteristics in shaping the labor process. Analyses made at the industry rather than the organizational level, in particular, rely on the assumption of a close correspondence between occupational properties and organizational structure. Bureaucratic differences between construction and mass production and automated process production industry "types" have been explained by task variabilities and technological complexities which foster craft administration of work.

Upon analysis, however, factors related to antagonistic union-employer labor relations and management control emerge as the salient determinants of work structure in construction. That size, bureaucratization, and position in the management hierarchy are the principle organizational influences on autonomy indicates some basic continuities across industrial sectors in their underlying logic of organization. Moreover, it suggests that logic to be informed by an organizational political economy reflecting employers' needs to control organizational operations.

The connection between work structure and labor relations bears this out. Organizational sociologists have tended to treat collective bargaining and labor relations processes as tangential or even irrelevant to the structural of work organizations. The academic division of labor between the Sociology of Organizations and Occupations on the one side, and Industrial and Labor Relations and Labor Studies on the other, reflects this parochialism. The present analysis suggests the importance of recognizing the areas of interrelation. Specifically, if the outcomes of labor bargaining increase the likelihood of noncooperation among the workforce, the mechanisms of management control are likely to be strengthened. Greater managerial surveillance of the workforce maximizes compliance when antagonistic interests in the labor process become prominent.

Thus, while interindustry differences may partially reflect effectiveness imperatives according to which organizations adapt to environmental, market, and task contingencies, the labor process also bears the stamp of the imperatives of management control. The confluence of effectiveness and control imperatives means that differences in organizational form should not be taken as necessarily signifying shifts in infrastructural power relations. Stating it somewhat more bluntly, employers facing variable product markets do not cede control to a "professionalized" workforce; rather, they alter the manner in which they exercise it.

In conclusion, I wish to raise a final point concerning the relation between sociological theory and research. This study has been, in part, an attempt to assess a theoretical perspective on craft production and, by extension, on the differences among capitalist work organizations generally. The craft-professional model, accepted in the literature for the past 30 years, has been complemented consistently by empirical methodologies which largely mirror the basic assumptions of the model. Bolstered by the historical analogy to precapitalist guild associations and the contemporary formalistic comparison to professional associations, craft production has been a priori considered a uniform process organized according to occupationally controlled principles of craft administration. In consequence, reliance on noncomparative microsociological field studies of craft culture and interindustry comparative research designs has allowed interpretations favorable to the perspective.

On the other hand, as we have seen, the craft-professional model of craft production does not stand up quite so well under the scrutiny of a critical empirical appraisal focused explicitly on its basic assumptions. Its longevity can thus be partially explained by the fact that subsequent research bearing upon the perspective has unquestioningly built on a theoretical foundation without first testing its soundness. The lesson, I think, is that as social scientists pursuing greater understanding of social processes, we have to maintain the delicate balance between carefully conceived theoretical orientations and appropriately critical empirical research. This means strict attention to how we define concepts and derive operational measures, but attention also to the questions we actually propose for empirical analysis. In short, we must be careful not to wed our research methods so closely to our theoretical orientations that they become mere reflections of the ideas we find comfortable.

PART V

CLIENT CONTEXT

THE FOCUS OF the following chapter is client control of occupations at the group and role levels. In addition to societal and cultural norms, the organizational milieu and the organization of the occupation itself, client control is particularly important in a participatory society.

Clients enhance or reduce role autonomy, and they do reflect societal and cultural norms. In some states today, for example, clients are encouraged to ask for a "second opinion" before consenting to various treatment modalities by physicians. Unnecessary surgery is a concern not only for those insurance companies who pay for them, but also for a society which appears to be shifting from a norm supporting illness to a norm supporting wellness. At the role level, the autonomy of the patient is enhanced if and when knowledge is shared so that a considered decision can be made by the patient. Some large insurance companies are advertising the need for second opinions through the media, with hopes of getting patients to request them. These opinions are paid for by the insurance companies. At this time, some companies are reporting that savings have already accrued from this effort.

Throughout the literature there is evidence that the client for the service of an occupation either *should* have or *does* have some influence both on the product produced and/or the way individuals perform in their occupational roles. Client control is considered more by those interested in professionals and artists than by those who study industrial workers. Service orientation to a client and direct interaction with a client have often been defined as characteristics of true professions, as contrasted to other occupations. Obviously, the communicator and artist have to be communicating to some audience, however small, in order to continue their artistic production

(Cantor, 1980). The number of clients, their social class, and the frequency with which they use the services or buy the product are only a few of the clients' ways of influencing occupational roles.

For some occupations which are employed mainly in large complex organizations, it is not always clear *who* is the client. This issue becomes more important for our understanding of occupational autonomy because the number of such occupations seems to be increasing as professionals continue to seek work in these organizations.

Scientists and engineers employed in larger industries, or even governments, may have several clients. For example, the public may be considered the client for some research and development specialists employed in the federal government, even though they may not be in direct contact with the researchers. Other scientists and engineers employed as researchers in private corporations may consider the organization as the client. In this case, contact is direct and frequent. Researchers employed in military organizations may consider the specific servicemen and -women as their clients, as they may benefit immediately from the specific development.

In some of the above examples, the professional may be in a different situation if he/she feels the organization is acting contrary to the good of the public or to the benefit of the professional. Being a professional means you are less than completely loyal to the organization. A phenomenon which manifested itself in the 1970s is "whistle blowing." This involves the worker taking his grievance of organizational misconduct outside the organization after having exhausted organizational channels without satisfaction (Westin, 1980). Consequently, legal protection has been extended mainly to employees in government organizations who seek to report organizational misconduct perceived to harm the worker or the public. In these circumstances, the worker, usually a professional, adapts to the conflict by being disloyal to the organization and loyal to the general client, the public.

Another type of adaptation is found when direct interaction between client and worker exists in a bureaucratic structure where rules and roles are formally arranged. Lewis Mennerick's study of client typologies addresses the issue of how service workers negotiate to maintain autonomy in the workplace. He examines one mechanism, social typing, used by service workers in the correctional system. The processing of clients, criminal offenders, is one task where all correctional workers interact. The conflict experienced by both the client and the workers results in continual negotiation and typing of each by the other. Direct interaction between client and worker in this organizational milieu is likely to increase the struggle between these two groups for control of the other.

Some unanswered questions remain in the area of client control of occupational autonomy at the group and role levels.

(1) Is client control more problematic for professionals than nonprofessionals? Does this vary by the setting in which the workers are employed?

(2) Who benefits from a high degree of client control? The client? The purchaser? The citizen? The consumer?

(3) How much can the autonomy of an occupation be reduced by client control without modifying standards of excellence?

These are empirical questions of particular importance in a changing economic, social, and technological era. As more knowledge is gained, further specialization within and among occupations is likely to occur. Also, some occupations may become obsolete because of technological developments. These constant changes in the workplace and within occupations suggest that negotiation and compromise will be necessary between workers and clients in order for some production standards to continue. Such negotiations and interactions between clients and workers will be of most importance in situations where client and worker interact directly. It is likely that client control will be high in those circumstances.

In a rapidly changing post-industrial society, with multiple new and old forms of service occupations, "cui bono" (who benefits) when the client has control over worker power is an important question from many dimensions.

CHAPTER FOURTEEN

CLIENT TYPOLOGIES AND OCCUPATIONAL ROLE AUTONOMY
Correctional System Personnel

Lewis A. Mennerick

OCCUPATIONAL ROLE AUTONOMY—that is, the ability or opportunity to carry out tasks according to the workers' definition of the occupational role—is dependent on various factors that can either enhance or threaten such autonomy.[1] Workers in service occupations confront one particular threat to autonomy that is inherent in the nature of their occupations. The threat is the client. As Howard Becker (1951: 136) has noted, service occupations are unique in that workers interact on a relatively direct, personal basis with the clients for whom (or on whom) they render services. Accordingly, service workers confront the problem of having clients who can drastically influence their work activities: clients who tend to be variable and unpredictable, thus introducing many uncertainties into the work scene (Becker, 1951: 136; Hasenfeld and English, 1974: 13-14, 282; Mennerick, 1974c). Clients possess the potential to influence workers' control of the work scene and thereby affect workers' autonomy in carrying out their occupational roles (Stewart and Cantor, 1974).

Given such conditions, how do service workers attempt to maintain autonomy and control of the situation? The social typing of clients constitutes one major mechanism. The process of social typing—the process of categorizing individuals, social interactions, and social settings—is a part of everyday life. Without the ability to categorize such stimuli and thus bring some semblance of order to our daily activities, we would find it difficult to function. I argue, however, that the use of such typing is *not* equally common among all social actors in all social settings. Rather, social typing is more pronounced, more critical, for some actors—service workers, specifically —than for others. Further, as I have demonstrated previously, such typing occurs among a diverse array of service occupations, ranging from "deviant" and low status occupations such as prostitute and topless barmaid to high status occupations such as physician and lawyer (see Mennerick, 1974c).

The present study extends this conceptualization by exploring the use of social types among members of different occupations, but within one institutional context: the *correctional system*. The correctional system constitutes a unique site for examining autonomy and the typing process. The system encompasses a variety of occupational roles—such as prison guard, caseworker, psychiatrist, and parole officer—which may differ dramatically in terms of specific work tasks, level of training required, and prestige, and which may reflect differing occupational/organizational goals. Yet, given their service orientation, these roles are bound together by the common tasks of interacting with and processing clients: criminal offenders. It is important to emphasize that probationers, prison inmates, and parolees *are* clients of the system, even though they may *not* perceive of themselves as clients and may *not* approve of the services rendered. Indeed, it is well-documented that corrections personnel frequently confront substantial conflict, fear, hostility, and uncertainty in their relations with offenders (see Guenther and Guenther, 1974; Irwin, 1980; Jacobs and Retsky, 1975; New York State Special Commission on Attica, 1972: 80; Weinberg, 1942).[2]

In the following discussion, I first lay the ground work by making more explicit what is meant by social typing. I then review factors—societal conceptions of offenders and organizational/occupational goals, constraints, and concerns—that also influence worker autonomy but at the same time constitute underlying bases of the typing process.

CLIENT TYPOLOGIES

Although the roles of service worker and client both incorporate implicitly agreed upon expectations and obligations, formal role prescriptions do not always provide adequate information to guide worker-client interaction. Where information is lacking, social types frequently fill the void (Mennerick, 1974c: 398). On a more general level, Klapp notes that social types allow individuals to fill the gap between merely knowing "a person's formal status" and being well acquainted; in short, the social type is a "substitute for really knowing the person" (Klapp, 1958: 674; also see Klapp, 1971; Strong, 1943, 1946). Social typing assists service workers in ordering their expectations of client behavior. Typing informs workers as to the particular "kinds" of clients they are confronting and to the problems certain types of clients may cause.

The process can be summarized as entailing at least four stages (see Mennerick, 1974c: 400).

Service workers → Workers anticipate → Workers utilize → Workers employ
confront clients   potential conflict   client typologies   tactics or
                                                                  strategems to
                                                                  cope with
                                                                  different types
                                                                  of clients

In sum, the *social typing* of clients constitutes one means frequently utilized by service workers—including corrections personnel—in attempting to order their work scene, to reduce uncertainty about clients, and to cope with client variability and worker-client conflict (Mennerick, 1974c; Hasenfeld and English, 1974: 13-14, 282). Typing assists workers in managing worker-client interaction. It assists workers in identifying those types of clients who accept and support the workers' definitions of their occupational roles and those types whose behavior threatens worker autonomy.[3]

FACTORS INFLUENCING OCCUPATIONAL ROLE AUTONOMY

Thus far, I have argued that criminal offenders pose a major threat to the autonomy of correctional system personnel. Workers are influenced most immediately by the conflict and uncertainty inherent in *worker-client interaction*. However, as Stewart and Cantor (1974: 17-20) suggest, it is important to place the worker in a broader context and to examine factors on various levels—including societal, organizational, and client—that can influence worker autonomy.

To some extent, work roles in corrections are shaped by *societal conceptions* of the offender and how such individuals should be handled. These notions of what constitutes a "criminal" influence worker autonomy by defining "legitimate" work roles within the system. For example, the role of prison guard would not exist were it not for widely shared beliefs that certain kinds of criminals require secure confinement. Likewise, the occupation of prison psychiatrist would not be viable if all offenders were viewed as psychologically normal.

For each role, these conceptions also define the general parameters of appropriate work behavior, thereby reducing autonomy of the individual worker. Thus, guards in a maximum security prison should neither "coddle" inmates nor utilize inhumane tactics. Societal conceptions are often manifested in *organizational goals:* segregation of "criminals" from "law-abiding citizens," custody versus treatment, and so forth. Indeed, worker autonomy can be reduced further as organizational goals and dictums define the more specific parameters of appropriate work behavior. Finally, *organizational constraints* and *occupational concerns,* including the need to process large numbers of clients and to maintain social order within the system, frequently serve to reduce worker autonomy even more. For corrections workers, these various factors constitute a continuum.

	Societal	Organizational	Worker-Client	
Most General	Conceptions	Goals/Constraints	Interaction	Most Specific
Influence on				Influence on
Autonomy ◄ — ►				Autonomy

FACTORS UNDERLYING WORKERS' TYPOLOGIES OF OFFENDERS

Societal conceptions and organizational/occupational goals and constraints shape occupational roles and influence worker autonomy. However, these factors also relate to the social typing process by which workers seek to manage the third factor affecting worker autonomy: namely, worker-client interaction. Specifically, workers' typologies of offenders are based in part on societal conceptions that influence the workers' general orientation toward offenders. Typing also reflects organizational and occupational constraints and concerns, primarily the concern for maintenance of order and control. Finally, still other forms of typing reflect workers' moral evaluations of offenders. These moral assessments are influenced, in turn, both by societal conceptions of criminals and by organizational and occupational concerns, such as the need to justify the conditions to which they subject their clients. The following discussion, based on a review and synthesis of relevant litera- ture, focuses on each of these three dimensions: (1) societal conceptions of the convicted criminal, (2) organizational and occupational concerns for maintenance of order/control, and (3) workers' evaluations of their clients' moral character. I examine ways in which correctional system personnel who process adult offenders further define convicted criminals into an array of more specific types, thereby facilitating their work activities.

Societal Conceptions of the Convicted Criminal

That prisons and other correctional agencies do not develop and function in a vacuum, isolated from the broader society, has been well noted (see Cressey, 1965; Irwin, 1980; Jacobs, 1977; Rothman, 1971). Thus, implicit in the structure of these organizations and in the activities associated with corrections-related occupations are broad societal images of what kind of a person a criminal is and of the appropriate ways of dealing with those individuals so conceived (see Cressey, 1965: 1025). Historically, such conceptions are reflected in differing correctional strategies, ranging from corporal punishment and public humiliation, through discipline and isolation through imprisonment, to more recent concerns for community "treatment" and reintegration.

Societal conceptions of offenders are not restricted to prisons. Rather, broad social types reflecting evaluations of dangerousness, susceptibility to and appropriateness of different "rehabilitation" techniques, and relative need for supervision are implicit in the structure of various segments of the correctional system: maximum versus minimum security prisons, probation and parole agencies, half-way houses, and so forth. Corrections personnel, then, operate in settings in which societal conceptions of convicted criminals as approximating one social type or another have been formalized through legal/political/administrative processes and in turn have influenced organizational structure and work activities (see Arditi et al., 1973). Theoretically, such conceptions could define all offenders as similar and as requiring similar handling. However, societal conceptions more commonly distinguish among various kinds of criminals and suggest "appropriate" strategies for dealing with those offenders so defined.[4]

In summary, day-to-day work activities of corrections personnel and workers' perceptions of offenders are influenced to the extent that societal conceptions structure the situation by providing indicators of the kinds of criminals with whom workers must interact and of the ways in which such types should be handled. Thus, societal conceptions affect worker autonomy by influencing expectations of appropriate work role behavior. Societal conceptions also influence workers' perceptions and typing of offenders. But such typing, in turn, allows workers to order the work scene and thereby assists in reducing any additional threats to autonomy that offenders may present.

Organizational/Occupational Goals and Constraints: Maintenance of Order and Control

Occupational role autonomy can be influenced by conflicting organizational goals, such as custodial versus treatment orientations, and by organizational and occupational constraints and concerns. Foremost is the need to process relatively large numbers of offenders and to maintain order and control. A disproportionate emphasis on security, combined with a rapid turnover of inmates, for example, can dramatically influence the work roles of treatment personnel (see Mennerick, 1972).

However, in addition to affecting autonomy, organizational and occupational goals, concerns, and constraints also constitute bases underlying the social typing of offenders. More specifically, corrections personnel frequently confront a work scene that stresses the need to maintain order and control. They confront a work scene in which worker-offender interaction is commonly characterized by conflict, uncertainty, and unpredictability. The emphasis on maintenance of order and control is multifaceted. For some corrections workers, such as guards in a maximum security prison, order and control refer in part to internal order, as in preventing fights or other disturbances that might threaten the safety of both inmates and prison personnel and disrupt prison routine. Likewise, order and control refer to the prevention of escapes that might threaten public safety and impune the integrity of the institution.

Yet, for all corrections personnel, whether their duties be broadly categorized as custodial or treatment, control also refers to the need to successfully manage interactions with clients on the day-to-day work scene. Offenders possess the potential to pose an immediate and direct threat to worker autonomy. Through recalcitrance and subterfuge, offenders can dramatically influence the workers' ability to carry out their tasks according to the workers' definition of the occupational role. Social typing, then, is one means of providing a structure that lessens uncertainty in the worker-client relationship. Typing permits workers to "know" the kinds of offenders with whom they are dealing. It allows workers to identify "good" clients, who facilitate their work activities, and "bad" clients, who threaten worker autonomy. Thus, social typing reflects organizational and occupational concerns, and at the same time contributes to the workers' control of the situation and ultimately to worker autonomy. Because such typing and re-typing occurs throughout the correctional system from entry to exit, it is useful to examine typing during each of three major stages in the correctional process.

Stage 1: Typing upon entry into the corrections system. Following arrest, legal *and* social definitions often determine where and with whom the offender will be housed. *Jail personnel* frequently confront a very heterogeneous clientele whose length of stay in the jail is uncertain. To bring greater structure to their work, such personnel often classify offenders into various types, depending upon the ways in which different "kinds" of offenders can be expected to affect the workers' activities. For example, they may distinguish between "unsentenced inmates," who are perceived as potential troublemakers, and "sentenced inmates," who are seen as much more settled and trustworthy (Mennerick, 1971). Similarly, social typing of offenders allows *probation officers* to more readily categorize clients, and thereby aids both in dealing with the organizationally induced problem of processing large numbers of presentence reports (see Blumberg, 1974: 157-167) and in attempting to predict the supervisability of potential probationers (see Irwin,

1970: 42-43). Finally, such conceptions also come into play among *prison personnel* during the initial classification process at reception-guidance centers (see Irwin, 1970: 40-43). Familiarity with typifications lessens the time required by *correctional caseworkers* to interview particular offenders and to write reports (Shover, 1974: 353) and assists *correctional officers* in "sizing-up" inmates for housing and work placement (see Heffernan, 1972: 49; Powelson and Bendix, 1951: 76).

Stage 2: Typing during incarceration. Throughout their period of confinement, inmates continue to be subject to classification and social typing by prison personnel. *Prison administrators* are sensitive to the need for an orderly functioning institution, and social typing plays an important role in helping administrators identify and deal with those prisoners who might cause "trouble" (see Irwin, 1977: 30). Typing also occurs in prison adjustment-center *classification committee* decision making. As Doran (1977: 44-63) points out, once the inmate has been typed, the committee is in a better position to determine how he should be handled. Finally, social typing constitutes one means utilized by *prison guards* in their attempt to maintain control (see Guenther and Guenther, (1974: 44-50). Guards frequently distinguish between "good" and "bad" inmates, not on the basis of the inmate's past criminal activities, but rather on the inmate's willingness to "conform to authority" (Jacobs and Retsky, 1975: 26-27; see also Heffernan, 1972: 63, 161; Giallombardo, 1966: 81).

Stage 3: Typing related to release from prison. Social typing also occurs among corrections personnel engaged in parole decision making and parolee supervision. *Parole board* members frequently resort to broad social types, based on a few salient cues or behavioral images, to categorize prospective parolees rather than systematically considering the unique features of each individual case (see President's Commission, 1967: 63). Such typing is implicit when, for example, parole boards employ different standards in evaluating black inmates and white inmates or "militant" and "nonmilitant" inmates (see Carroll and Mondrick, 1976: 104-105). *Parole officers*, in turn, may type parolees—as "dangerous men" or "noncriminals"—largely in terms of the amount of trouble they might cause the officer in his day-to-day work routine (McCleary, 1978: 103-128; also see Irwin, 1970: 130, 189). Thus, as with other corrections personnel, social typing contributes to worker autonomy for both parole boards and parole officers. For parole board members, who often confront heavy caseloads, social typing provides a form of shorthand that allows them to more readily categorize inmates as suitable or unsuitable for parole. Social typing, in turn, alerts parole agents to both "good" parolees and to those from whom they can anticipate problems.

Societal Conceptions and Organizational/Occupational Concerns: Assessments of Moral Character

Typing of offenders extends beyond the general processes of decision making and maintenance of control within the correctional system. Specifically, corrections personnel, like workers in other service occupations, often confront clients who violate the workers' standards of morality, and they categorize such clients accordingly (see Becker, 1952: 461; Jacobs and Retsky, 1975: 24; Mennerick, 1974c: 405-406).

Social typing, based on moral assessments of their clients, occurs among many different occupational roles within the correctional system. *Prison administrators* often view confrontations between individual inmates and violence among prison gangs as reflections of the prisoners' low moral character (see Irwin, 1977: 38). Further, typing by prison personnel sometimes focuses on specific racial/ethnic groups, characterizing them as being violence prone, untrustworthy, and lacking in moral character (see Davidson, 1974: 60-61).

Given the "deviant" sexual activities of some prisoners and the generally demeaning status to which all inmates are relegated, *prison guards* and *correctional officers* also frequently type inmates as morally inept (see Giallombardo, 1966: 82; Heffernan, 1972: 97; Jacobs and Retsky, 1975: 24-26; Weinberg, 1942: 721). Similarly, conceptions of prisoners as abnormal, morally degenerate, or "less honest" are found among *caseworkers, psychiatric* and *educational personnel,* and *parole officers* (see Shover, 1974: 356; Powelson and Bendix, 1951: 82; Mennerick, 1971: 26-31; Irwin, 1970: 182).

Such moral assessments of offenders indicate the repugnance with which many corrections workers view criminal offenders: repugnance that is also shared by many laymen. Thus, to some extent, this typing mirrors societal conceptions of offenders as being morally inadequate.

However, the moral typing of offenders is also based on organizational and occupational concerns. Such typing indirectly assists workers in at least two ways. First, by reducing inmates to a morally inferior status, corrections personnel can routinize the processing of offenders (see Giallombardo, 1966: 82, 90). The key issue is that by morally discrediting the offender, corrections workers need not bother to accord the same considerations as would be accorded the morally correct individual (see Goffman, 1963: 8-9).

Second, this form of typing also establishes and reinforces the workers' own moral credibility. Social typing facilitates work by supporting the workers' self concepts and ultimately by justifying dealing with offenders in ways which many people would otherwise find unconscionable (see Goffman, 1961: 87; Irwin, 1977: 38; Powelson and Bendix, 1951: 85; Shover, 1974: 356).

In the end, moral typing does not merely reflect the workers' value system and their conceptions of appropriate and inappropriate behavior. Rather, such typing also contributes to the workers' control of the situation, which in turn contributes to occupational role autonomy.

CONCLUSION

Correctional system personnel, like workers in other service occupations, confront clients who tend to be variable and unpredictable; clients who frequently pose a threat to worker autonomy. Workers, in turn, commonly employ social typologies of their clients in an attempt to reduce uncertainty and to bring greater structure to the work scene. Social types assist workers in creating a social world in which they "know" the kinds of clients with whom they must deal. Thus, workers go beyond the initial label of "convicted criminal" and type offenders in more specific ways, depending on how different kinds of offenders can be expected to influence their work activities. Having categorized the offender, corrections personnel are then in a better position to utilize various tactics or strategems to deal with those types of inmates who might adversely affect worker autonomy and the routine functioning of the system.

While I have emphasized that social typing is beneficial to workers, it is also important to stress that the typing of clients may be either functional or dysfunctional, depending on several factors, including the level of analysis and the accuracy of the typing. In the correctional system, for example, the typing of inmates may be functional for prison guards, by facilitating their daily work routine, but dysfunctional for the community at large to the extent that it interferes with the rehabilitation of offenders. Similarly, while accurate typing may assist guards, *mistyping* of inmates may actually compound the problems of uncertainty and conflict. Finally, what is functional for those doing the typing may be either functional or dysfunctional for those being typed.

Future research should explore the relative importance of variables intrinsic to the system and variables that can be viewed as external. Thus, in what ways is the typing of offenders influenced by the structure of particular work settings? For example, many questions remain as to the extent to which the social typing of offenders varies due to differing organizational goals (see Street et al., 1966: 159-161). Similarly, do variables such as workers' rank or position and length of time on the job affect their perceptions of clients? Equally important is the question of the influence of external variables which corrections personnel import into the work scene. In their study of attitudes of black and white prison guards, Jacobs and Kraft (1978: 307) found, for example, that the guards tended to be about equally divided in agreement/

disagreement with the statement that "most inmates lack morals." On the other hand, their findings failed to support the hypothesis that "black guards, especially those who are younger and less 'institutionalized,' will feel less social distance from the prisoners and be more likely to accept the prisoners' moral worth and humanity." Additional research, then, should also examine the relevance of external variables such as age, education, race, and social class of corrections personnel.

NOTES

1. In the present work, I use the terms "occupational role autonomy" and "worker autonomy" interchangeably.

2. Correctional system personnel actually serve two sets of clientele: criminal offenders and the public at large. They serve the public to the extent that they contribute to the effective operation of the particular correctional institution or agency and ultimately to the control and rehabilitation of lawbreakers.

Criminal offenders, in turn, are more direct recipients of services provided by corrections workers. Within prisons, examples range from education and counseling programs for inmates to security and surveillance activities intended to reduce violence and the physical threats that inmates may pose toward one another. Whether offenders are receptive to the services (and in effect accept the client role) varies among inmates and also varies over time. (For a description of inmates' changing attitudes toward treatment services, see Irwin, 1980: 56-63.)

Further, criminal offenders (usually) become clients of the correctional system not by choice but through the power of the state. This involuntary status can extend to various inmate activities. For example, even when prison inmates "voluntarily" engage in treatment programs, such participation is often motivated by the concern that lack of participation will damage the prospect for early parole.

The present study focuses on criminal offenders as the primary clientele and on those corrections workers who engage directly in service-oriented activities requiring face-to-face interaction with criminal offenders.

3. One can argue that corrections personnel may employ various mechanisms to enhance autonomy. For example, workers may stress the professionalization of their occupations and the "rights" that accrue to individuals recognized as professionals. Yet, in order for "professional stature" to contribute to occupational role autonomy in the context of worker-client interaction, we must make the very dubious assumption that offenders actually accept the *legitimacy* of corrections workers' occupational roles—much less the legitimacy of such workers as professionals. The mechanism of social typing, in contrast, requires no such assumption.

4. Societal conceptions do change over time. Further, the salience of conceptions of particular "types" of criminals can change relatively quickly. This is due in part to news reporting and to the portrayal of actual and fictional criminals through the mass media. For example, prevalent conceptions in the late 1960s and early 1970s focused on "violent social protesters" and "political radicals." Today, conceptions again focus on more "traditional" criminal types such as "murderers" and "rapists."

Also, societal conceptions usually affect corrections personnel in a relatively indirect fashion: for example, by influencing the structure of work organizations and the definition of work roles. However, the impact can be more immediate, as when societal conceptions influence the *specific* conceptions of offenders that corrections personnel develop and then bring into the work scene.

PART VI

CONCLUSIONS

THIS BOOK, FOLLOWING *Varieties of Work Experience* (Stewart and Cantor, 1974), develops and applies a perspective for examining the social control of occupational groups and roles by investigating four sources of such control on occupations: cultural and societal, organizational, occupational, and client control. The empirical studies included here illustrate how these sources modify or enhance group and role autonomy separately or in combination. Each essay in this book is either an update of a chapter which appeared in our earlier volume or a new essay written especially to be included here. This book differs from the earlier one in several important ways: first, more emphasis is placed on how historic and economic factors enhance or limit autonomy. As an example, we emphasize how the changing patterns of women in the labor force, in both traditional and nontraditional occupations, have made gender an important variable in analyzing power in work. Second, fewer research articles were available on the scientific, professional, and artistic workers, than on craft workers and those classified as nonprofessionals. While the issue of autonomy and control over work has been and still is very important to professions, it has been and continues to be important for most workers in the 1980s.

AUTONOMY, POWER, AND CONTROL

The issue of autonomy for workers may not be the most important problem of the near future. The most important problem may be finding work at all. In other words, employment and unemployment may be more important than any other work-related problem (see Jenkins and Sherman,

269

The Collapse of Work, 1979). However, once workers are employed, having control over their work is salient. A general theme of this book has been that occupations and work are not static but change as material conditions, government policies, and the consciousness of workers change. Literal power and autonomy in the workplace and in the larger society (for an occupational group) depend on a number of interactive forces. The case studies we have presented show how the changing social organization of work affects workers at the role level and as members of occupational groups. As work has changed, so has the issue of autonomy over work. For the greater part of the last century, autonomy has primarily been an issue for those in professional and craft occupations. More recently, since World War II, other kinds of workers, especially those doing routine factory work, have been concerned about autonomy and control over their work as well. Surveys show that most Americans want meaningful work and independent working conditions (Burns et al., 1979; Kanter, 1978b; Yankelovich, 1981; U.S.A. Today, 1981). Young workers expect self-fulfillment and meaning through work and are concerned about their autonomy and control over their own work.

Many researchers and critics believe that such desires of workers cannot be realized under present conditions. For example, Richard Edwards (1979) views control and autonomy in the context of the larger class struggle that is an outgrowth of capitalist development. His analysis is very pessimistic, where he strongly suggests that control rests with those who control the large bureaucratic organizations that have developed under monopoly capital. He explains the changes in work organizations since World War II by contending that these are not the inevitable consequences of modern technology or of industrial society, but have their roots in the basic arrangements of capitalist production. Although we, like O'Toole (1977) and others, have some disagreements with Edwards, we also have several agreements. Like Edwards, we agree that control is always problematic and that power is embodied in people, who have their own interests and needs and who often resist being treated like a commodity (Edwards, 1979: 12).

We also agree that there has been a growth of large, bureaucratic organizations with hierarchical control (pyramidic organization), where work is highly differentiated. In such organizations, many workers are in narrow jobs, requiring little skill or training. Even technical and white collar work is often organized in such a way that workers are left with little discretion over their tasks. Under such conditions, work is routinized, dull, and often meaningless (Braverman, 1974; Kanter, 1977c).

In contrast, some work, while becoming specialized, requires a great deal of knowledge and expertise. The tension between researcher scientists, for example, and the organizations which hire them has been well documented (Stewart, 1968; Loether, 1974; Miller, 1974). The type of organizational structure in which scientists perform their work is an important condition affecting the way in which they react to their work (Miller, 1974: 114). The basic dilemma of autonomy versus integration is negotiated within the interdependence relationship of the professionals and the employing organization. In other words, autonomy remains a variable even in the large organization. As Perrow (1979) has pointed out, organizations also exist within the larger framework and change as societal conditions and values change.

Occupational autonomy at both the group and role levels for most occupations does depend upon the workplace, which for many occupations is the large conglomerate, corporation, or government. Our case studies suggest that organizational control (workplace control) is a most important source limiting occupation autonomy at group and role levels. Autonomy may be limited or enhanced primarily because of how the organizational setting and the occupational group interact. Housewives are an interesting exception. They have role autonomy but not group autonomy. They are not controlled directly at the workplace, but they are also unorganized and therefore powerless at the group level.

Others who also recognize the power of organizations to control workers have suggested that it is necessary to redesign jobs and working arrangements so that the quality of work (Davis and Cherns, 1975) and worker control will be enhanced (O'Toole, 1977; Kanter, 1977b). Although we are sympathetic with such suggestions, we are not providing a blueprint for the future. Rather, we simply show here that work autonomy has changed as more people work in organizations, and that these changes have affected the higher status as well as the lower status occupations.

AUTONOMY AND WORK GROUPS

Most researchers who have been interested in mass production workers and lower status occupational groups have focused on the problems of alienation and job satisfaction. These problems follow from the questions and assumptions which were brought up in the nineteenth century as the Western countries were becoming industrialized. Both Marx and Weber were concerned about the workers' lack of control over their product in industrial and bureaucratic settings. Modern studies show that lack of control leads to dissatisfaction, alienation, and according to some, even low productivity (see O'Toole, 1977; Trist, 1981; Peterson, 1981). In contemporary American society, some unions, citizen groups, and social scientists are concerned with changing societal conditions in order to remove barriers of authority and compliance so that individuals and work groups will have the right to be more involved in their work.

The study of work groups and worker control over the work process has two major antecedents: One is the human relations school of industrial relations, and the second is from the more radical perspective of socialism and syndicalism in Europe (Vanek, 1974). Both traditions hold that workers who control their work are likely to be more productive, happier, and less alienated workers. The literature, however, is vast and not without contradictions. In reviewing the literature briefly on the subject, Ivar Berg (1979), from a human relations perspective, says that workers are demonstrably more satisfied when they enjoy some "codeterminative" rights in establishing the conditions under which they work.

Eric Trist (1981) goes further and says that western industrial structures are weak in the middle, and that only if work is reorganized in a way that workers will have more control can production increase and workers be satisfied. According to Trist, no worker in any organization can be completely autonomous. Workers can be only conditionally or semi-autonomous. There are, nevertheless, several dimensions and degrees of worker autonomy. Susman (1976) identifies three classes of decisions which relate to autonomy at work: those concerning task independence (close to our definition of role autonomy); those concerning self-governance; and those concerning self-regulations of members of the work group. The last two are close to our definition of group autonomy.

Trist (1981) believes that autonomous groups, rather than individuals doing differentiated tasks as in most factories, tend to absorb certain maintenance and control functions in the workplace. They become able to set their own machines, and are able to solve problems on day-to-day issues. Because they are also learning systems, more of their members acquire more of the relevant skills. Under these conditions, workers become multiskilled and can interchange jobs. In his review, Trist also notes that autonomous groups do not always succeed. However, he contends that the most common reason for failure is lack of support in the surrounding organization. Nonetheless, his optimism for worker autonomy suggests that the work arrangements which disturb so many sociologists of varying theoretical persuasions are not the only ones possible in a capitalist system (see also Peterson, 1981, for a discussion of innovation in organizational structures). For workers, autonomous work groups provide a map of the total process and a sense of control over the work itself. Although he cites several examples of major, multinational companies adopting a system similar to the one he proposes, there is little evidence that such autonomy for many workers is possible in the near future. Yet his concern with this issue and the concern of so many others, including several major unions, suggest to us that worker autonomy and control is an important issue for the 1980s. Many major American companies, e.g., Hewlett-Packard, American Airlines, and General Electric, are experimenting with the "quality circle concept," also called Participation Action Circles and Quality Work Life Groups. This concept includes the development of a small team or program in which decision making is shared among the workers doing the work. It is a process by which an organization attempts to release the creative abilities of its workers by involving them in decisions affecting their work lives. Not all companies are ready to innovate following these models, but they are watching carefully the results from these programs.

AUTONOMY AND PROFESSIONAL AND TECHNICAL WORKERS

Although there are a number of definitions of what constitutes a profession (see Stewart and Cantor, 1974), all definitions include the notion of autonomy, both at the group and task level. The more professionalized an occupation, the more likely the people practicing that occupation will have task or role autonomy. Such workers will be freer from organizational directives and from client control than others who are less professionalized. The more professionalized occupations are also more likely to govern themselves as a group, rather than being governed by management or by bureaucratic rulings. The occupation ideally decides who is qualified to practice, what appropriate fees or salaries should be, and which institutions are best able to train or socialize new members. Some occupations have a monopoly over the skills associated with the work. Along with setting the rules of membership, skills, and recruitment and training, a profession polices and regulates its members.

From the nineteenth century on, arguments have developed for increasing occupational professionalism. The rationale can be summarized as follows: as the division of labor increases, occupations become specialized and require a specific knowledge base. Due to the expansion of knowledge and the growth of technology, workers need more skill rather than less. This condition has led certain occupational groups to work for improved status within the labor force by trying to become professionalized. Whereas the mass production worker used the union as the type of organization to improve worker status and control, those occupations seeking professional status organized differently. The professional association, which limits membership by setting entry and socialization standards, has an opposite philosophy from the trade union. The union's chief strength lies in its power to shut down the factory or shop by organizing all workers to participate. The guild or professional association has strength only when membership is limited to those the occupational group defines as desirable and competent, and when employers and clients only recognize such members as qualified to perform the tasks associated with the work.

Rather than the labor force becoming more professionalized, the opposite seems to be true. This "deprofessionalization of almost everyone" is evident from two obvious structural changes in the nature of work and occupations. The first is that the distinction between unions and guilds is no longer viable. Many unions have become closer to guilds, especially craft unions, and many guilds and professional associations encourage their members to strike, to bargain collectively, and to organize in a manner which is similar to union practices. Unions and professional associations are converging in their methods of operation. Many of the large unions (not all) are working for more autonomy for their members, while almost all of the so-called professional associations are now essentially unions (the American Medical Association and The American Bar Association are, of course, exceptions.)

The second structural change is that more and more workers classified as technical and professional are working in large bureaucracies. This trend has been documented elsewhere (Larson, 1977). Most professionals, including those who are primarily client-oriented (doctors, nurses, and teachers) and those who are science and technology-oriented (research scientists, engineers, and computer specialists), are not always in control of resources, nor do they participate freely in central decision making when they work in large organizations. The research on professionals in bureaucracies is far too vast and complex to be reviewed here. However, one generalization can be made: The potential for conflicts exists, even though most professionals adapt to the organizational constraints.

For small numbers of the population, the self-employed professionals, the nature of their work is less defined by the battle for autonomy in the workplace. Many of these professionals (physicians, lawyers, and dentists, in particular) won the battle for autonomy several generations ago when they gained a monopoly from the state. This battle is well documented (see Gilb, 1966) and shows how difficult it is for an occupational group to control its own work and the members of its profession. (The case of lawyers and advertising is a case in point.) Some members of the occupation become dissident with too much occupational control from the guild, and more important, other occupations try to encroach on the hard-won monopoly. Therefore, the free professionals have to be continuously vigilant and politically active to maintain power.

TECHNOLOGY AND WORKER AUTONOMY

In *Varieties of Work Experience,* we looked at the ways in which the adoption of new technologies might change the nature of several categories of occupations: in particular, physicians and professional elites working in the communication industries. We noted that in a high technology, post-industrial society, the future of work is uncertain. Many questions were left unanswered. Six years is not enough time to answer the questions we raised then. In considering the professional autonomy of physicians, we noted that the process of establishing subspecialities as means of control within medicine is likely to be followed by other occupations. The traditional professions are often models for other occupations to follow. Physicians have more to lose than others with less autonomy. While reduction of role autonomy may be slow to change, the combination of several conditions may result in physicians sharing autonomy with other roles with the result that new spheres of control may be defined:

(1) *Increased technological development* and knowledge may result in decreased physician knowledge necessary to order and interpret test procedures and results.

(2) *Increased development of technical specialists* within the occupation of medicine may lead to further fragmentation of the field, with consequent struggles for domain.

(3) *Increase in the growth of large-scale organizations* providing medical service may result in conflicts and reduced autonomy for physicians at the *role* level.

(4) *Increase in the growth of skill capabilities of paraprofessionals,* such as physicians' extenders, nurse practitioners who are capable of functioning in many settings, at lower fees, may encroach on some physician domains. This will be more crucial if a so-called "glut" of physicians occurs in the late 1980s.

(5) *Increase in medical knowledge made available to the public* through mass media forms may result in a public wanting to participate more fully in determining treatment regimes. Patients may want to have more control over what happens to them and compliance relationships may change.

These are just a few of the factors that might be combined into a process model to examine how power and control in medicine, like many other occupations, is changing. While acknowledging that the structure of medicine is complex, the use of a process model (rather than a static model) provides a way to learn (1) the power of various medical occupations in providing services; (2) the role of the organizations vis-à-vis the practitioners, and (3) how much influence or power the patient may have over his/her treatment as newer technologies are adopted.

It is in the communications industries that the adoption of technology may be causing a revolution. The most important questions of the 1980s will not be how audiences might be affected by television content (e.g., sex and violence, alcohol and drug use, sexism, and so forth) but rather how the distribution of information and entertainment to home audiences will be affected by advances in transmission. Since the 1930s, when radio became a mass medium, social scientists, policy-makers, and citizens have been concerned over the limited range of programs offered. The newer concern will be over the future structure and public accountability of an even greater communications industry to be made possible by cable and satellites (Business Week, 1981). Will the now-few program suppliers and distributors continue their control? Will that power shift to a few industrial conglomerates? Or will creators become more powerful? The power and control of writers, actors, and other creators who must work for organizations in order to work is now limited (Cantor, 1980). Because there will be more audience choice, professionals may become freer and more autonomous, but control could still rest with the few large production companies, thus limiting the freedom of the creators to act independently. These are empirical questions at this time.

In conclusion, there are some generalizations that can be made. The United States has become an advanced industrial society (some say post-industrial). This economy is characterized by a number of features, including the adoption of new technologies in all areas of work. A large and growing proportion of adult women are employed outside the home; most paid workers are employed in either service occupations (usually professional, technical, and clerical) or in manufacturing occupations (although the number of manufacturing jobs is declining, partly from the adoption of automation); work in agriculture has declined steadily since the early 1900s as farms became mechanized; since 1970 there is a growing reserve of unemployed and part-time workers; and a few hundred corporations (conglomerates and multinationals) with extensive market power control the employment of hundreds of thousands of employees.

The work that people do changes with social and economic climates. In an advanced industrial-technological society, work in certain sectors of the economy has expanded (white collar work, especially work in knowledge, information, and entertainment industries) and contracted in others (farming, blue collar work, especially in automobile, clothing, and equipment manufacturing). Also, this changing economy has resulted in larger work organizations and corporations which control the work process, define tasks, and generally limit the power of most workers. Only those who monopolize skills in demand (medicine and engineering, for example) have some autonomy and control over the work process.

Entering the 1980s, the indications are that the trends of the past several decades will continue. More workers will want jobs than will be available. As the use of the computer and automation become more widespread, even more workers will be employed in service rather than manufacturing jobs. A higher technology society will be seen by some as liberating and by others as a means for greater exploitation.

Almost everyone agrees that social and economic conditions will continue to change at a rapid rate, and optimists such as Alvin Toffler (1980) and Daniel Yankelovich (1981) believe work will continue to be important to people, with self-fulfillment and self-improvement also keys to success. More will be free to choose their work, to retire early, or to work intermittently, and to participate in decision making on the job. Toffler (1980) also believes that computer technology will enable over 20 percent of the people to work in their homes, as a new cottage industry develops to free people from routine, daily tasks.

The more pessimistic predict a different future. They also believe a higher technology economy will result in drastic changes, but not in a society where individual self-fulfillment will be the norm. According to the pessimists, e.g., Edwards (1979) and Braverman (1974), the population will be further divided between those employed in creative, autonomous jobs and those relegated to powerless positions in monotonous, routine, low-level jobs that barely provide a living wage.

POSTSCRIPT

Our purpose has not been to predict the future but to present the sociology of work from the occupational perspective, rather than from a class or management perspective. Our discussions have been limited to autonomy, power, and control. We believe now as we believed earlier that autonomy from the worker's perspective is important politically and ideologically, especially in the United States, where there are so many conflicts at the occupational level rather than the class level. The case of PATCO, the air controllers' union, is only one of many recent conflicts that was confined to an occupational group and those who employed them, the U.S. government. Actors, baseball players, school teachers, and nurses have all had strikes in the last two years.

We have not covered the complexities, contradictions, and difficulties inherent in analyzing the division of labor in an advanced, high technology society. In presenting the empirical studies and some theoretical interpretation, we know that some people will disagree with our selections and approach. Sometimes we disagree with each other and our authors. However, we do agree on several important concerns.

(1) Occupations are an important area for study, one that is often neglected in the study of work. Furthermore, occupations are important by themselves, and a theory of occupations can be developed.

(2) Power and control over work and the work process is one of the key concerns for workers and employers alike.

(3) Our approach allows students and unfunded scholars ideas for doing research on meaningful topics in the future.

We see this book not as a completed work but rather as a work in process. Both of us hope that in five years we will be able to bring together another volume to continue our explorations and present the research of others. If we are unable to do so, we hope others will take up the topics and bring together more occupational studies. Possibly other volumes should not focus only on autonomy but on broader issues concerning employment and the meaning of work and occupations. We hope the ideas in this book will stimulate others to continue this effort.

REFERENCES AND SELECTED BIBLIOGRAPHY

Abel, Bruce
    1963   "The firms: what do they want?" Harvard Law Record 37 (December 12): 1ff.
Akers, Ronald L.
    1968   "The professional association and the legal regulation of practice." Law and Society Review 2 (May): 463-482.
Aldrich, Howard E.
    1979   Organizations and Environments. Englewood Cliffs, NJ: Prentice-Hall.
Alper, Benedict S.
    1974   Prisons Inside-Out: Alternatives in Correctional Reform. Cambridge, MA: Ballinger.
American Nurses Association
    1941   Facts About Nursing. New York: American Nurses Association.
    1967   Facts About Nursing. New York: American Nurses Association.
    1972   Facts About Nursing. New York: American Nurses Association.
Andelin, Helen
    1980   Fascinating Womanhood. New York: Bantam Books.
Anderson, Bernard E.
    1979   "Minorities and work: the challenge for the next decade." Pp. 92-110 in Clark Kerr and Jerome M. Roscow (eds.) Work in America. New York: D. Van Nostrand.
Anderson, Jack
    1971   "Pension benefits for housework." Washington Post (November 7): B07.
Anderson, Nels
    1964   Dimensions of Work: The Sociology of a Work Culture. New York: David McKay.
André, Rae
    1981   Homemakers: The Forgotten Workers. Chicago: University of Chicago Press.
Arditi, Ralph R., Frederick Goldberg, Jr., M. Martha Hartle, John H. Peters, and William R. Phelps
    1973   "The sexual segregation of American prisons." Yale Law Review 82 (May): 1229-1273.
Arnowitz, Stanley
    1973   False Promises. New York: McGraw-Hill.
Ashworth, Kenneth H.
    1979   American Higher Education in Decline. College Station: Texas A & M University Press.

Backes, Clarus
1969   "The cabbies: a front seat view." Chicago Tribune, Sunday Magazine, (February 23): 21-28.
Banton, Michael P.
1964   The Policeman in the Community. New York: Basic Books.
Baran, Paul A. and Paul M. Sweezy
1966   Monopoly Capital: An Essay on the American Economic and Social Order. New York: Monthly Review Press.
Barnes, Craig
1980   "Denver: a case study." Pp. 125-137 in B. Bullough (ed.) The Law and the Expanding Nursing Role. New York: Appleton-Century-Crofts.
Becker, Howard S.
1951   "The professional dance musician and his audience." American Journal of Sociology 57 (September): 136-144.
1952   "Social class variations in the teacher-pupil relationship." Journal of Educational Sociology 25 (April): 451-465.
1963   Outsiders: Studies in the Sociology of Deviance. New York: The Free Press.
Becker, Howard S. and James Carper
1956   "The elements of identification with an occupation." American Sociological Review 21 (June): 341-348.
Becker, Howard S. and Anselm L. Strauss
1956   "Careers, personality, and adult socialization." American Journal of Sociology 62 (November): 253-263.
Becker, Howard S., Blanche Geer, Everett C. Hughes, and Anselm L. Strauss
1961   Boys in White: Student Culture in Medical School. Chicago: University of Chicago Press.
Bell, Daniel
1973   The Coming of Post-Industrial Society: A Venture in Social Forecasting. New York: Basic Books.
Bell, Raymond, Elizabeth Conrad, Thomas Laffey, J. Gary Lutz, Paul VanReed Miller, Christine Simon, Anne E. Stakelon, and Nancy Jean Wilson
1979   Correctional Education Programs for Inmates. Washington, DC: U.S. Government Printing Office.
Ben-David, Joseph
1976   "Science as a profession and scientific professionalism." Pp. 874-888 in Jan. J. Loubser et al. (eds.) Explorations in General Theory in the Social Sciences. Vol. 2. New York: The Free Press.
Bensman, Joseph and Robert Lilienfeld
1973   Craft and Consciousness: Occupational Technique and the Development of World Images. New York: John Wiley.
Benson, J. Kenneth
1977   "Organizations: a dialectical view." Administrative Science Quarterly 22: 1-21.
Berg, Ivar E.
1970   Education and Jobs: The Great Training Robbery. New York: Praeger.
1979   Industrial Society. Englewood Cliffs, NJ: Prentice-Hall.
Bergmann, Barbara
1981   "The economic risks of being a housewife." American Economics Association Papers and Proceedings 71 (May): 81-86.

Bernard, Jessie
   1942   American Family Behavior. New York: Harper & Row.
   1971a   "Changing lifestyles: one role, two roles, shared roles." Issues in Industrial Society 2 (January): 21-28.
   1971b   Women and the Public Interest: An Essay on Policy and Protest. Chicago: Aldine-Atherton.
   1972   The Future of Marriage. New York: World.
   1974   The Future of Motherhood. New York: Dial.
   1978   "Models for the relationship between the world of women and the world of men." Pp. 219-338 in L. Kriesberg (ed.) Research in Social Movements, Conflict, and Change: An Annual Compilation of Research. Vol. 1. Greenwich, CT: JAI Press.
   1981a   The Female World. New York: The Free Press.
   1981b   "The good provider role: its rise and fall." American Psychologist 36 (January): 1-12.
   1981c   "The female world and technology in 2020." National Forum (Summer): 8-10.
Bernstein, Paul
   1980   Workplace Democratization. New Brunswick, NJ: Transaction Books.
Bishop, Jerry E.
   1980   "The personal and business costs of 'job burn out.' " Wall Street Journal (November 11): 31, 36.
Bittner, Egon
   1967   "The police on Skid Row: a study in peacekeeping." American Sociological Review 32 (October): 699-715.
   1970   The Functions of the Police in Modern Society. Chevy Chase, MD: National Institute of Mental Health.
Black, Donald
   1980   The Manners and Customs of the Police. New York: Academic Press.
Blau, Peter
   1960   "Orientation toward clients in a public welfare agency." Administrative Science Quarterly 5 (December): 341-361.
   1973   The Organization of Academic Work. New York: John Wiley.
Blauner, Robert
   1964   Alienation and Freedom: The Factory Worker and His Industry. Chicago: University of Chicago Press.
Bloch, Peter B., Deborah Anderson, and Pam Gervais
   1973a   D.C. Policewomen Evaluation. Vol. III. Instruments. Washington, DC: Urban Institute.
   1973b   Policewomen on Patrol: Major Findings: First Report. Washington, DC: Urban Institute.
Bloch, Peter B. and Deborah Anderson
   1974a   Policewomen on Patrol: Final Report: Methodology, Tables, and Measurement Instruments. Washington, DC: Urban Institute.
   1974b   Policewomen on Patrol: Final Report. Washington, DC: Urban Institute.
Blumberg, Abraham S.
   1974   Criminal Justice. New York: Franklin Watts.
Blundell, William E.
   1981   "The days of a cowboy are marked by danger, drudgery, and low pay." Wall Street Journal (June 10): 1, 20.

Bohen, Halcyone H. and Annamaria Viveros-Long
  1981   Balancing Jobs and Family Life: Do Flexible Work Schedules Help? Phila-
          delphia: Temple University Press.
Bottomore, T. B.
  1963   Karl Marx: Early Writing. New York: McGraw-Hill.
Bowles, Samuel and Herbert Gintis
  1976   Schooling in Capitalist America: Educational Reform and the Contradictions
          of Economic Life. New York: Basic Books.
Braude, Lee
  1975   Work and Workers: A Sociological Analysis. New York: Praeger.
Braverman, Harry
  1974   Labor and Monopoly Capital: The Degradation of Work in the Twentieth
          Century. New York: Monthly Review Press.
Brown, D. J. and J. H. Atkinson
  1981   "Cash and share renting: an empirical test of the link between entrepre-
          neurial ability and contractual choice." Bell Journal of Economics 12
          (Spring): 296-299.
Brown, Esther Lucile
  1948   Nursing for the Future. New York: Russell Sage Foundation.
Brown, George W. and Tirril Harris
  1978   Social Origins of Depression: A Study of Psychiatric Disorder in Women.
          New York: The Free Press.
Brubacher, John S. and Willis Rudy
  1976   Higher Education in Transition: A History of American Colleges and Univer-
          sities, 1636-1976. 3rd Edition. New York: Harper & Row.
Bryant, Clifton D., John P. King, and Kenneth B. Perkins
  1980   Work and Career in Poultry Processing: A Pilot Study of Morale and
          Disaffection in a Rural Industry. Blacksburg: Virginia Polytechnic Institute
          and State University.
Bucher, Rue and Anselm Strauss
  1961   "Professions in process." American Journal of Sociology 66 (January):
          325-334.
Building Trades Employers' Association of the City of New York
  1973   Handbook. New York: Building Trades Employers' Association.
Bulkeley, William M.
  1981   "The attractions of starting a new venture prove irresistible to some entre-
          preneurs." Wall Street Journal (June 9): 56.
Bullough, Bonnie
  1971   "The new militancy in nursing: collective bargaining activities by nurses in
          perspective." Nursing Forum 10(3): 273-288.
  1978   "The struggle for women's rights in Denver: a personal account." Nursing
          Outlook 26 (September): 566-567.
  1980   The Law and the Expanding Nursing Role. New York: Appleton-Century-
          Crofts.
Bullough, Vern and Bonnie Bullough
  1978   The Care of the Sick: The Emergence of Modern Nursing. New York: Neale
          Watson.
Bunzel, John H.
  1974   "Collective bargaining in higher education." Pp. 157-178 in Sidney Hook,
          Paul Kurtz, and Miro Todorovich (eds.) The Idea of a Modern University.
          Buffalo, NY: Prometheus Books.

Burns, Tom R., Lars Erik Karlsson, and Veljko Rus
1979   Work and Power: The Liberation of Work and the Control of Political Power. Beverly Hills, CA: Sage.
Business Week
1980a   "Deregulation weakens the Teamsters' clout." July 28: 80-81.
1980b   "A steep downgrade for truckers." August 11: 28.
1981   "Window on the world: the home information revolution." June 29: 74-83.
Butler, Suellen and James K. Skipper, Jr.
1981   "Working for tips: an examination of trust and reciprocity in a secondary relationship of the restaurant organization." Sociological Quarterly 22 (Winter): 15-27.
Cantor, Muriel G.
1980   Prime-Time Television: Content and Control. Beverly Hills, CA: Sage.
Caplow, Theodore
1964   The Sociology of Work. New York: McGraw-Hill.
Carnoy, Martin and Derek Shearer
1980   Economic Democracy. White Plains, NY: M. E. Sharpe.
Carr-Saunders, Alexander M.
1928   Professions: Their Organization and Place in Society. Oxford, Eng.: Clarenden Press.
Carr-Saunders, Alexander M. and P. A. Wilson
1933   The Professions. Oxford, Eng.: Clarenden Press.
Carroll, Leo and Margaret E. Mondrick
1976   "Racial bias in the decision to grant parole." Law and Society Review 11 (Fall): 93-107.
Cherniss, Cary
1980   Staff Burnout: Job Stress in the Human Services. Beverly Hills, CA: Sage.
Cherry, Mike
1974   On High Steel: The Education of an Ironworker. New York: Ballantine Books.
Chinoy, Ely
1955   Automobile Workers and the American Dream. Garden City, NY: Doubleday.
Christiansen, Hal
1977   "The 'long night' of a Nashville cab driver." Nashville Magazine (May): 35-36, 44.
Clark, Burton R. and Ted I.K. Youn
1976   Academic Power in the United States: Comparative Historic and Structural Perspectives. Washington, DC: American Association for Higher Education.
Cohen, Michael D., James G. March, and Johan P. Olsen
1972   "A garbage can model of organizational choice." Administrative Science Quarterly 17 (March): 1-25.
Cole, Jonathan R.
1971   "American men and women of science." Presented at the annual meetings of the American Sociological Association, Denver, Colorado (September 1).
Coleman, Milton
1978   " 'Imbalance' seen among D.C. police blacks, women." Washington Post (July 11): B1.
Collins, Randall
1979   The Credential Society: An Historical Sociology of Education and Stratification. New York: Academic Press.

Conte, Michael and Arnold S. Tannenbaum
  1978   "Employee-owned companies: is the difference measurable?" Monthly Labor Review 101 (July): 23-28.
Conway, J. T.
  1965   "Poverty and public health—new outlooks, part 4. The beneficiary, the consumer—what he needs and wants." American Journal of Public Health 55 (November): 1757-1786.
Cressey, Donald R.
  1965   "Prison organizations." Pp. 1023-1070 in James G. March (ed.) Handbook of Organizations. Chicago: Rand McNally.
Dahrendorf, Ralf
  1959   Class and Class Conflict in Industrial Society. Stanford, CA: Stanford University Press.
Davidson, R. Theodore
  1974   Chicano Prisoners: The Key to San Quentin. New York: Holt, Rinehart & Winston.
Davis, Alan J.
  1980   "Sexual assaults in the Philadelphia prison system." Pp. 102-113 in David M. Peterson and Charles W. Thomas (eds.) Corrections: Problems and Prospects. Englewood Cliffs, NJ: Prentice-Hall.
Davis, Fred
  1959   "The cabdriver and his fare: facets of a fleeting relationship." American Journal of Sociology 65: 158-165.
Davis, Kingsley and Wilbert Moore
  1945   "Some principles of stratification." American Sociological Review 10 (April): 242-249.
Davis, Louis E. and Albert B. Cherns (eds.)
  1975   The Quality of Working Life. Volume One: Problems, Prospects, and the State of the Art. New York: The Free Press.
  1975   The Quality of Working Life. Volume Two: Cases and Commentary. New York: The Free Press.
Davis, Stanley M. and Paul R. Lawrence
  1977   Matrix. Reading, MA: Addison-Wesley.
Doeringer, Peter B. and Michael J. Piore
  1971   Internal Labor: Markets and Manpower Analysis. Lexington, MA: D. C. Heath.
Doran, Robert E.
  1977   "Organizational stereotyping: the case of the adjustment center classification committee." Pp. 41-68 in David F. Greenberg (ed.) Corrections and Punishment. Beverly Hills, CA: Sage.
Dubin, Robert, R. Alan Hedley, and Thomas C. Taveggia
  1976   "Attachment to work." Pp. 281-341 in R. Dubin (ed.) Handbook of Work, Organization and Society. Chicago: Rand McNally.
Durkheim, Emile
  1947   The Division of Labor in Society. Glencoe, IL: Free Press
  1957   Professional Ethics and Civic Morals. London: Routledge and Kegan Paul.
  1964   The Division of Labor in Society. New York: The Free Press.
Edelwich, Jerry and Archie Brodsky
  1980   Burn-out: Stages of Disillusionment in the Helping Professions. New York: Human Sciences Press.

Edwards, Alba M.
 1943   Comparative Occupational Statistics for the United States, 1870-1940. Washington, DC: U.S. Government Printing Office.
Edwards, Richard C.
 1975   "The social relations of production in the firm and labor market structure." Pp. 3-26 in Richard C. Edwards et al. (eds.) Labor Market Segmentation. Lexington, MA: D. C. Heath.
 1979   Contested Terrain: The Transformation of the Workplace in the Twentieth Century. New York: Basic Books.
Elbaum, Bernard and Frank Wilkinson
 1979   "Industrial relations and uneven development: a comparative study of the American and British steel industries." Cambridge Journal of Economics 3 (September): 275-303.
Elifson, Kirk W.
 1968   "Job satisfaction of taxicab drivers." Master's Thesis, Vanderbilt University.
Epstein, Cynthia Fuchs
 1968   "Women and professional careers: the case of the woman lawyer." Ph.D. dissertation, Columbia University.
 1970a   "Encountering the male establishment: sex limits on women's careers in the professions." American Journal of Sociology 75 (May): 965-982.
 1970b   Woman's Place: Options and Limits in Professional Careers. Berkeley: University of California Press.
Fanning, D. M.
 1967   "Families in flats." British Medical Journal 4 (November): 382-386.
Feigelman, William
 1974   "Peeping: the pattern of voyeurism among construction workers." Urban Life and Culture 3 (April): 35-49.
Feld, Sheila
 1963   "Feelings of adjustment." Pp. 331-352 in Lois N. Wladis Hoffman and F. Ivan Nye (eds.) The Employed Mother in America. Chicago: Rand McNally.
Fern, Fanny
 1870   Ginger Snaps.
Flynn, Edith Elisabeth
 1973   "Jails and criminal justice." Pp. 49-85 in Lloyd E. Ohlin (ed.) Prisoners in America. Englewood Cliffs, NJ: Prentice-Hall.
Foner, Philip S.
 1977   The Factory Girls: A Collection of Writings on Life and Struggles in the New England Factories of the 1840's. Urbana: University of Illinois Press.
Form, William H. and Joan A. Huber
 1976   "Occupational power." Pp. 751-806 in Robert Dubin (ed.) Handbook of Work, Organization and Society. Chicago: Rand McNally.
Freedman, Marcia
 1976   Labor Markets: Segments and Shelters. Montclair: Allanheld, Osmun.
Freeman, Christopher
 1974   The Economics of Industrial Innovation. Baltimore: Penguin Books.
Freidson, Eliot
 1970a   Profession of Medicine: A Study of the Sociology of Applied Knowledge. New York: Dodd, Mead.
 1970b   Professional Dominance: The Social Structure of Medical Care. New York: Atherton Press.

Garino, David P.
  1981   "Jerry Wilson, cab magnate, keeps driving." Wall Street Journal (January 14): 29.
George, Paul S. and Gary Krist
  1980   "A unique educational experience: teaching in a correctional institution." Corrections Today 42 (July-August): 58-60.
Gerstl, Joel and Glenn Jacobs (eds.)
  1976   Professions for the People: The Politics of Skill. Cambridge, MA: Schenkman.
Giallombardo, Rose
  1966   Society of Women: A Study of a Women's Prison. New York: John Wiley.
Gilb, Corrine Lathrop
  1966   Hidden Hierarchies: The Professions and Government. New York: Harper & Row.
Gilman, Charlotte P.
  1968   "Economic basis of the woman question." Pp. 331-352 in Aileen S. Kraditor (ed.) Up from the Pedestal. Chicago: Quadrangle.
Ginzberg, Eli
  1980   Employing the Unemployed. New York: Basic Books.
Glazer, Nona
  1981   "The invisible intersection: women's unwaged work outside the household." Unpublished.
Goffman, Erving
  1961   Asylums: Essays on the Social Situation of Mental Patients and Other Inmates. Garden City: Anchor Books.
  1963   Stigma: Notes on the Management of Spoiled Identity. Englewood Cliffs, NJ: Prentice-Hall.
Goldthorpe, John H., David Lockwood, Frank Bechhofer, and Jennifer Platt
  1968   The Affluent Worker: Industrial Attitudes and Behavior. Cambridge, Eng.: Cambridge University Press.
Goode, William J.
  1957   "Community within a community: the professions." American Sociological Review 22 (April): 194-200.
  1960a   "A theory of role strain." American Sociological Review 25 (August): 483-496.
  1960b   "Encroachment, charlatanism, and the emerging professions: psychology, sociology, and medicine." American Sociological Review 25 (December): 902-914.
  1969   "The theoretical limits of professionalization." Pp. 226-314 in Amitai Etzioni (ed.) The Semi-Professions and Their Organization: Teachers, Nurses and Social Workers. New York: The Free Press.
Gouldner, Alvin W.
  1957-   "Cosmopolitans and locals: toward an analysis of latent social roles."
  58   Administrative Science Quarterly 2 (December): 281-306 and 2 (March): 444-480.
Gray, Thomas C.
  1975   "Selecting for a police subculture." Pp. 46-56 in J. H. Skolnick and T. C. Gray (eds.) Police in America. Boston: Little, Brown.
Greenberg, Edward S.
  1980   "Participation in industrial decision-making and work satisfaction: the case of producer cooperatives." Social Sciences Quarterly 60: 551-569.

1981 "Industrial self-management and political attitudes." American Political Science Review 75: 29-42.

Gronseth, Erik
1970 "The dysfunctionality of the husband provider role in industrialized societies." Presented to the Seventh World Congress of Sociology, Varna, Bulgaria.

Gross, Edward
1958 Work and Society. New York: Thomas Y. Crowell.
1968 "Plus ca change . . . ? The sexual structure of occupations over time." Social Problems 16 (Fall): 198-208.

Guenther, Anthony L. and Mary Quinn Guenther
1974 "Screws vs. thugs." Society 11 (July/August): 42-50.

Haas, Jack
1972 "Binging—educational control among high-steel ironworkers." American Behavioral Scientist 16 (September/October): 27-34.
1974 "The stages of the high-steel ironworkers apprentice career." The Sociological Quarterly 15 (Winter): 93-108.
1977 "Learning real feelings—a study of high-steel ironworkers' reactions to fear and danger." Sociology of Work and Occupations 4 (May): 147-170.

Hall, Oswald
1946 "The informal organization of the medical profession." Canadian Journal of Economics and Political Science 22 (February): 30-44.

Hall, Richard H.
1975 Occupations and the Social Structure. Englewood Cliffs, NJ: Prentice-Hall.

Harmon, L. R.
1965 "High school ability patterns: a backward look from the doctorate." Scientific Manpower Report # 66. Washington, DC: National Research Council.

Harris, Richard N.
1973 The Police Academy: An Inside View. New York: John Wiley.

Harris, Roy J., Jr.
1981 "Dave Brown finds joy along the steel girders over the streets of L.A." Wall Street Journal (May 11): 1, 24.

Hart, William
1980 "L.A.'s giant jail is a giant headache." Corrections Magazine 6 (December): 32-37.

Hasenfeld, Yeheskel and Richard A. English
1974 Human Service Organizations: A Book of Readings. Ann Arbor: University of Michigan Press.

Haug, Marie R. and Marvin B. Sussman
1969 "Professional autonomy and the revolt of the client." Social Problems 17 (Fall): 153-161.

Hayden, Dolores
1981 The Grant Domestic Revolution: A History of Feminist Designs for American Homes, Neighborhoods and Cities. Cambridge, MA: MIT Press.

Heffernan, Esther
1972 Making It in Prison: The Square, the Cool, and the Life. New York: Wiley-Interscience.

Henslin, James M.
1967 "The cab driver: an international analysis of an occupational culture." Ph.D. dissertation, Washington University (St. Louis, Missouri).

1974   "The underlife of cabdriving: a study in exploitation and punishment." Pp. 67-79 in Phyllis L. Stewart and Muriel Cantor (eds.) Varieties of Work Experience. 1st Edition. New York: John Wiley.

Hepburn, John R. and Celesta Albonetti
1980   "Role conflict in correctional institutions: an empirical examination of the treatment custody dilemma among correctional staff." Criminology 17 (February): 445-459.

Hinings, C. R., D. J. Hickson, J. M. Pennings, and R. E. Schneck
1974   "Structural conditions of intraorganizational power." Administrative Science Quarterly 19 (March): 22-44.

Hirshey, Gerri
1980   "Uneasy riders—the taxi perplex." New York Magazine 13 (May 5): 22-27.

Hodge, Robert W., Paul M. Siegel, and Peter Rossi
1964   "Occupational prestige in the United States, 1925-1963." American Journal of Sociology 70: 286-302.

Holter, Harriet
1970   Sex Roles and Social Structure. Oslo: Universitetsforlaget.

Homans, George C.
1961   Social Behavior: Its Elementary Forms. New York: Harcourt Brace Jovanovich.

Hughes, Everett C.
1944   "Dilemmas and contradictions of status." American Journal of Sociology 50: 353-359.
1958   Men and Their Work. Glencoe, IL: The Free Press.
1971   The Sociological Eye: Selected Papers. Chicago: Aldine-Atherton.

Hurtwood, Lady Allen of
1968   Planning for Play. Cambridge, MA: MIT Press.

Irwin, John
1970   The Felon. Englewood Cliffs, NJ: Prentice-Hall.
1977   "The changing social structure of the men's prison." Pp. 21-40 in David F. Greenberg (ed.) Corrections and Punishment. Beverly Hills, CA: Sage.
1980   Prisons in Turmoil. Boston: Little, Brown.

Jacobs, James B.
1977   Stateville: The Penitentiary in Mass Society. Chicago: University of Chicago Press.

Jacobs, James B. and Lawrence J. Kraft
1978   "Integrating the keepers: a comparison of black and white prison guards in Illinois." Social Problems 25 (February): 304-318.

Jacobs, James B. and Harold G. Retsky
1975   "Prison Guard." Urban Life: A Journal of Ethnographic Research 4 (April): 5-29.

Jaffe, Abram J. and Charles D. Stewart
1951   Manpower Resources and Utilization: Principles of Working Force Analysis. New York: John Wiley.

Jamous, H. and B. Peloille
1970   "Changes in the French university hospital system." Pp. 111-152 in J. A. Jackson (ed.) Professions and Professionalisation. Cambridge, Eng.: Cambridge University Press.

Jaroslav, Vanek
1975   Self-Management: Economic Liberation of Man. Middlesex, Eng.: Penguin.
Jenkins, C. and B. Sherman
1979   The Collapse of Work. London: Eyre Methuen.
John Howard Association
1973   Survey Report: Cook County Jail. Chicago: John Howard Association.
Johnson, Terence J.
1972   Professions and Power. London: Macmillan.
Jones, Larry and Franz A. Nowotny (eds.)
1979   New Directions for Higher Education: Preparing for the New Decade. San Francisco: Jossey-Bass.
Kahn, Robert L.
1967   "The meaning of work," in The Worker in the New Industrial Environment. Ann Arbor, MI: Foundation for Research on Human Behavior.
Kalleberg, Arne L.
1977   "Work values and job rewards: a theory of job satisfaction." American Sociological Review 42: 124-143.
Kalleberg, Arne L. and Larry J. Griffen
1978   "Positional sources of inequality in job satisfaction." Sociology of Work and Occupations 5: 371-401.
Kanter, Rosabeth Moss
1972   Commitment and Community: Communes and Utopias in Sociological Perspective. Cambridge, MA: Harvard University Press.
1977a   "Some effects of proportions on group life: skewed sex ratios and responses to token women." American Journal of Sociology 82 (March): 965-990.
1977b   Men and Women of the Corporation. New York: Basic Books.
1977c   Work and Family in the United States: A Critical Review and Agenda for Research and Policy. New York: Russell Sage Foundation.
1978a   "Powerlessness." The New York Times (April 6): A21.
1978b   "Work in a new America." Daedalus 107 (Winter): 47-78.
1979   "Power failure in management circuits." Harvard Business Review 57 (July-August): 65-75.
Kanter, Rosabeth Moss and Marilyn Halter
1973   "The de-housewifing of women: equality between the sexes in urban communes." Presented at the annual meetings of the American Psychological Association.
Kantrow, Alan M.
1980   "The strategy-technology connection." Harvard Business Review 58 (July-August): 6-20.
Katz, F. E.
1968   Autonomy and Organization. New York: Random House.
Kerr, Clark
1950   "Labor markets: their character and consequences." American Economic Review 40 (May): 278-291.
1979a   "Key issues for higher education in the 1980's." Pp. 1-11 in Jones and Nowotny (eds.) New Directions for Higher Education: Preparing for the New Decade. San Francisco: Jossey-Bass.

1979b "Introduction." Pp. ix-xxvii in Clark Kerr and Jerome Rosow (eds.) Work in America. New York: D. Van Nostrand.

Kilby, Peter
1971 "Hunting the heffalump." Pp. 1-40 in Peter Kilby (ed.) Entrepreneurship and Economic Development. New York: The Free Press.

Klapp, Orrin E.
1958 "Social types: process and structure." American Sociological Review 23 (December): 674-678.
1971 Social Types: Process Structure and Ethos. San Diego, CA: Aegis.

Kohn, Melvin L.
1976 "Occupational structure and alienation." American Journal of Sociology 82: 111-130.

Kottkamp, John H.
1957 "Master and servant-employee or independent contractor-right to control as the test of relationship." Oregon Law Review 37: 88-92.

Kraft, Philip
1979 "The routinizing of computer programming." Sociology of Work and Occupations 6: 139-155.

Krause, Elliott A.
1971 The Sociology of Occupations. Boston: Little Brown.

Kreckel, Reinhard
1980 "Unequal opportunity structure and labor market segmentation." Sociology 14 (November): 525-550.

Kronus, Carol L.
1976 "The evolution of occupational power." Sociology of Work and Occupations 3 (February): 3-37.

Kucera, Daniel J.
1963 "Women unwanted." Harvard Law Record 37 (December 12): 1ff.

Kusterer, Ken C.
1978 Know-How on the Job: The Important Working Knowledge of "Unskilled" Workers. Boulder, CO: Westview Press.

Larson, Erik
1981 "On top of the hump: key railwayman feels on top of the world." Wall Street Journal (May 25): 1, 17.

Larson, Magali Sarfatti
1977 The Rise of Professionalism: A Sociological Analysis. Berkeley: University of California Press.

Laumann, Edward O. and John P. Heinz
1979 "The organization of lawyer's work: size, intensity and co-practice of the fields of law. American Bar Foundation Research Journal. (Spring): 217-246.

Lawrence, Paul R. and Jay W. Lorsch
1967 Organization and Environment: Managing Differentiation and Integration. Boston: Division of Research, Graduate School of Business Administration, Harvard University.

Lazarsfeld, Paul F. and Wagner Thielens, Jr.
1958 The Academic Mind: Social Scientists in a Time of Crisis. Glencoe, IL: The Free Press.

Lees, D. S.
1966 Economic Consequences of the Professions. London: Institute of Economic Affairs.

Le Masters, E. E.
  1975   Blue-Collar Aristocrats: Life-Styles at a Working Class Tavern. Madison: University of Wisconsin Press.
Lenski, Gerhard E. and Jean Lenski
  1978   Human Societies: An Introduction to Macrosociology. 3rd Edition. New York: McGraw-Hill.
Lipset, Seymour Martin, Martin Trow, and James Coleman
  1962   Union Democracy: The Internal Politics of the International Typographical Union. Garden City, NY: Anchor Books.
Lipsky, Michael
  1980   Street-Level Bureaucracy: Dilemmas of the Individual in Public Services. New York: Russell Sage Foundation.
Lockmiller, David A.
  1969   Scholars on Parade: Colleges, Universities, Costumes and Degrees. New York: Macmillan.
Loether, Herman J.
  1974   "Organizational stress and the role orientations of college professors." Pp. 159-172 in Phyllis L. Stewart and Muriel G. Cantor (eds.) Varieties of Work Experience. New York: John Wiley.
Lopata, Helena
  1971   Occupation: Housewife. New York: Oxford University Press.
Lynd, Robert S. and Helen M. Lynd
  1929   Middletown: A study in Contemporary American Culture. New York: Harcourt Brace Jovanovich.
Macrae, Norman
  1976   "The coming entrepreneurial revolution: a survey." The Economist 261 (December 25): 41-44, 53-65.
Mann, Michael
  1973   Consciousness and Action Among the Western Working Class. London: Macmillan.
Manning, Peter K.
  1977   Police Work: Essays on the Social Organization of Policing. Cambridge, MA: MIT Press.
Martin, Susan Ehrlich
  1980   "Breaking and Entering": Policewomen on Patrol. Berkeley, CA: University of California Press.
Marx, Karl and Frederick Engels
  1959   "Manifesto of the Communist Party." In Lewis S. Feuer (ed.) Marx and Engels. New York: Doubleday.
Mattick, Hans W.
  1974   "The contemporary jails of the United States: an unknown and neglected area of justice." Pp. 777-848 in Daniel Glaser (ed.) Handbook of Criminology. Chicago: Rand McNally.
McCleary, Richard
  1978   Dangerous Men: The Sociology of Parole. Beverly Hills, CA: Sage.
McClelland, David C.
  1961   The Achieving Society. Princeton, NJ: D. Van Nostrand.
Mennerick, Lewis A.
  1971   "The county jail school: problems in the teacher-student relationship." Kansas Journal of Sociology 7 (Spring): 17-33.

1972   "External control of recruits: the county jail school." American Behavioral Scientist 16 (September/October): 75-84.

1974a   "The county jail school teacher: social roles and external constraints." Pp. 143-158 in Phyllis L. Stewart and Muriel G. Cantor (eds.) Varieties of Work Experience: The Social Control of Occupational Groups and Roles. New York: John Wiley.

1974b   "The county jail school: custody-security as a constraint." Kansas Journal of Sociology 10 (Spring): 29-41.

1974c   "Client typologies: a method of coping with conflict in the service worker-client relationship." Sociology of Work and Occupations 1 (November): 396-418.

Merton, Robert K.
1957a   "The role set: problems in sociological theory." British Journal of Sociology 8 (June): 106-120.

1957b   Social Theory and Social Structure. Glencoe, IL: The Free Press.

Merton, Robert K. and Elinor Barber
1963   "Social ambivalence." Pp. 91-120 in Edward Tiryakian (ed.) Theory, Values and Sociocultural Change. New York: The Free Press.

Miles, Herbert J.
1953   "The taxi driver." Ph.D. dissertation, University of Missouri–Columbia.

Miller, Delbert C. and William H. Form
1980   Industrial Sociology: Work in Organizational Life. New York: Harper & Row.

Miller, E. Eugene
1978   Jail Management: Problems, Programs and Perspectives. Lexington, MA: Lexington Books.

Miller, Gale
1981   It's a Living: Work in Modern Society. New York: St. Martins.

Miller, George A.
1974   "Aerospace scientists and engineers: some organizational considerations." Pp. 114-127 in Phyllis L. Stewart and Muriel G. Cantor (eds.) Varieties of Work Experience. New York: John Wiley.

Miller, J. D. and S. M. Shortell
1969   "Hospital unionization: a study of the trends." Hospitals 43 (August 16): 67-72.

Miller, Joanne
1980   "Individual and occupational determinants of job satisfaction." Sociology of Work and Occupations 7: 337-366.

Miller, Ronald M.
1971   "The hospital-union relationship: part I. The multiparty nature of collective bargaining in the voluntary hospital." Hospitals 45 (May): 49-54.

Millerson, Geoffrey
1964   The Qualifying Associations: A Study in Professionalization. London: Routledge & Kegan Paul.

Mills, C. Wright
1951   White Collar: The American Middle Classes. New York: Oxford University Press.

Mintzberg, Henry
1979   The Structuring of Organizations: A Synthesis of the Research. Englewood Cliffs, NJ: Prentice-Hall.

Montagna, Paul D.
    1977   Occupations and Society: Toward a Sociology of the Labor Market. New York: John Wiley.

Montgomery, David
    1979   Workers' Control in America: Studies in the History of Work, Technology and Labor Struggles. New York: Cambridge University Press.

Moore, Wilbert E.
    1970   The Professions: Roles and Rules. New York: Russell Sage Foundation.

Morgan, D.H.J.
    1975   "Autonomy and negotiation in an industrial setting." Sociology of Work and Occupations 2 (August): 203-226.

Morris, Charles N.
    1951   "Some characteristics of occupational choice and adjustment in a sample of New York City taxi drivers." Ph.D. dissertation, Columbia University.

Morris, Richard and Raymond J. Murphy
    1959   "The situs dimension in occupational structure." American Sociological Review 24 (April): 231-239.

Morse, Dean
    1969   The Peripheral Worker. New York: Columbia University Press.

Mortimer, Kenneth P. and Michael L. Tierney
    1979   The Three "R's" of the Eighties: Reduction, Reallocation and Retrenchment. Washington, DC: The American Association for Higher Education.

Myers, Richard R.
    1946   "Interpersonal relations in the building industry." Human Organization 5 (Spring): 1-7.

National League for Nursing
    1981   Nursing Data Book, 1980. New York: NLN.

Newman, Charles L. and Barbara R. Price
    1977   Jails and Drug Treatment. Beverly Hills, CA: Sage.

New York State Special Commission on Attica
    1972   Attica: The Official Report of the New York State Special Commission on Attica. New York: Bantam Books.

Noble, David F.
    1977   America by Design: Science, Technology and the Rise of Corporate Capitalism. Oxford: Oxford University Press.

Olesen, Virginia L. and Frances Katsuranis
    1978   "Urban nomads: women in temporary clerical services." Pp. 316-338 in Ann H. Stromberg and Shirley Harkness (eds.) Women Working: Theories and Facts in Perspective. Palo Alto, CA: Mayfield.

Olson, Mancur, Jr.
    1968   "Economics, sociology and the best of all possible worlds." The Public Interest 12 (Summer): 96-118.

Orzack, Louis H.
    1977   "Competing professions and the public interest in the European Economic Community: drugs and their quality control." Pp. 95-129 in Stuart S. Blume (ed.) Perspectives in the Sociology of Science. London: John Wiley.

O'Toole, James
    1977   Work, Learning and the American Future. San Francisco: Jossey-Bass.

O'Toole, James and HEW Task Force
    1973   Work in America: Report of a Special Task Force to the Secretary of Health, Education and Welfare. Cambridge, MA: Massachusetts Institute of Technology Press.

Parenti, Michael
   1978   Power and the Powerless. New York: St. Martin's Press.
Parker, S. R., R. K. Brown, J. Child, and M. A. Smith
   1975   The Sociology of Industry. 3rd Edition. London: George Allen & Unwin.
Parkin, Frank
   1979   Marxism and Class Theory: A Bourgeois Critique. New York: Columbia University Press.
Parsons, Talcott
   1959   "The social structure of the family." Pp. 241-274 in Ruth Ashen (ed.) The Family: Its Function and Destiny. New York: Harper & Row.
   1968   "Professions." Pp. 536-547 in David L. Sills (ed.) International Encyclopedia of the Social Sciences 12. New York: Free Press and MacMillan.
Parsons, Talcott and Gerald M. Platt
   1973   The American University. Cambridge, MA: Harvard University Press.
Pavalko, Ronald M.
   1971   Sociology of Occupations and Professions. Itaska, IL: F. E. Peacock.
   1972   Sociological Perspectives on Occupations. Itaska, IL: F. E. Peacock.
Perkins, James A.
   1966   The University in Transition. Princeton, NJ: Princeton University Press.
Perrow, Charles
   1979   Complex Organizations: A Critical Essay. 2nd Edition. Glenview, IL: Scott, Foresman.
Perry, Stewart
   1978   San Francisco Scavengers: Dirty Work and the Pride of Ownership. Berkeley: University of California Press.
Persell, Caroline Hodges
   1977   Education and Inequality. New York: The Free Press.
Peterson, Richard A.
   1973   The Industrial Order and Social Policy. Englewood Cliffs, NJ: Prentice-Hall.
   1981   "Entrepreneurship and organization." Pp. 65-83 in Paul C. Nystron and William H. Starbuck (eds.) Handbook of Occupational Design. Volume 1. New York: Oxford University Press.
Peterson, Richard A. and John Schmidman
   1966   "Neo-entrepreneurs: a blue collar case." Presented at the 29th annual meetings of the Southern Sociological Society, New Orleans.
Peterson, Richard A. and Kirk W. Elifson
   1967   "Entrepreneurship as a mechanism of social mobility in a blue collar occupation." Presented at the 30th annual meetings of the Southern Sociological Society, Atlanta.
Peterson, Richard A. and David G. Berger
   1971   "Entrepreneurship in organizations: evidence from the popular music industry." Administrative Science Quarterly 16 (March): 97-106.
Pettigrew, Andrew M.
   1973   The Politics of Organizational Decision-Making. London: Tavistock.
Piore, Michael J.
   1975   "Notes for a theory of labor market stratification." Pp. 125-150 in Richard C. Edwards et al. (eds.) Labor Market Segmentation. Lexington, MA: D. C. Heath.

Piven, Frances F. and Richard A. Cloward
  1977   Poor People's Movements: Why They Succeed, How They Fail. New York: Random House.
Pollack, Ricki
  1979   "The abc's of prison education." Corrections Magazine 5 (September): 61-66.
Pope John Paul II
  1981   "Encyclical 'Laborem Exercens': On Human Work." Pp. 226-244 in Origins. Volume II: No. 15 (September 24). Washington, DC: National Catholic News Service.
Powelson, Harvey and Reinhard Bendix
  1951   "Psychiatry in prison." Psychiatry 14 (February): 73-86.
President's Commission on Law Enforcement and Administration of Justice
  1967   Task Force Report: Corrections. Washington, DC: U.S. Government Printing Office.
Reagen, Michael V. and Donald M. Stoughton (eds.)
  1976   School Behind Bars: A Descriptive Overview of Correctional Education in the American Prison System. Metuchen, NJ: Scarecrow Press.
Riemer, Jeffrey W.
  1979   Hard Hats—The Work World of Construction Workers. Beverly Hills, CA: Sage.
Riesman, David
  1958   "Work and leisure in post-industrial society." Pp. 363-385 in E. Larrabee and R. Meyersohn (eds.) Mass Leisure. Glencoe, IL: The Free Press.
  1964   "Introduction to 'Academic Women,' " in Jessie Bernard, Academic Women. University Park: Pennsylvania State University.
Riessman, Frank
  1969   Strategies Against Poverty. New York: Random House.
Ritzer, George
  1977   Working, Conflict and Change. Englewood Cliffs, NJ: Prentice-Hall.
Roberts, Albert R.
  1971   Sourcebook on Prison Education: Past, Present and Future. Springfield, IL: Charles C. Thomas.
Rogers, David and Ivar E. Berg
  1961   "Occupation and ideology: the case of the small businessman." Human Organization 20 (Fall): 103-111.
Rothman, David J.
  1971   The Discovery of the Asylum: Social Order and Disorder in the New Republic. Boston: Little, Brown.
Rothschild-Whitt, Joyce
  1979   "The collectivist organization: an alternative to rational-bureaucratic models." American Sociological Review 44 (August): 509-527.
Rottman, David B. and John R. Kimberly
  1975   "The social context of jails." Sociology and Social Research 59 (July): 344-361.
Rubin, Lillian
  1976   Worlds of Pain. New York: Basic Books.
Rubinstein, Jonathan
  1974   City Police. New York: Ballantine Books.

Ryan, John and Richard A. Peterson
　1982　" 'Product image': solving the problems of collaborative creativity in the media arts, the case of country music songwriters." Annual Review of Communication Research 10. In press.
Salaman, Graeme
　1974　Community and Occupation. London: Cambridge University Press.
Salaman, Graeme and Kenneth Thompson (eds.)
　1980　Control and Ideology in Organizations. Cambridge, MA: MIT Press.
Schmidman, John
　1979　Unions in Post-industrial Society. University Park: Pennsylvania State University Press.
Schneider, Eugene V.
　1980　Industrial Sociology: The Social Relations of Industry and the Community. Third Edition. New York: McGraw-Hill.
Schulder, Diane B.
　1970　"Does the law oppress women?" Pp. 139-157 in Robin Morgan (ed.) Sisterhood is Powerful: An Anthology of Writings From the Womens Liberation Movement. New York: Random House.
Schultz, Terri
　1980　"The untaxed millions." New York Times Magazine (March 16): 42ff.
Schumpeter, Joseph A.
　1934　The Theory of Economic Development: An Inquiry Into Profits, Capital, Credit, Interest and the Business Cycle. Cambridge, MA: Harvard University Press.
　1965　"Economic theory and entrepreneurial history." Pp. 45-64 in Hugh G. J. Aitken (Ed.) Explorations in Enterprise. Cambridge, MA: Harvard University Press.
Sears, Don W.
　1951　"A reappraisal of the employment status in social legislation." Rocky Mountain Law Review 23 (April): 392-415.
Seeman, Melvin and John W. Evans
　1962　"Alienation on learning in a hospital setting." American Sociological Review 27 (December): 772-782.
Sexton, Patricia C.
　1967　The American School: A Sociological Analysis. Englewood Cliffs, NJ: Prentice-Hall.
Sharp, Lawrence J. and F. Ivan Nye
　1963　"Maternal mental health." Pp. 309-319 in Lois N. Wladis Hoffman and F. Ivan Nye (eds.) The Employed Mother in America. Chicago: Rand McNally.
Sheppard, Harold L. and Neal Q. Herrick
　1972　Where Have All the Robots Gone? Worker Dissatisfaction in the '70's. New York: The Free Press.
Shimberg, Benjamin, Barbara F. Esser, and Daniel H. Kruger
　1973　Occupational Licensing: Practices and Policies. Washington: Public Affairs Press.
Shover, Neal
　1974　" 'Experts' and diagnosis in correctional agencies." Crime and Delinquency 20 (October): 347-358.
Silver, Marc L.
　1981a　"Organization and alienation in the construction industry." Ph.D. dissertation, Columbia University.

1981b "Craft relations of production: quality of employment in the construction industry." Prepared for the annual meetings of the Eastern Sociological Society.

Slater, Philip E.
1970 "What hath Spock wrought?—freed children, chained moms." Washington Post (March 1): H1, 10.

Slocum, Ken
1981 "A game warden's job offers lively scenery and abundant risks." Wall Street Journal (June 19): 1, 23.

Slocum, Walter L.
1966 Occupational Careers: A Sociological Perspective. Chicago: Aldine.

Smigel, Erwin O.
1964 The Wall Street Lawyer, Professional Organization Man? Bloomington: Indiana University Press.

Smith, Ralph E. (ed.)
1979 The Subtle Revolution. Washington, DC: The Urban Institute.

Solomon, David N.
1968 "Sociological perspectives on occupations." Pp. 3-13 in Howard S. Becker et al. (eds.) Institutions and the Person. Chicago: Aldine.

Soo, Chong
1969 "The monetary value of a housewife." American Journal of Economics and Sociology 28 (July): 271-284.

Staines, Graham L. and Pamela O'Connor
1980 "Conflicts among work, leisure, and family roles." Monthly Labor Review (August): 35-39.

Stannard, D. L.
1971 "White cabdrivers and black fairs." Transaction 8 (November/December): 44-46, 68.

Stauffer, James D.
1976 The Community, The County Prison and You. Lancaster, PA: Lancaster-Lebanon Intermediate Unit.

Stein, Barry A. and Rosabeth Moss Kanter
1980 "Building the parallel organization: toward structures for permanent quality of work life." Journal of Applied Behavioral Science 16 (July-August-September): 371-388.

Stein, Leonard I.
1967 "The doctor-nurse game." Archives of General Psychiatry 16 (6): 699-703.

Stewart, Phyllis L.
1968 "Organizational change in an advanced research and development laboratory: a study of attrition." Ph.D. Dissertation. University of California, Los Angeles.

Stewart, Phyllis L. and Muriel G. Cantor
1974 Varieties of Work Experience: The Social Control of Occupational Groups and Roles. New York: John Wiley.

Stinchcombe, Arthur L.
1959 "Bureaucratic and craft administration of production: a comparative study." Administrative Science Quarterly 4: 168-187.
1965 "Social structure and organizations." Pp. 142-193 in James G. March (ed.) Handbook of Organizations. Chicago: Rand McNally.

Strauss, Anselm L., Leonard Schatzman, Rue Bucher, Danuta Ehrlich, and Melvin Sabshin

1964   Psychiatric Ideologies and Institutions. New York: The Free Press.

Strauss, George
1958   Unions In the Building Trades: A Case Study. The University of Buffalo Studies 24 (2): June.

Street, David, Robert D. Vinter, and Charles Perrow
1966   Organization for Treatment: A Comparative Study of Institutions for Delinquents. New York: The Free Press.

Strong, Samuel M.
1943   "Social types in a minority group: formulation of a method." American Journal of Sociology 48 (March): 563-573.
1946   "Negro-white relations as reflected in social types." American Journal of Sociology 52 (July): 23-30.

Susman, Gerald I.
1976   Autonomy at Work: A Sociotechnical Analysis of Participative Management. New York: Praeger.

Swados, Harvey
1957   "The myth of the happy worker," in A Radical's America. New York: Atlantic-Little, Brown.

Talbot, Ross B.
1978   The Chicken War: An International Trade Conflict Between the United States and the European Economic Community, 1961-64. Ames: Iowa State University Press.

Terman, Lewis M. and Catherine C. Miles
1936   Sex and Personality: Studies in Masculinity and Femininity. New York: McGraw-Hill.

Thurow, Roger
1981   "Assembling computers means that happiness doesn't come til 4:30." Wall Street Journal (June 1): 1, 22.

Tilgher, Adriano
1958   Homo Faber: Work Through the Ages. Dorothy C. Fisher, trans. Chicago: Henry Regnery.

Titmuss, Richard M.
1971   The Gift Relationship: From Human Blood to Social Policy. New York: Pantheon Books.

Toffler, Alvin
1980   The Third Wave. New York: William Morrow.

Treiman, Donald and Kermit Terrell
1975   "Sex and the process of status attainment: a comparison of working women and men." American Sociological Review 40 (April): 174-200.

Tremblay, Kenneth, Don A. Dillman, and Joye J. Dillman
1977   Housing Satisfactions and Preferences of Washington Residents: A 1977 Statewide Survey. College of Agriculture Research Center, Washington State University, Pullman.

Trist, Eric
1981   "The evolution of socio-technical systems: a conceptual framework and an action research program." Occasional Paper 2 (June). Toronto: Associate of the Ontario Quality of Working Life Centre.

Turner, C. and M. N. Hodge
1970   "Occupations and professions." Pp. 19-50 in J. A. Jackson (ed.) Professions and Professionalization. Cambridge, MA: Cambridge University Press.

U.S. Department of Commerce, Bureau of the Census
  1960   Statistical Abstract of the United States. Washington, DC: U.S. Government Printing Office.
  1970a   Statistical Abstract of the United States. Washington, DC: U.S. Government Printing Office.
  1970b   1970 Census Users' Guide. Washington, DC: U.S. Government Printing Office.
  1970c   Current Population Reports; 24 Million Americans—Poverty in the United States: 1969. Washington, DC: U.S. Government Printing Office.
  1973   1970 Census of the Population; Subject Reports, Occupational Characteristics. Washington, DC: U.S. Government Printing Office.
  1979   Statistical Abstract of the U.S.: 100th Edition. Washington, DC: U.S. Government Printing Office.
U.S. Department of Health, Education and Welfare
  1978   Minorities and Women in the Health Fields: Applicants, Students, and Workers. Washington, DC: U.S. Government Printing Office.
U.S. Department of Labor, Bureau of Employment and Security
  1977   Dictionary of Occupational Titles. 4th Edition. Washington, DC: U.S. Government Printing Office.
U.S. Department of Labor, Bureau of Labor Statistics
  1976   Brief History of the American Labor Movement. Washington, DC: U.S. Government Printing Office.
  1980   Perspectives on Working Women. Washington, DC: U.S. Government Printing Office.
U.S. Public Health Service, National Center for Health Statistics
  1970a   Health Resources Statistics: Health Manpower and Health Facilities, 1969. Washington, DC: U.S.Government Printing Office.
  1970b   Selected Symptoms of Psychological Distress. Washington, DC: U.S. Government Printing Office.
  1977   Health Resources Statistics: Health Manpower and Health Facilities, 1976-77. Washington, DC: U.S. Government Printing Office.
U.S.A. Today
  1981   "Life in America: Demands on Working Women." (August): 1-3.
U.S. News and World Report
  1964   "Why capital's taxi drivers stay home at night." 56 (February 3): 8.
Vanek, Joann
  1974   "Time spent in housework." Scientific American 231 (November): 116-120.
Van Maanen, John
  1975   "Police socialization: a longitudinal examination of job attitudes in an urban police department." Administrative Science Quarterly 20 (June): 207-228.
Vaz, Edmund W.
  1955   "The metropolitan taxi driver: his work and self-conception." Master's Thesis, McGill University.
Walsh, Mary Roth
  1977   "Doctors Wanted: No Women Need Apply": Sexual Barriers in the Medical Profession, 1835-1975. New Haven, CT: Yale University Press.
Wax, Murray L., Rosalie H. Wax, and Robert V. Dumont, Jr.
  1964   Formal Education in an American Indian Community. Society for the Study of Social Problems, Supplement to Social Problems II (Spring).

Weber, Max
1958   The Protestant Ethic and the Spirit of Capitalism. Talcott Parsons, trans. New York: Charles Scribner.
1964   The Theory of Social and Economic Organization. A. M. Henderson and Talcott Parsons, trans. New York: The Free Press.

Weinberg, S. Kirson
1942   "Aspects of the prison's social structure." American Journal of Sociology 47 (March): 717-726.

Westin, Alan F. and Stephan Salisbury (eds)
1980   Individual Rights in the Corporation: A Reader of Employee Rights. New York: Pantheon.

Westley, William A.
1970   Violence and the Police: A Sociological Study of Law, Custom, and Morality. Cambridge, MA: MIT Press.

Who's Who of America Women
1958-
59   Chicago: A. N. Marquis

Wilensky, Harold L.
1964   "Varieties of work experience." Pp. 125-154 in Henry Borow (ed.) Man in a World at Work. Boston: Houghton Mifflin.

Wilken, Paul H.
1979   Entrepreneurship: A Comparative and Historical Study. Norwood, NJ: Ablex.

Wilson, James Q.
1973   Varieties of Police Behavior: The Management of Law and Order in Eight Communities. New York: Atheneum.

Wilson, Logan
1964   The Academic Man: A Study in the Sociology of a Profession. New York: Octagon Books.

Wright, Erik Olin
1978   "Race, class, and income inequality." American Journal of Sociology 83 (May): 1368-1397.

Yankelovich, Daniel
1979   "Work, values, and the new breed." Pp. 3-26 in Clark Kerr and Jerome M. Rosow (eds.) Work in America. New York: D. Van Nostrand.
1981   "New rules in American life: searching for self-fulfillment in a world turned upside down." Psychology Today 15 (April): 35-91.

Zald, Mayer N. (ed.)
1969   Power in Organizations: Proceedings, Vanderbilt Sociology Conference. Nashville: Vanderbilt University Press.

Zeitlin, Jonathan
1979   "Crafts control and the division of labor: engineers and compositors in Britain, 1890-1930." Cambridge Journal of Economics 3 (September): 263-274.

Zeitz, Gerald
1980   "Interorganizational dialectics." Administrative Science Quarterly 25: 72-88.

Zwerdling, Daniel
1978   Democracy at Work: A Guide to Workplace Ownership, Participation and Self-Management Experiments in the United States and Europe. Washington, DC: Association for Self-Management.

AUTHOR INDEX

SUBJECT INDEX

ABOUT THE AUTHORS

Jessie Bernard, Ph.D., 1935–Washington University. Research Scholar Honoris Causa at Pennsylvania State University. Numerous publications, including: *The Future of Marriage* (World, 1972); *The Future of Motherhood* (Dial, 1974); *The Female World* (Free Press, 1981).

Clifton D. Bryant, Ph.D., 1964–Louisiana State University. Professor and Head, Department of Sociology, Virginia Polytechnic University and State University. President of the Mid-South Sociological Association and a former president of the Southern Sociological Society. Publications include: *Khaki-Collar Crime: Deviant Behavior in Military Context* (Free Press, 1979); *Sexual Deviancy and Social Proscription* (Human Sciences Press, Spring, 1982).

Bonnie Bullough, R.N., Ph.D., 1968–University of California, Los Angeles. Dean, School of Nursing, State University of New York, Buffalo. Numerous publications, including: *The Law and the Expanding Nursing Role, The Management of Common Human Miseries,* and several works with Vern Bullough.

Vern Bullough, R.N., Ph.D.–University of Chicago. Dean, Natural and Social Sciences, State University College at Buffalo. Numerous publications, including: *Sexual Variance in Society and History, The Subordinate Sex,* and *Frontier of Sex Research.*

Muriel G. Cantor, Ph.D., 1969–University of California, Los Angeles. Professor, American University, Washington, D.C. Publications include articles in *Communication Research, Journal of Communication, Journalism Quarterly.* Books include: *The Hollywood TV Producer* (Basic Books, 1971), *Varieties of Work Experience* (with Phyllis L. Stewart; John Wiley, 1974) and *Prime-Time Television: Content and Control* (Sage, 1980).

Kirk W. Elifson, Ph.D., 1973—Vanderbilt University. Associate Professor of Sociology at Georgia State University, Atlanta. Co-author with Richard P. Runyon and Audrey Haber of *Essentials of Social Statistics* (Addison-Wesley, January 1982).

Cynthia Fuchs Epstein, Ph.D., 1968—Columbia University. Co-Director, Program in Sex Roles and Social Change, Columbia University. Numerous publications, including: *The Woman Lawyer* (University of Chicago, 1971); *The Other Half* (edited with W. J. Goode; Prentice-Hall, 1971) and *Women in Law* (Basic Books, 1981).

Eliot Freidson, Ph.D., 1952—University of Chicago. Professor, New York University. Numerous books and articles on professions, including: *Professional Dominance* (Atherton Press, 1970); *Profession of Medicine* (Dodd-Mead, 1970); *Doctoring Together* (Elsevier Scientific, 1975).

Rosabeth Moss Kanter, Ph.D., 1967—University of Michigan. Professor of Sociology and Organization and Management, Yale University. Numerous publications, including: *Commitment and Community* (Harvard University Press, 1972); *Men and Women of the Corporation* (Basic Books, 1977); and over 70 articles in books and scholarly journals.

Herman J. Loether, Ph.D., 1955—University of Washington. Professor, California State University, Dominguez Hills. Numerous publications, including: *Descriptive and Inferential Statistics: An Introduction* (with Donald G. McTavish; 2nd edition, Allyn and Bacon, 1980) and *Problems of Aging* (2nd edition, Dickinson, 1975).

Susan E. Martin, Ph.D., 1977—American University, Washington, D.C. Study Director of Panel on Sentencing Research, National Academy of Sciences, National Research Council. Publications include: *"Breaking and Entering": Policewomen on Patrol* (University of California Press, 1980) and *New Directions in the Rehabilitation of Criminal Offenders* (National Academy Press, 1981; with Lee Sechrest and Robin Redner).

Lewis A. Mennerick, Ph.D., 1971—Northwestern University. Associate Professor, University of Kansas, Lawrence, Kansas. Numerous articles published in *American Behavioral Scientist, Sociology of Work and Occupations* and *Administrative Science Quarterly.*

Kenneth B. Perkins is a doctoral student in the Department of Sociology at Virginia Polytechnic Institute and State University. He is completing his thesis, titled "Occupational Communities in Modern Society."

Richard A. Peterson, Ph.D., 1961—University of Illinois. Professor, Vanderbilt University, Tennessee. Publications include: *The Industrial Order and Social Policy* (Prentice-Hall, 1973); *The Production of Culture* (Sage, 1976); and "Measuring Culture, Leisure and Time Use," in the *Annals of the Academy of Political and Social Sciences,* 1981.

Jeffrey W. Riemer, Ph.D., 1975—University of New Hampshire. Associate Professor, Wichita State University, Kansas. Numerous articles published in sociological journals. *Hard Hats—The Work World of Construction Workers* (Sage, 1979).

John T. Schmidman, Ph.D., 1968—University of Wisconsin. Associate Professor, Department of Labor Studies, Pennsylvania State University. Publications include: *British Unions & Economic Planning* and *Unions in Post-Industrial Society* (1979).

Marc L. Silver, Ph.D., 1981—Columbia University. Adjunct Assistant Professor, Queens College, New York and affiliated with the Center for the Social Sciences, Columbia University, New York.

Phyllis L. Stewart, Ph.D., 1968—University of California, Los Angeles. Professor and Chairman, Department of Sociology, George Washington University, Washington, D.C. Co-author, with Muriel G. Cantor, of *Varieties of Work Experience* (John Wiley, 1974).